OUR THEATRES IN THE NINETIES

LONDON
PUBLISHED BY
Constable and Company Ltd.
10–12 ORANGE STREET W.C.2

•

INDIA
Longmans, Green and Company Ltd.
BOMBAY   CALCUTTA   MADRAS

•

CANADA
Longmans, Green and Company Ltd.
TORONTO

OUR THEATRES IN THE NINETIES BY BERNARD SHAW

IN THREE VOLUMES

VOLUME II

LONDON

CONSTABLE AND COMPANY

LIMITED

Revised and reprinted for this Standard Edition 1932
Reprinted 1948

PRINTED IN GREAT BRITAIN
BY R. & R. CLARK, LIMITED, EDINBURGH

These criticisms were contributed week
by week to THE SATURDAY REVIEW from
January 1895 to May 1898

OUR THEATRES IN THE NINETIES

NEW YEAR DRAMAS

A WOMAN'S REASON. By Charles H. E. Brookfield and F. C.
   Philips. Shaftesbury Theatre, 27 December 1895.
THE LATE MR CASTELLO. A new and original farce in three acts.
   By Sydney Grundy. Comedy Theatre, 28 December 1895.

[4 *January* 1896]

IT was such pleasure to see Mr Lewis Waller and his company
divested of the trappings of Manxmanity and in their right minds
again, that we all received A Woman's Reason with more gaiety
and enthusiasm than can easily be justified in cold blood. The
play has been produced, as far as I can guess, by the following
process. One of the authors, whom I take to be Mr Philips, wrote
a commonplace Froufrou play, in a style so conscientiously and
intolerably literary that the persons of the drama do not hesitate to remark familiarly to their nearest and dearest that "Convention speaks one thing, whilst some sweeter voice whispers
another." The sweeter voice in the composing of the play, I
assume, was Mr Brookfield's. Mr Brookfield is an assiduous col-
lector of conversational *jeux d'esprit*, and is witty enough to be
able to contribute occasionally to the museum himself. Such a
collection, from its very miscellaneousness, is better for ordinary
theatrical purposes than a complete philosophy reduced to aphorisms; and by sticking its plums into Mr Philips's literary dough
with reckless profusion, Mr Brookfield has produced a sufficiently
toothsome pudding.

The worst of it is that the Brookfieldian plums digest and are
forgotten, whilst the Philipian suet remains heavy on soul and
stomach. I cannot now remember a single one of Mr Brookfield's
sallies, not even the one in which I recognized a long-lost child
of my own. On the other hand, I do recollect, with a growing
sense of injury, the assumption that the relation between a British
officer and a cultivated Jewish gentleman who makes a trifle of

seventy thousand a year or so in the City is the relation between Ivanhoe and Isaac of York, with its offensiveness somewhat accentuated by modern snobbery. When Captain Crozier proceeded to explain haughtily to Mr Stephen D'Acosta that it was useless for two persons in their respective conditions to discuss a question of honor, as they could not possibly understand one another, I seemed to hear a voice from my boyhood—the voice of Howard Paul—singing:

> I'm Captain Jinks of the Horse Marines;
> And I feed my horse on kidney beans:
> Of course it far exceeds the means
>   Of a captain in the army.

It is to this rustic conception of "a captain in the army" that we owe Crozier. And yet—would you believe it?—the performance at the Shaftesbury leaves one with a stronger sense of the reality of Captain Crozier than of any other person in the drama. This is largely due, no doubt, to Mr Coghlan, who, having given himself a complete rest from acting during his assumption of the part of Mercutio at the Lyceum, now resumes it at the Shaftesbury with all the vigor of a man who has had a thorough holiday. I do not say that Mr Coghlan's effects are made with the utmost economy of time and weight; but then it is perfectly in the character of the part and in the interest of the drama that Captain Crozier should be a comparatively slow, heavy person, in contrast to the keen, alert Jew. The presentation of a British officer as an over-eating, under-thinking person, professionally the merest routineer, one who by dint of sincere aspiration and conscientious plodding has learnt to play cards and billiards, to shoot, to bet, to do the correct thing in social emergencies, and in an irreproachably gentlemanly way to make women aware of his readiness to accept any degree of intimacy they may care to admit him to, is fair criticism of life; for wherever the social soil is manured by "independent incomes," it still produces large crops of such men (very pleasant fellows, many of them), though certainly the army has of late years become a much less eligible career for them than it was in the days of Captain Rawdon Crawley. The difficulty of giving the authors of A Woman's Reason credit for a clever study of an officer of this type lies in the fact that, as I have already hinted, his speeches to D'Acosta shew a quite romantic ignorance of the healthy promiscuity by which English society protects itself against all permanent Faubourg-St Germain formations. Thanks to the truly blessed institution of primogeniture constantly thrusting down the great bulk of our aristocratic stock into the ranks of the commoners, we are the most republican country in the world; and the ideas expressed by Captain Crozier at the Shaftesbury, though they might pass as part of the established currency on the Continent, and even in America, are here only the affectations of dukes' housekeepers and Hampton Court pensioners. Nor can we, when the Captain foolishly hides in the lady's bedroom from her husband, believe much more in him than in the domestic architecture which cuts that sacred apartment off from all ingress and egress save through the drawing room. In fact, the bedroom incident elicited one of those jeers from the audience which will soon force even the most conservative west end manager to abjure through terror of the gallery that insane faith in worn-out stage tricks which seem proof against the printed persuasion of the stalls. There is much else in Captain Crozier's part which is differentiated from the conventional seducer and villain business of melodrama rather by Mr Coghlan's acting than by the words put into his mouth; but the final touch, where he "does the right thing" by telling the usual divorce-court lie as to the lady's spotlessness, and offering to marry her when he perceives that he runs no risk of being accepted in view of her imminent reconciliation with her husband, is a genuine stroke of comedy and character.

Mr Coghlan created the part, like a true actor, by the simple but very unusual method of playing it from its own point of view. The tradition of the stage is a tradition of villains and heroes. Shakespear was a devout believer in the existence of the true villain—the man whose terrible secret is that his fundamental

3

moral impulses are by some freak of nature inverted, so that not only are love, pity, and honor loathsome to him, and the affectation of them which society imposes on him a constant source of disgust, but cruelty, destruction, and perfidy are his most luxurious passions. This is a totally different phenomenon from the survivals of the ape and the tiger in a normal man. The average normal man is covetous, lazy, selfish; but he is not malevolent, nor capable of saying to himself, "Evil: be thou my good." He only does wrong as a means to an end, which he always represents to himself as a right end. The case is exactly reversed with a villain; and it is my melancholy duty to add that we sometimes find it hard to avoid a cynical suspicion that the balance of social advantage is on the side of gifted villainy, since we see the able villain, Mephistopheles-like, doing a huge amount of good in order to win the power to do a little darling evil, out of which he is as likely as not to be cheated in the end; whilst your normal respectable man will countenance, connive at, and grovel his way through all sorts of meanness, baseness, servility, and cruel indifference to suffering in order to enjoy a miserable twopennorth of social position, piety, comfort, and domestic affection, of which he, too, is often ironically defrauded by Fate. I could point to a philanthropist or two—even to their statues—whom Posterity, should it ever turn from admiring the way they spent their money to considering the way they got it, will probably compare very unfavorably with Guy Fawkes.

However, these reflections are beside the present purpose, which is only to shew how our actors have been placed at cross-purposes with our authors by the traditional stage villain being a monster, or perversion of nature, like Iago; whilst the gentleman who serves as a foil to the hero in a modern west end play is not a villain at all, but at worst a comparatively selfish, worthless fellow. As far as he is taken from life at all, he is suspiciously like the average man of the world as portrayed by Thackeray. Indeed, in the best modern plays, and even in the best modern melodramas (for example, Held by the Enemy), there is no wicked person at all. Ever since Milton struck the popular fancy by changing the devil into a romantic gentleman who was no-body's enemy but his own, and thereby practically abolished the real devil, or god of villains, as a necessary figure in the world drama, playgoers have been learning to know themselves well enough to recognize that quite mischief enough for the plot of any ordinary play can be made by average ladies and gentlemen like themselves. Captain Crozier is not the least bit of a villain. He shews abject weakness in allowing Mrs D'Acosta to ruin him and make him ridiculous by dragging him out of a seventy-thousand-a-year mansion in which he is most comfortably in-stalled as tame cat, with the certainty that she will throw him over without scruple as a moral outcast the moment she is tired of him; but one feels that, after all, it does not greatly matter, since the elopement is only a stage convention—one of those events which you let pass in the theatre because they lead to in-teresting scenes, on the understanding that nobody is to be held morally responsible for them. (Otherwise, it may be remarked, Mrs D'Acosta's treatment of Captain Crozier must be condemned as severely as her treatment of her husband.) Crozier, in all the points at which he can reasonably be regarded as exercising free will, behaves like a gentleman according to his lights; and when I say that Mr Coghlan's success was due to his taking the char-acter from its own point of view, I mean that he so played it as to make clear, when Crozier finally walked out, that he was filled with the most complete sense of having done everything that the most exacting social critic could have expected of him, and done it handsomely and adroitly. And the effect left upon us was that of having made the acquaintance of Captain Crozier, instead of merely seeing Mr Coghlan with a new suit of clothes on.

The part of Stephen D'Acosta fitted Mr Lewis Waller so closely that it was not necessary for him to make any great im-personative effort; and the same may be said of Miss Florence West, who happily obliterated all memory of her struggles with the Manxwoman. The pleasant personal qualities with which we are familiar carried Mr Waller through sympathetically; and though there was one speech in which the authors evidently in-

5

tended him to play much more forcibly—that in which Stephen D'Acosta gives his father-in-law a piece of his mind—I cannot blame him for refusing to exert himself violently for its sake, since it was hardly equal to, say, the exhortation which Molière puts into the mouth of Don Juan's father on the subject of the true gentleman. Still, the underplaying was a little hard on Mr Brookfield, whose elaborate exit, as of a man utterly crumpled up, would have been more effective had Mr Waller done the crumpling with due energy. Mrs Beerbohm Tree, to whom some malignant fairy godmother must have denied the gifts of empty-headed sentimentality and hysterical incontinence which are essential to success in our drama, substituting for them the fatal disqualifications of brains, individuality, and positiveness of character, gave an amazingly ingenious imitation of the conventional Froufrou. Only once, through the genius of another member of the company, was she carried into a sincere bit of acting. This talented colleague was a Mr Stewart Dawson, an actor not yet in his teens, but with a pleasant voice, a blarneying smile, a simplicity of manner all irresistible. The house took to him as if he were its own son; and so apparently did Mrs Tree. I can only say that if Mr Dawson's fascination increases with his years, it is a grave question whether he ought to be allowed to grow up. Mrs Tree, by the way, was announced as appearing "by arrangement," as if all the rest had dropped in by accident. What has had to be arranged is evidently either Mrs Tree's objection to appear "by kind permission of Mr Tree," or Mr Tree's objection to give the kind permission. This observation is, of course, not serious; but I make it for the sake of calling attention to the absurdity, and indeed the indelicacy, of the "kind permission" formula by which managers insist on publicly asserting proprietary rights in artists who are under engagement to them. Imagine one of the Reviews announcing an article on the theatre by Mr Clement Scott as "by kind permission of the Editor of the Daily Telegraph"! Why should the manager of a theatre have worse manners than an editor?

Of the other characters, Lord Bletchley, half convention, half burlesque, is cleverly played by Mr Brookfield. He should be warned, however, that his tricky diction occasionally prevents his sentences from being quite clearly caught. The Rev. Cosmo Pretious, all burlesque, and unenlightened burlesque at that, is very well played by Mr Henry Kemble, whose sense of character and artistic feeling have been too much wasted on plays with no characters in them. Agatha Pretious, also a burlesque figure, is a part quite unworthy of Miss Maude Millett. She has evidently been cast for it merely to drag another popular name into the bill.

I have forgotten to mention, by the way, that A Woman's Reason is a play with a purpose—the same purpose as that of Daniel Deronda. All the Jews in it are heroes and heroines, and all the Christians the meanest and feeblest wretches conceivable. Serve them right!

And now for The Late Mr Castello, which has replaced The Benefit of the Doubt at the Comedy. In this work Mr Sydney Grundy has—but on second thoughts I think I will confine myself to offering Mr Grundy and Mr Comyns Carr and Miss Winifred Emery and Miss Rose Leclercq and everyone else concerned, my devoted compliments. We shall meet again soon—very soon.

PLAYS OF THE WEEK

THE PRISONER OF ZENDA. A romantic play in a prologue and four acts. Adapted from Anthony Hope's story by Edward Rose. St James's Theatre, 7 January 1896.

THE SIGN OF THE CROSS. In four acts. By Wilson Barrett. Lyric Theatre, 4 January 1896.   [11 *January* 1896]

MR ANTHONY HOPE's Prisoner of Zenda was an amusing attempt to get a Scott-Dumas romance out of modern life. To take the nineteenth-century hero, give him a sword and a horse, a forest to gallop through and a castle to besiege, enemies to pursue him, persons with wrists of steel to fence with, princesses to love and rescue, and all the other luxuries of a D'Artagnan, was a laudable enterprise, in pursuit of which Mr Hope went to the shores of the Baltic, and carved an imaginary State of Ruritania out of

Mecklenburg. He was so far successful that the book made pleasant reading up to within a few chapters of the end. Then the reader's heavily taxed powers of make-believe gave out. At least, that was my experience. At about the point where Rassendyl began his swimming exploits in the moat, I found it impossible any longer to forget that the whole book was a great piece of nonsense. Mere incident in a romance is not interesting unless you believe in the reality of the people to whom the incidents occur. Scott and Dumas could create real men and women for you: their merest supernumeraries, from the innkeepers whom the Musketeers cheat to Higg the son of Snell, are more solid acquaintances than Mr Hope's heroes. Rassendyl is really nothing but a pasteboard pattern of manly attitudes to be struck in the act of doing one's duty under difficult circumstances, a figure motived by conventionalities, without individual will, and therefore without reality or humanity. If it were not for Mr Hope's light touch and sense of fun, the whole book would be as dull and mechanical a rigmarole of adventure as its last chapters. As it is, all the attempts to indicate the serious worth and rarity of the qualities which Rassendyl carries so lightly, bore and jar us by threatening to awake our common sense, which, if aroused, must immediately put a summary stop to the somewhat silly Ruritanian gambols of our imagination.

This weakness of characterization is perpetuated in the play with some added disadvantages. The liveliest character in the book is Captain Hentzau, because, though he is not a very possible scoundrel, at least his conduct is wilful, and not obviously made to order for the British Wholesale Association for the Supply of Moral Fiction. On the stage he acquires possibility, but loses fascination. The flimsiness of Rassendyl is terribly exposed by the footlights. The notion that in England every futile, harum-scarum, goodnaturedly selfish Johnny is a hero who only needs opportunity to display the noblest qualities, and have his hand kissed by veterans and high-souled ladies, is as popular, because as widely flattering, as that other idea that our yachts constitute a reserve fleet, and our shopmen a reserve army which in case of invasion would rush from behind the counter to hurl the foe back in confusion from the soil of England. It is, of course, pleasant to think that valuable qualities are dirt cheap in our own country; but I, unluckily, am constitutionally sceptical as to the heroism of people who never do anything heroic. However disgusting this cynicism of mine may appear, I noticed that Rassendyl pleased the audience at the St James's in all the passages where he appears as a reckless young gentleman impersonating the King of Ruritania for a lark, and rubbed it the wrong way in all his attempts to pose as a king of men. The only qualities needed for his exploit are impudence and the not very uncommon sort of dare-devilry that induces young men to risk breaking their necks at bodily exercises for the mere excitement of the thing. The real author and hero of it is Colonel Sapt, who risks his life as much as Rassendyl, besides taking his chance of the English stranger breaking down or backing out. All the anxiety is his, as well as all the serious purpose and contrivance. When he addresses the sham king as "You damned young fool!" for exposing himself idly to an unnecessary risk of discovery, the audience is sympathetic and satisfied. When he kneels down and kisses Rassendyl's hand in homage to the innate princeliness which that gentleman has in no wise displayed, it is impossible not to feel revolted. And there you have the false note of the play.

Perhaps the most serious consequence of this mistake is the Prologue. Mr Rose knows far too much about the theatre to suppose that the resemblance of Rassendyl to the King of Ruritania needed any explanation. An audience will always accept a resemblance with eagerness as a freak of nature. What Mr Rose wanted to do was to place Rassendyl under a moral obligation to risk his life for the red Elphberg because the red Elphberg's grandfather sacrificed his life for Rassendyl's grandmother. Now, I submit not only that the motive appeals to that bogus-kingly side of Rassendyl's character which had better have been left out, but that even so its compulsion is ridiculously unconvincing. If a gentleman were to ask me to lend him half a crown on the strength of a relationship based on the following circumstances:

9

to wit, that his grandfather had seduced my grandmother; fought a duel with my grandmother's husband, in the course of which he had been run through during a moment of inattention caused by the entry of the lady; declared with his last breath that he had died for her; and finally walked out of the house in his blood-stained shirt in apparently robust health, I should refer that gentleman to the Charity Organization Society.

Besides, Mr Rose has written the Prologue in the spirit of the nineteenth-century fancier of the eighteenth century rather than in that of the eighteenth century itself. It is a pomandering sort of Prologue, thrown in, not by dramatic necessity, but for the sake of hoops and patches, snuff-boxes and silk coats—above all, a duel by candlelight, without which no eighteenth-century drama would be complete. Mr Rose has often written pleasantly about these and other more remote and lavendery antiquities; but in giving way to them on the stage he has been beset by the temptation to lay the scene out not only for obsolete dresses and incidents, but for obsolete acting, and even obsolete drama. I should not be surprised to learn that he had pleaded hard with Mr Alexander to have a door knocked through the proscenium in order that Miss Mabel Hackney might enter through it with two black pages carrying her train, as the stage custom was in those days. The Prologue, in short, exhibits Mr Rose as the man of sentimental fancies and antiquarian learning rather than as the playwright. It will be useful as a curtain-raiser; but it is not essential to the comprehension or enjoyment of the play.

The play itself, as far as the novel will let it, brings into action Mr Rose's best qualities as a dramatist: his humor, his intelligence in the more generous issues of human feeling, and his insight, which is engagingly disabled—especially in the case of his feminine characters—by a certain shy anxiety to apologize to the lady for the intrusion, and present her with a favorable construction for what he has discovered. It is a thousand pities that the novel contained no figures sufficiently rounded and solid to make the drama really live. Still, unsubstantial as they are, they are superficially natural; and the play hops genially and adventurously along to the final speeches of Flavia and Rassendyl, which make a very pretty ending. A strong ending could only have been achieved by throwing the novel over, and changing the drunken imbecile of a king into an able but unlovable man, as whose consort Flavia might reasonably feel that her high destiny (rather a sentimental fancy, by the way, that high destiny!) would be better fulfilled than with the lovable but feather-brained Rassendyl.

The performance is a curiously haphazard one, considering its costliness and elaboration. Though the prevalent style of play is in the usual quiet St James's key, some of the characters rush on the stage supercharged with dramatic excitement, and momentarily upset all congruity of style. Mr Cautley or Mr Alexander will certainly either kill or be killed some night, unless the sabre fight at the end is more carefully preconcerted than it was on the first night. What is called the coronation scene—meaning the scene in which Rassendyl goes off the stage to be crowned and comes back when the ceremony is over—seems a very quiet little drawing room party business to a musical critic nursed on Le Prophète and the Wagnerian music drama; but it is enjoyable in its unsensational way. The dresses are recklessly expensive and not unhandsome. If I had never been taught to use my eyes as a critic of pictures, I might, perhaps, have been satisfied with the sunset scene in the forest of Zenda: as it was, the hopeless absurdity of the foreground light where Mr Alexander lay at the foot of the tree, set me speculating as to when some serious attempt will be made to produce any of the subtler effects of open air on the stage. The acting was mostly very easy. Mr Vernon, as Colonel Sapt, had the best part—indeed, in a sense the only part—and he left all the rest far behind in it. Mr Alexander was capital in the comedy passages, and delivered his speeches in the last scene finely, but was bad in the drunken episode, which he played like a seasoned teetotaller. The rest of his part, or rather parts, was the wrong side of Rassendyl, which nothing could make really effective. Mr Waring did what was possible to give an air of substance to the nullity called Duke Michael; and Mr Lawrence Cautley had not the material in his lines for producing the dashingly diabolical effect of the Hentzau of the novel. The truth is that half the company are doing nothing but "supering," although they are of course neither lineless nor nameless. Miss Millard has apparently taken the most heroic measures to transform herself into a true red Elphberg. She played with a touch of passion in the later scenes; but she was a little flat in the second act through her deficiency in comedy, her sense of humor resolutely refusing to express itself artistically. Miss Olga Brandon had nothing to do but embody the description of the Mayor's wife as a pretty woman; but though the part is nothing, Miss Brandon certainly got the last inch out of it, and something over, making more of her curtsey than a good many actresses make of a speech. Miss Lily Hanbury was fairly successful in grappling with Antoinette de Mauban; and Miss Mabel Hackney, not as yet a very finished executant, conceived her part in the Prologue excellently.

Mr Wilson Barrett has given me such unbounded delight by his feat of persuading the London critics that several of the most characteristic passages in his Sign of the Cross are quotations from the Bible that I have nothing but praise for him. Sterne's "tempering the wind to the shorn lamb" need never again be quoted as the champion instance of scripturization. It is true that Mr Wilson Barrett, following the universal law of art development, has founded his Sermon on the Mount to some extent on the original one; but I can assure the public that the text of The Sign of the Cross is essentially original; and if Mr Wilson Barrett writes to the papers to assure us, in the usual terms, that so far from his having taken his play from the Bible, he has never even read that volume, I am quite prepared to believe him. His literary style is altogether different. The play is a monument of sacred and profane history. The influence of Ibsen is apparent throughout, the Norwegian keynote being struck by Mr Barrett himself in the words: "How many crimes are committed under the cloak of duty!" With scathing, searching irony, and with resolute courage in the face of the prejudiced British public, he has drawn a terrible contrast between the Romans ("Pagans, I regret to say,"

12

as Mr Pecksniff remarked of the sirens), with their straightforward sensuality, and the strange, perverted voluptuousness of
the Christians, with their shuddering exaltations of longing for
the whip, the rack, the stake, and the lions. The whole drama lies
in the spectacle of the hardy Roman prefect, a robust soldier and
able general, gradually falling under the spell of a pale Christian
girl, white and worn with spiritual ecstasy, and beautiful as Mary
Anderson. As she gradually throws upon him the fascination of
suffering and martyrdom, he loses his taste for wine; the cour-
tezans at his orgies disgust him; heavenly visions obsess him; un-
dreamt-of raptures of sacrifice, agony, and escape from the world
to indescribable holiness and bliss tempt him; and finally he is
seen, calm and noble, but stark mad, following the girl to her
frightfully voluptuous death. It is a tremendous moral lesson;
and though I am pagan enough to dislike most intensely the
flogging and racking and screaming on the stage (I really am
such a bloodless creature that I take no delight in torture), yet
no doubt it helps to drive the irony of the theme home.

On the intellectual side, Christianity hardly receives justice
from Mr Wilson Barrett. "Christianity is not in itself a crime,"
says Marcus to Nero. "Marcus argues strongly, Cæsar," is
Poppea's comment. I must say I think Poppea is rather too easily
satisfied. But, after all, we do not want to hear the case argued at
this time of day. What we enjoy is being so familiarly in Rome
that it sounds quite natural when such directions to wayfarers
as "Fourth on the right from the statue of Hercules" are given by
the lictors. We come into the presence of Nero, and hear him
ordering a set of living torches for that evening, and boasting of
what an artist he is. We see the Roman ladies at home sticking
pins into their slaves, and the Roman diner-out exhausted by his
second vomit. We hear the thunder of the chariot race, and see
the gladiator enter the arena. And we have, as aforesaid, whips
and racks, chains and dungeons, uplifted crosses and Christian
martyrs, not to mention plenty of music well handled by Mr
Edward Jones, with hymns for the Christians, waltzes for the
Romans, and Sullivan's Thou'rt passing hence, my brother, and

13

Gounod's Nazareth on the cornet and sackbut between the acts.

The mounting is handsome, and the stage management good and unselfish, all the parts being played with quite extraordinary spirit, and in no way sacrificed to the actor-manager's. I have never seen better work got out of a company. Mr Wilson Barrett has honestly sunk the actor in the author, and done his best for the play, instead of for himself personally. Indeed, the one conspicuous and laughable oversight is in Mr Barrett's own make-up. Instead of wearing the proper cropped Roman wig, he wears his own hair in his old familiar feminine fashion, with the result that when he first steps on the stage he presents such an amazing resemblance to Miss Victor that, instead of applauding him, I stared with a shocked conviction that I had that lady before me in the costume of a Roman warrior. The effect is amusing; but it spoils an otherwise manly picture.

MICHAEL AND HIS LOST ANGEL

MICHAEL AND HIS LOST ANGEL. A new and original play of modern English life. In five acts. By Henry Arthur Jones. Lyceum Theatre, 15 January 1896.   [18 *January* 1896]

ONE of the great comforts of criticizing the work of Mr Henry Arthur Jones is that the critic can go straight to the subject matter without troubling about the dramatic construction. In the born writer the style is the man; and with the born dramatist the play is the subject. Mr Jones's plays grow: they are not cut out of bits of paper and stuck together. Mr Grundy or Sardou, at their respective worsts, perform such feats of carpentry in constructing show-cases for some trumpery little situation, that the critics exhaust all their space in raptures over the mechanical skill displayed. But Mr Jones's technical skill is taken as a matter of course. Nobody ever dreams of complimenting him about it: we proceed direct to abusing his ideas without delay. This is quite right and natural. If you invent a mechanical rabbit, wind it up, and set it running round the room for me, I shall be hugely entertained, no matter how monstrously unsuccessful it may be as a representation of nature; but if you produce a real rabbit which begins running about without being wound up at all, I simply say "Why shouldnt it?" and take down my gun. Similarly, on Mr Jones producing a live play, which starts into perfectly natural action on the rising of the curtain without being wound up during an act or two of exposition, I say "Why shouldnt it?" and, as aforesaid, take down my gun.

When I respond to the appeal of Mr Jones's art by throwing myself sympathetically into his characteristic attitude of mind, I am conscious of no shortcoming in Michael and his Lost Angel. It then seems to me to be a genuinely sincere and moving play, feelingly imagined, written with knowledge as to the man and insight as to the woman by an author equipped not only with the experience of an adept playwright, and a kindly and humorous observer's sense of contemporary manners, but with that knowledge of spiritual history in which Mr Jones's nearest competitors seem so stupendously deficient. Its art is in vital contact with the most passionate religious movement of its century, as fully quickened art always has been. On comparing it in this relation with the ordinary personal sentiment of Mr Grundy, and with those grotesque flounderings after some sort of respectably pious foothold which have led Mr Pinero to his rescue of the burning Bible from Mrs Ebbsmith's stove, and his redemption of Mrs Fraser by the social patronage of the Bishop's wife, I unhesitatingly class Mr Jones as first, and eminently first, among the surviving fittest of his own generation of playwrights.

But when, instead of throwing myself sympathetically into Mr Jones's attitude, I remain obstinately in my own, I find myself altogether unable to offer to Michael that final degree of complete sympathy and approval which is implied in the conviction that I would have written the play myself if I could. As to the first two acts, I ask nothing better; but at the beginning of the third comes the parting of our ways; and I can point out the exact place where the roads fork. In the first act Michael, a clergyman, compels a girl who has committed what he believes to be a deadly sin to confess it publicly in church. In the second act he commits that sin himself. At the beginning of the third he meets the lady who has been his accomplice; and the following words pass between them:

AUDRIE. Youre sorry?

MICHAEL. No. And you?

AUDRIE. No.

Now, after this, what does the clergyman do? Without giving another thought to that all-significant fact that he is not sorry— that at the very point where, if his code and creed were valid, his conscience would be aching with remorse, he is not only impenitent, but positively glad, he proceeds to act as if he really were penitent, and not only puts on a hair shirt, but actually makes a confession to his congregation in the false character of a contrite sinner, and goes out from among them with bowed head to exile and disgrace, only waiting in the neighborhood until the church is empty to steal back and privily contradict his pious imposture by picking up and hiding a flower which the woman has thrown on the steps of the altar. This is perfectly true to nature: men do every day, with a frightful fatalism, abjectly accept for themselves as well as others all the consequences of theories as to what they ought to feel and ought to believe, although they not only do not so feel or believe, but often feel and believe the very reverse, and find themselves forced to act on their real feeling and belief in supreme moments which they are willing with a tragically ridiculous self-abnegation to expiate afterwards even with their lives.

Here you have the disqualification of Michael and his Lost Angel for full tragic honors. It is a play without a hero. Let me rewrite the last three acts, and you shall have your Reverend Michael embracing the answer of his own soul, thundering it from the steps of his altar, and marching out through his shocked and shamed parishioners, with colors flying and head erect and unashamed, to the freedom of faith in his own real conscience. Whether he is right or wrong is nothing to me as a dramatist: he must follow his star, right or wrong, if he is to be a hero. In Hamlet one cannot approve unreservedly of the views of Fortinbras; but, generations of foolish actor-managers to the contrary notwithstanding, what true Shakespearean ever thinks of Hamlet without seeing Fortinbras, in his winged helmet, swoop down at the end, and take, by the divine right of a born "captain of his soul," the crown that slips through the dead fingers of the philosopher who went, at the bidding of his father's ghost, in search of a revenge which he did not feel and a throne which he did not want? Fortinbras can, of course, never be anything more than an Adelphi hero, because his bellicose instincts and imperial ambitions are comfortably vulgar; but both the Adelphi hero and the tragic hero have fundamentally the same heroic qualification— fearless pursuit of their own ends and championship of their own faiths *contra mundum*.

Michael fails to satisfy this condition in an emergency where a heroic self-realization alone could save him from destruction; and if this failure were the subject of Mr Jones's last three acts, then the play without a hero might be as tragic as Rosmersholm. But Mr Jones does not set Michael's situation in that light: he shares his fatalism, accepting his remorse, confession, and disgrace as inevitable, with a monastery for the man and death for the woman as the only possible stage ending—surely not so much an ending as a slopping up of the remains of the two poor creatures. The last act is only saved from being a sorry business by the man's plucking a sort of courage out of abandonment, and by a humorous piteousness in the dying woman, who, whilst submitting, out of sheer feebleness of character, to Michael's attitude, is apologetically conscious of having no sincere conviction of sin. When the priest offers his services, she replies, "No, thanks, Ive been dreadfully wicked—doesnt much matter, eh? Cant help it now. Havnt strength to feel sorry. So sorry I cant feel sorry." This gives a pleasant quaintness to the hackneyed pathos of a stage death; but it does not obliterate the fact that Audrie is dying of nothing but the need for making the audience cry, and that she is a deplorable disappointment considering her promise of force and originality in the first two acts. A play without a hero may still be heroic if it has a heroine; and had Mr Jones so laid out his play as to pose the question, "What will this woman do when she discovers that the saint of Cleveheddon is nothing but a hysterical coward, whose religion is a morbid perversion of his sympathetic instincts instead of the noblest development of them?" the answer of a capable woman to such a question might have given the last three acts the attraction of strength and hope, instead of their present appeal *ad misericordiam* of sentimental despair and irrelevant bodily disease. But Audrie, though she has a certain salt of wit in her, is as incapable of taking her fate into her own hands as Michael; and the two, hypnotized by public opinion, let themselves be driven abjectly, she to the shambles and he to the dustbin, without a redeeming struggle.

It is clear, I think, that if the public were of my way of thinking, the play, good as it is of its kind, would fail; for the public is not sympathetic enough to throw itself into Mr Jones's attitude, and enjoy the play from his point of view, unless it can do so without going out of its own way. And I cannot help thinking that the public dislike a man of Michael's stamp. After all, stupid as we are, we are not Asiatics. The most pigheaded Englishman has a much stronger objection to be crushed or killed by institutions and conventions, however sacred or even respectable, than a Russian peasant or a Chinaman. If he commits a sin, he either tells a lie and sticks to it, or else demands "a broadening of thought" which will bring his sin within the limits of the allowable. To expiation, if it can possibly be avoided, he has a wholesome and energetic objection. He is an individualist, not a fatalist: with all his apparent conventionality there is no getting over the fact that institutions—moral, political, artistic, and ecclesiastical—which in more Eastern lands have paralysed whole races, making each century a mere stereotype of the one before, are mere footballs for the centuries in England. It is an instinct with me personally to attack every idea which has been full grown for ten years, especially if it claims to be the foundation of all human society. I am prepared to back human society against any idea, positive or negative, that can be brought into the field against it. In this—except as to my definite intellectual consciousness of it—I am, I believe, a much more typical and popular person in England than

18

the conventional man; and I believe that when we begin to produce a genuine national drama, this apparently anarchic force, the
mother of higher law and humaner order, will underlie it, and
that the public will lose all patience with the conventional col-
lapses which serve for last acts to the serious dramas of today.
Depend upon it, the miserable doctrine that life is a mess, and
that there is no way out of it, will never nerve any man to write a
truly heroic play west of the Caucasus. I do not for a moment suspect Mr Jones of really holding that doctrine himself. He has
written Michael as a realist on the unheroic plane, simply taking
his contemporaries as he finds them on that plane.

Perhaps it is unfair to Mr Jones to substitute to this extent a
discussion of the philosophy of his play for a criticism of its
merits on its own ground. But the performance at the Lyceum
has taken all the heart out of my hopes of gaining general assent
to my high estimate of Michael and his Lost Angel. The public
sees the play as it is acted, not as it ought to be acted. The sooner
Mr Jones publishes it the better for its reputation. There never
was a play more skilfully designed to fit the chief actors than this
was for Mr Forbes Robertson and Mrs Patrick Campbell. But
though Mr Jones was able to write for Mrs Campbell such a part
as she is not likely to get the refusal of soon again, he had to depend on Mrs Campbell's own artistic judgment to enable her to
perceive the value of the chance. The judgment was apparently
not forthcoming: at all events, Mrs Patrick Campbell vanished
from the bills as the day of battle drew nigh. In such an emergency
your London manager has only one idea—send for Miss Marion
Terry. Miss Marion Terry was accordingly sent for—sent for to
play the bad angel; to be perverse, subtly malign, infernally
beautiful; to sell her soul and her lover's to the Devil, and bite
her arm through as a seal to the bargain; to do everything that is
neither in her nature, nor within the scope of her utmost skill in
dissimulation. The result was a touching little sham, very charming in the first act, where her entry rescued the play just as it was
staggering under the weight of some very bad acting in the opening scene; and very affecting at the end, where she died consider-

ately and prettily, as only an inveterately amiable woman could.
But not for the most infinitesimal fraction of a second was she
Audrie Lesden; and five acts of Michael and his Lost Angel without Audrie Lesden were not what the author intended. As to Mr
Forbes Robertson, Mr Jones had undertaken to make the actor's
outside effective if he in return would look after the inside of the
Reverend Michael. Mr Jones kept to his bargain: Mr Forbes
Robertson was unable to fulfil his. He made the mistake—common in an irreligious age—of conceiving a religious man as a
lugubrious one. All the sympathy in the first act depended on his
making it clear that the force that swept Rose Gibbard to the
altar to confess was the priest's rapturous faith in the gladness of
an open and contrite heart, natural to a man made over-sanguine
by spiritual joy. Mr Forbes Robertson threw away all this sympathy, and set the audience against him and against the play from
the outset by adopting the solemn, joyless, professional manner
and the preachy utterance of the Low-Church apostle of mortifi-
cation and wrath. It is quite impossible to exaggerate the disastrous effect of this initial mistake on the performance. The more
saintly Mr Robertson looked, the slower, gloomier, more de-
pressingly monotonous he became, until at last, in spite of Miss
Terry's spoonfuls of sweet syrup, I half expected to see the infuriated author rush on the stage and treat us to a realistic tableau
of the stoning of St Stephen. What is the use of the dramatist har-
monizing the old Scarlet-Letter theme in the new Puseyite mode
if the actor is to transpose it back again into the old Calvinistic
minor key?

As to the rest, their woodenness is not to be described, though
woodenness is hardly the right word for Mr Mackintosh, in whose
performance, however, I could discover neither grace nor verisimilitude. Miss Brooke need not be included in this wholesale
condemnation; but her part was too small to make any difference
to the general effect. The melancholy truth of the matter is that
the English stage got a good play, and was completely and igno-
miniously beaten by it. Mr Jones has got beyond the penny novel-
ette conventions which are actable in our theatre. I fear there is no

future for him except as a dramatic critic.

The play is well mounted, though the church scene is an appalling example of the worst sort of German "restoration." And it has the inevitable defect of all stage churches: the voices will not echo nor the footsteps ring through its canvas naves and aisles. Mr Forbes Robertson has been specially generous in the matter of the band. Mr Armbruster was able to give between the acts a genuine orchestral performance of the slow movement from Raff's Im Walde Symphony, and as much of the andante of Mendelssohn's Italian Symphony as there was time for.

CHURCH AND STAGE

[25 *January* 1896]

A LITTLE squall of controversy has been raised by the church scene in Michael and his Lost Angel at the Lyceum. It is contended by gentlemen who get their living by going to the theatre and reporting or criticizing performances there, that Church ritual, and indeed anything of a sacred character, is out of place on the stage, and its dramatic representation a breach of good taste and an offence against public decency. Let us see exactly what this means.

Of all the vile places on earth that are not absolutely contrary to law, the vilest is a convict prison. The vilest thing in the prison is the gallows; and the vilest thing done there is an execution. Yet the prison has its chaplain; and his prayers are an indispensable part of the disgusting business of hanging a man. The most heathenish and wasteful, not to say bestial civic celebration now tolerated is a City dinner. Men go there with the intention of eating too much and drinking too much; and many of them exceed their intention. But the proceedings always commence with the ritual called "grace before meat." For wrath and violence, terror and ferocity, on a scale of the most frightful magnitude, nothing can compare with a battle, especially when the victims are poor men tempted by a shilling a day to fight for the glorification of bloodthirsty fools and cowards who sit at home at ease and gloat over sensational "special correspondence." Yet no victory is complete without the "Te Deum" by which Christian combatants assume that their God is an accomplice in their crime, and praise Him for it. But, if you please, there is one lawful place worse than the gallows and the battlefield, one tolerated pursuit filthier than gluttony and more damnable than wholesale murder. That place is the theatre; that pursuit, playgoing. We may drag the symbols of our religion through seas of blood, waste, riot, and rapine, if only we spare it the final outrage of mentioning it on the stage of the Lyceum. If I am to accept this as good sense—if actors are infamous wretches prostituting themselves to the desire of the audience to indulge a detestable vice, then pray what am I, the critic, who sell myself to advertize such abomination by writing seductive descriptions and eulogies of the plays with which I am especially pleased? And what are those still more abandoned colleagues of mine who lard the managers with flatteries which even Mr Wilson Barrett's Nero might find a trifle hyperbolical? Clearly we are baser than Molière, to whom Christian burial was refused in France, baser than the ballet dancer to whom the Bishop of London refused the Sacrament (though this certainly occurred a few years before the knighting of Sir Henry Irving) by as much as the pandar is baser than his employer.

Let us look at the case from another point of view. It is said that "some things" are too sacred to be represented on the stage. The phrase "some things" is highly characteristic: it recalls the intelligent member of Parliament who supported the attempt to exclude the late Charles Bradlaugh from the House of Commons on the ground that "a man ought to believe in something or another." But since it is just as well not to be frivolously vague in speaking of sacred things, let us replace "some things" by the mysteries of religion, which is what the objectors would mean if, on this subject, they were earnest enough to mean anything at all. Pray what are the mysteries of religion? Are they faith, hope, love, heroism, life, creation; or are they pews and pulpits, prayer-books and Sunday bonnets, copes and stoles and dalmatics? Even that large section of the population of these islands whose religion

22

is the merest idolatry of material symbols will not deny that the former are the realities of religion. Then I ask the gentlemen who think that the pews and prayer-books are too sacred to be represented on the stage, why it is that they have never protested against the fact that all our dramas deal with faith, hope, love, and the rest of the essentials? The most sacred feelings and the holiest names are never long out of the mouths of our stage heroes and heroines. In the last Adelphi melodrama but two the heroine recited the service for the dead on the stage, whilst her father danced round her in a frenzy, trying to make up his mind to shoot her before the Indians took the place by storm. The critics who are protesting against the procession in the fourth act of Michael and his Lost Angel did not protest against that. Of course it is possible that they did not recognize it because Miss Millward did not wear a surplice during the passage, just as they mistook a homily of Mr Wilson Barrett's the other day for the Sermon on the Mount because the actor stood on a hill in a long gown, and gave it out like a clergyman reading the lessons. But I could easily find instances for which that unpresentable excuse cannot be alleged. The real objection to Mr Jones's play is the objection to Michael's treatment of religion as co-extensive with life: that is, as genuinely catholic. To the man who regards it as only a watertight Sunday compartment of social observance, such a view is not only inconvenient but positively terrifying. I am sorry for him; but I can assure him that the British drama is annexing steadily the territory on which he feels so uncomfortable. And whoever tries to obstruct that advance will be inevitably ground into the mud. When I want to exhibit the might of criticism, I may throw an express train off the line; but you do not catch me trying to stop the imperceptibly slow march of a glacier.

Yet another point of view. It is argued that a stage representation is only a pretence, a mockery, a sham, a thing made to simulate something that it is not by tricks of light and paint and feats of mimicry. Granted; but what, then, is to be said of the pictures in the National Gallery, in which canvas and colored clay are made to simulate, not only churches and priests, but the very persons

23

of the Trinity themselves? Is a crucifix an offence against the sacredness of what it represents? Are religious fictions, such as Barabbas and The Sorrows of Satan at one extreme, and Goethe's Faust at the other, to be suppressed? The Cromwellian Puritans would have said "Yes" to all this. Those of them who believed, like the Reverend Michael, that life and religion are coextensive, were for destroying, not only theatres, but images, pictures, statues, symbols, and simulations of all kinds. Those who held the more convenient watertight-compartment theory, thus dividing life into the sacred and profane, encouraged and rejoiced in profane art, but would not have sacred art on any terms. They would have family portraits, but no pictures of saints and virgins: they were musicians, but would not have music in church. They would have sacked the National Gallery, and burnt its most precious treasures in Trafalgar Square; and they actually did enter cathedrals, smash everything they could get at that was in the nature of statuary, pulled the organs to pieces, and tore up the music-books. In short, though they were too fond of art to want to exterminate it, they excommunicated it. Are our watertight-compartment critics willing to take the same line? Are they prepared to excommunicate art altogether, or do they wish to excommunicate the theatre only, leaving the cathedral, the picture gallery, the library, untouched? If so, this also involves them in the conclusion that some quite peculiar infamy and disgrace attaches to the theatre; and I am again compelled to submit that, since they have voluntarily chosen theatregoing as a means of livelihood, they fall under their own condemnation as infamous and disgraceful persons, unworthy as such to lead public opinion on this or any other matter. Having no such unfriendly opinion of them, I had rather coax them to retreat from their position than see them impale themselves on either horn of so inhuman a dilemma. For what alternative is left to them, except, perhaps, to follow the example of Sheridan Knowles by abandoning their profession and spending the rest of their lives in warning others against it?

The public, consisting as it does of many who do not go to the theatre, is in no way bound, as a critic is, to be loyal to it or else leave it. But the playgoing, art-supporting public may reasonably be called on to make up its mind whether religion is to be denied the services of art or not. Something may be learnt from past follies on this subject. Music, for instance, has always been highly privileged in the popular imagination. No other art has ever been conceived as practised in Heaven. Prophets may have been inspired to write books on earth; and St Luke is supposed to have painted a portrait of the Virgin; but who ever dreamt of easels and inkbottles, or typewriters, in Heaven? Yet what would Heaven be without its harps, and trumpets, and choir of angels? It was owing to this association of ideas that Handel met with no opposition when he popularized the oratorio. He gave us, in the concert-room, Samson and Delilah, and Manoah, and the rest of the persons in the Bible story; and no one was scandalized. But when Salvini came over here, a hundred and thirty years later, he found that Samson was out of the question in a theatre. The playgoing public was perfectly willing—and, indeed, highly curious—to see him walk off with the gates of Gaza, throw his father across his shoulder with one hand and carry him away, and finally perish between the pillars under a shower of dummy Philistines. But the people who never go to the theatre might have been offended; and so Samson had to be reserved for a much more Puritan country—America. Even music itself has had to make absurd concessions to pietistic prudery. Beethoven composed an oratorio called The Mount of Olives; and immediately the question arose whether the Handelian privilege extended to the New Testament. After about thirty years consideration we made up our minds the wrong way, and turned The Mount of Olives into Engedi, with David for the principal figure. Thirty years more, and the original work was performed at the Leeds Festival, with such complete impunity that it was evident the Engedification had been an act of gratuitous folly. We were kept for a long time out of one of the world's great possessions, Bach's St Matthew Passion, on the same grounds. If it had been an acre of blue dirt, with a few handfuls of trumpery diamonds in it, we should have

gone to war about it. Let nobody suppose that our ultimate
emancipation from these silly restrictions was the result of any
growth or change in public opinion on the matter. There was no
such growth and no such change. On the contrary, the sort of
people who were supposed to object to The Mount of Olives
when it was first performed as a Lenten oratorio at Drury Lane
in 1814 are much more numerous at present than they were then.
And they are just as free to stay away from performances they
disapprove of as they were then. The restrictions are always the
work of half a dozen busybodies, actuated less by cowardice than
by a desire to make an officious display of the undesirable quality
they call "good taste."

Goethe's taste being even worse than that displayed by Mr
Henry Arthur Jones in the fourth act of Michael and his Lost
Angel, he placed the scene of the prologue to his best known
drama, not in Cleveheddon church, but in Heaven itself, with the
Almighty conversing with Satan on easy terms, as in the Book of
Job. Some of our dramatic critics (especially those who are not
suspected of reading Goethe, and who see no difference between
the literary styles of St Matthew and Mr Wilson Barrett) will be
shocked at this, and will exult in the fact that no attempt was made,
or could have been made, to introduce the prologue on the English stage when the Lyceum Faust provided the opportunity. But
I, having graduated as a musical critic, can assure my colleagues
that I have seen this prologue repeatedly on no less English a
stage than that of Covent Garden, under no less respectable a
manager than Sir Augustus Harris. And nothing could have been
more English than the manner in which the scene was represented. There was a front cloth with clouds painted on it. In the
right-hand top corner (from the spectator's point of view) there
was a large hole irradiated with white light, and in the left-hand
bottom corner a similar hole, glowing with red light. Satan appeared bodily in the red hole and sang his speeches. Nothing but
the white glory could be seen through the higher rift in the
clouds; and the speeches were sung by the chorus, as in the case
of the words "Saul, why persecutest thou me?" in Mendelssohn's

oratorio. This has occurred as often as Boïto's Mefistofele has been performed; and I have not heard up to the present that any grave social consequences have ensued, or that any person has been shocked, hurt, injured, demoralized, or other than edified and delighted—except, perhaps, when the chorus sang flat, as choruses behind the scenes are apt to do.

When there is anything artistic to be done in England, all that is necessary is to do it as a matter of course without saying anything about it. If you raise the question whether it is permissible, there will be an outcry against it as impossibly scandalous, especially if it is something that has been done over and over again for hundreds of years. If the proprietors of the French Gallery had asked the leave of the British press and public before they exhibited Van Uhde's picture of Christ sitting in a room speaking to people in tall hats and frock coats, a horror-stricken prohibition would have been voiced by writers who would have tried their utmost to get a private peep at the picture. The proprietors of the French Gallery wisely said nothing. They exhibited the picture; and all the genuinely religious visitors were greatly touched and pleased by it. If any sculptor were to ask public permission to exhibit a figure of a lady or gentleman with nothing on at Burlington House, that permission would be sternly refused. But the thing is done every year without permission, and nobody is any the worse. The man who submits a moral syllabus of a work of art to the public is a fool. Submit the work of art itself, and then the public can judge. Of course, if they dislike it they will beat it with any stick they can lay hold of. If the drama of Michael had pleased the critics who imagined they were scandalized by the fourth act, Mr Jones might have introduced not only a consecration, but a baptism, a confirmation, a marriage, and a communion, as safely as the Adelphi authors introduced the service for the dead.

I do not lay down the law on this subject according to any canon of taste or theory of permissibility. I take things as I find them. I have seen not only Michael and his Lost Angel, but Parsifal at Bayreuth, and the Passion Play at Ober Ammergau. I found them good, and should be glad to see them brought within the reach of English playgoers. I have also seen Gentleman Joe; and I have no doubt that some of my colleagues whom Mr Jones has shocked would be glad to see that piece brought within the reach of Bavarian playgoers. And with this reminder that you cannot attack the freedom of the plays you do not like without equally endangering the freedom of those you like, and that it is better to tolerate the catholicly religious people who are claiming for the theatre its share in the common spiritual heritage than to put a weapon into the hands of the sectarianly religious people who would make an end of the theatre altogether if they could, I leave the subject until the next week in which there happens to be nothing else to write about.

DEAR HARP OF MY COUNTRY!

The Colleen Bawn; or, the Brides of Garryowen. Dion Boucicault's Great Drama (*sic*), in three acts. Princess's Theatre, 25 January 1896. [*1 February* 1896]

I have lived to see The Colleen Bawn with real water in it; and perhaps I shall live to see it some day with real Irishmen in it, though I doubt if that will heighten its popularity much. The real water lacks the translucent cleanliness of the original article, and destroys the illusion of Eily's drowning and Myles na Coppaleen's header to a quite amazing degree; but the spectacle of the two performers taking a call before the curtain, sopping wet, and bowing with a miserable enjoyment of the applause, is one which I shall remember with a chuckle whilst life remains.

When I imply, as above, that the Irishmen in The Colleen Bawn are not real Irishmen, I do not mean for a moment to challenge the authenticity of Mr Richard Purdon, who succeeds Dion Boucicault as Myles. Nor do I even accuse him of demonstrating the undeniable fact that the worst stage Irishmen are often real Irishmen. What I mean is that Dion Boucicault, when he invented Myles, was not holding the mirror up to nature, but blarneying the British public precisely as the Irish car-driver, when he is '"cute" enough, blarneys the English tourist. To an Irish-man who has any sort of social conscience, the conception of Ire-land as a romantic picture, in which the background is formed by the Lakes of Killarney by moonlight, and a round tower or so, whilst every male figure is "a broth of a bhoy," and every female one a colleen in a crimson Connemara cloak, is as exasperating as the conception of Italy as a huge garden and art museum, in-habited by picturesque artists' models, is to a sensible Italian. The Kerry peasant is no more a Myles na Coppaleen (his real name is Smith, or, at most, Ryan) than the real Wiltshire peasant is a Mark Tapley; and as for Eily, Dolly Varden as a typical English tradesman's daughter is a masterpiece of realism in comparison. The occupation of the Irish peasant is mainly agricultural; and I advise the reader to make it a fixed rule never to allow himself to believe in the alleged Arcadian virtues of the half-starved drudges who are sacrificed to the degrading, brutalizing, and, as far as I can ascertain, entirely unnecessary pursuit of unscientific farming. The virtues of the Irish peasant are the intense melancholy, the surliness of manner, the incapacity for happiness and self-respect that are the tokens of his natural unfitness for a life of wretched-ness. His vices are the arts by which he accommodates himself to his slavery—the flattery on his lips which hides the curse in his heart; his pleasant readiness to settle disputes by "leaving it all to your honor," in order to make something out of your generosity in addition to exacting the utmost of his legal due from you; his instinctive perception that by pleasing you he can make you serve him; his mendacity and mendicity; his love of a stolen advantage; the superstitious fear of his priest and his Church which does not prevent him from trying to cheat both in the temporal trans-actions between them; and the parasitism which makes him, in domestic service, that occasionally convenient but on the whole demoralizing human barnacle, the irremovable old retainer of the family. Of all the tricks which the Irish nation have played on the slow-witted Saxon, the most outrageous is the palming off on him of the imaginary Irishman of romance. The worst of it is, that when a spurious type gets into literature, it strikes the imagination of boys and girls. They form themselves by playing up to it; and thus the unsubstantial fancies of the novelists and music-hall song-writers of one generation are apt to become the unpleasant and mischievous realities of the next. The obsoletely patriotic Englishman of today is a most pestilent invention of this sort; and ever since the formation of the German Empire, the German has been dramatized with such success that even the Emperor spends most of his time in working up the character. Ireland, always foremost in the drama, may claim the credit of having invented the Irishman out of nothing—invented him without the stimulus of empire, national independence, knowledge of her own history, united population, common religion, or twopennorth of prestige of any sort, her very rebellions having only attained eminence by giving the national genius for treachery an opportunity of surpassing all recorded achievements in that important department of revolutionary politics. Fortunately the same talent that enabled Ireland to lead the way in inventing and dramatizing national types now keeps her to the front in the more salutary work of picking them to pieces, a process which appeals to her barbarous humor on the one hand, and on the other to her keen common sense and intelligent appreciation of reality. Of course it sacrifices the advantages which the imposture secured, as I have good reason to feel; for nobody can be better aware than I am of the convenience to an Irishman in England of being able, by an occasional cunning flourish of his nationality, to secure all the privileges of a harmless lunatic without forfeiting the position of a responsible member of society. But there is a point at which shams become so deadly tiresome that they produce ungovernable nausea, and are rejected at all risks. There are signs that Ireland, never very tolerant of the stage Irishman within her own coasts, is disaffected to him even in the literature by which her scribes habitually impose on England and America. Quite lately a London publisher, Mr Arnold, sent me a novel with the suggestive title of Misther O'Ryan, who turned out to be the traditional blend of Myles na Coppaleen, Robert Emmett, Daniel O'Connell, Thomas Moore, Fin McCoul, and Brian Boru, as

30

compounded and impersonated by a vulgar rascal—an Irish Silas Wegg—whose blackguardism and irremediable worthlessness the writer, evidently that very rare literary bird, an Irish author living in Ireland, had sketched with a vengeful zest that was highly refreshing and, I should say, very wholesome just at present. Take any of the pictures Balzac or Maupassant have painted for us of the spiritual squalor of the routine of poor middle-class life, in which the education, the income, the culture of the family are three-quarters abject pretence; and you will not find it more depressing and even appalling than those which break through the usually imaginative atmosphere of Mr T. P. O'Connor's reviews when the book in hand happens to touch Irish life. I shewed my own appreciation of my native land in the usual Irish way by getting out of it as soon as I possibly could; and I cannot say that I have the smallest intention of settling there again as long as the superior attractions of St Helena (not to mention London) are equally available; but since I cannot disguise from myself the helpless dependence of the British Empire on us for vital elements of talent and character (without us the English race would simply die of respectability within two generations), I am quite ready to help the saving work of reducing the sham Ireland of romance to a heap of unsightly ruins. When this is done, my countrymen can consider the relative merits of building something real in the old country, or taking a hint from that other clever people, the Jews, and abandoning their Palestine to put on all the rest of the world as a shepherd putteth on his garment, beginning with English journalism and American politics as a convenient intermediary stage to soften the transition from their present habits.

These considerations, though they bear more or less on the performance at the Princess's, are not absolutely indispensable to a reasonable enjoyment of it. I have always had a special respect for Mr Richard Purdon because his father was Lord Mayor of Dublin when I was an impressionable boy; and I am, therefore, probably apt to overrate his talent as a comedian. Still, I can see that his Myles is not the inimitable Myles of Dion

Boucicault. It is a case of the words of Mercury being harsh after the songs of Apollo. Boucicault had a charming brogue: not even the speech of the eminent journalist and M.P. named in a former paragraph of this article is more musical in sound or irresistible in insinuation—"sloothering" would be the right word, were it current here—than his. But Mr Purdon unhappily did not learn to speak in Galway or Kerry. He bewrays the respectable Dublin citizen, whose knowledge of the brogue is derived from domestic servants drawn chiefly from the neighboring counties, and corrupted by the tongue of Dublin itself, which, like all crowded capitals, somehow evolves a peculiar villainous accent of its own. With such opportunities Mr Purdon, having a strong sense of fun, and being a born mimic, has no difficulty in producing a brogue; but it is not a pretty one. Further, his voice, a little coarsened, perhaps, by many years' vigorous exploitation in the interests of the aforesaid sense of fun, which seems unchastened by any very vigilant sense of beauty, is rougher than that of the late author. He has to omit the song in which Boucicault effortlessly persuaded us to accept the statement that "old Ireland was his country, and his name it was Molloy," as a complete and satisfying *apologia pro sua vita*. And the attempt to humbug Father Tom is an obvious and blundering evasion instead of what it used to be—an artless outpouring of the innocence of a poor lad who had not the wit to understand what the priest was asking, much less tell a lie to his reverence. Boucicault was a coaxing, blandandhering sort of liar, to whom you could listen without impatience long enough to allow the carpenters time to set the most elaborate water-scene behind the front cloth. Mr Purdon is just half a trifle too grating and boisterous, though of course the generation which does not recollect Boucicault hardly feels this. On the other hand, Miss Beaumont Collins is a much better Eily than Mrs Boucicault, who now plays Mrs Cregan, used to be. Mrs Boucicault was always hopelessly ladylike, and usually made Hardress Cregan's complaints of her rusticity ridiculous by being more refined than he. Miss Collins speaks the part, which is really an engaging and almost poetic one, very prettily, and is always right about the feeling of it. Mr Cockburn does nothing with Father Tom; but as the character happens to suit his personality, his performance passes, and is even highly praised. Mr Tom Terriss does capitally for Hardress, besides being in earnest about his work, and so sustaining the reputation of his name. Miss Agnes Hewitt does all that can be done with the part of Anne Chute, an Irish edition of Lady Gay Spanker, and therefore one of the dreariest of Boucicault's pet vulgarities. Miss Clifton as Shelah, and Messrs Kenney and Rochelle as Corrigan and Danny Mann, were fully equal to the occasion, though Danny did not shew any of Charles II's sense of the tediousness of a prolonged death agony. Mrs Boucicault's competence in the stagey work to which Mrs Cregan is condemned goes without saying. The play, as a whole, in spite of an obsolete passage or two, and of the stupid mutilations imposed by the censorship of its day, is so far superior to the average modern melodrama, that I shall not be surprised if it repays the management handsomely for reviving it.

I regret to say that the patrons of the gallery at the Princess's, being admitted at half the usual west end price, devote the saving to the purchase of sausages to throw at the critics. I appeal to the gentleman or lady who successfully aimed one at me to throw a cabbage next time, as I am a vegetarian, and sausages are wasted on me.

I see that Mr Charles Hudson, the Tigellinus of Mr Wilson Barrett's Sign of the Cross, has written a long letter in defence of that play against the adverse opinion of an eminent colleague of mine. I hope that his example will be followed. Not only ought actors to write occasionally, so as to shew the critics their ideas of dramatic criticism; but the critics ought to act from time to time, so as to shew the actors their notions of acting. If Mr Hudson perseveres for a few years he will make a fair average critic. At present he is hardly abreast of the times. He tries, for instance, to catch the fashionable tone by speaking of Ibsen's dramas as unclean and indecent. That is quite out of date now: it belongs to the period when Mr Hudson was distinguishing himself by creating the part of Ulrik Brendel, in Rosmersholm. One has to be careful about these little things at first; but the trick of them soon comes. Go on, Mr Hudson: go on improving us, even chastening us: we are always willing to be instructed.

Michael and his Lost Angel, the best play its school has given to the theatre, has been withdrawn. And Mr Forbes Robertson has improved the occasion at the Playgoers' Club. After eloquently paraphrasing an interesting circular recently issued by Miss Dorothy Leighton, of the Independent Theatre Society, he goes on to say: "I would ask dramatic authors to continually remind themselves that a play is not finished, not complete, when the last word is written at the desk. A play must have an audience, must be acted, or it is no play." How true! There can be no doubt that Mr Forbes Robertson is right; that the three things necessary are the play, the audience, and the acting. At the Lyceum Mr Jones supplied the play; and the public eagerly supplied the audience. There was something missing; but why ask the dramatic author about it, since the deficiency did not occur in his department?

ANOTHER FAILURE

THE FOOL OF THE FAMILY. A new and original comedy in three acts. By Fergus Hume. Duke of York's Theatre, 30 January 1896. [8 *February* 1896]

THE tragically sudden disappearance of The Fool of the Family from the stage is attributed by the management to the failure of the play to please the public. Alas! plays are not so easily got rid of on that account, in spite of an apparent instance at the Lyceum, as to which I shall have something particular to say presently. I suspect that a favorable opportunity of letting the Duke of York's Theatre had more to do with the fate of The Fool of the Family than the feelings of the public, not to mention those of the performers and the author. However, the play was not what one would call brilliant. Some of the scenes

exhibited a foolish middle-aged spinster making love to a handsome young man, who submitted to her caresses with many wry
faces, and finally consented to marry her for her money. About
a dozen people laughed: the rest of the audience stared with stony
disfavor. What they felt I do not know: as for myself, I was
disgusted; and I beg Mr Fergus Hume and all other authors
whom it may concern to remember that modern audiences are not
so callous in these matters as those forbears of ours with whom,
a century ago, the merciless marriage scene in Hogarth's Rake's
Progress passed as a comic picture. Otherwise the piece, in spite
of sundry makeshifts and absurdities, rattled along inoffensively
enough, not carrying ballast enough to be heavy. Mr Cartwright,
made up so as to present a convulsing resemblance to the Editor
of the Daily Chronicle, enjoyed, as far as I was concerned, a
sort of *succès de scandale*. To me, the gentleman who was kissing
Miss Lena Ashwell, or conversing fatuously with a sentimental
bulldog, or getting himself locked up in a safe full of diamonds,
or sallying forth from hiding-places in bedrooms to snatch at
glasses of whisky-and-soda, and being always baffled in the
attempt, was not Mr Charles Cartwright, not Peter Adolphus
Grison, but Mr H. W. Massingham, the pillar of Nonconformity,
the holder of the scales between the Old World and the New,
the hammer of Rhodes, the monitor of the Liberals, the editorial
Man of Destiny. So strong was the illusion, that when he at last
went to the length of drinking ardent spirits out of a large
tumbler, I was on the point of rising to remonstrate with him
for thus recklessly throwing away a reputation dear to the forces
of Temperance in this country. Even when I recollected myself,
the question rose in my mind repeatedly whether this thing
should be allowed—whether it was lawful for one man to assume
another's aspect, as Siegfried assumed Gunnar's, and blast his
fair fame by doing things incompatible with the public's high
ideal of him. It was appalling to see how aptly Mr Massingham's
personality adapted itself to the proceedings of Peter Grison—
how naturally he handled that siphon and spirit bottle, how
inevitably he kissed Kitty Trevor. Before the 30th of last month

I could no more have conceived Mr Massingham doing such things than I can now conceive the Archbishop of Canterbury doing them: since then I find it difficult to imagine him doing anything else. I ask, Has a man no property in his own personal appearance; or is his character to be at the mercy of the accidents of an actor's make-up—for I of course do not suggest that Mr Cartwright did it on purpose? Which of us can feel sure that he will not be the next victim?

Mr Cartwright is prodigiously better in comedy than in the melodramatic business which he more usually affects. The very fact that he is always within a hair's breadth of dropping into the hollow resonance and pumped-up emotion of what he regards as his serious style (a classification which I find myself unable to endorse) forces him to play in comedy with exceptional discretion, and to place his effects with remarkable nicety. What he lacks is the true comedian's faith in comedy. He may think a little of it all very well for the first act; but clearly he will die in the belief that when it comes to the really important point of the play he must sink his voice to the evangelical diapason, and be locked up in a safe to discomfit villainy or rescue beauty in distress. This is fundamentally a lack of faith in human intelligence. I do not blame an actor for it: a life spent in contemplating the folly and childishness of playgoers is enough to destroy the staunchest belief in the shrewdness of Voltaire's Mr Everybody. But it is dangerous to know that the average playgoer is a fool unless you also know that there is, somehow, hardly any surer way to failure than by treating him according to his folly. When I was a child, certain persons used to adapt themselves to my childishness by talking in what they thought a childish way to me; and I remember how I resented and despised that unbecoming and offensive imposture. They all made the same mistake. Instead of being natural, in which condition they would have been quite childish enough to put me at my ease, they affected imbecility—a very different thing to childishness, and open to instant detection by any sane infant. I cannot help thinking that Mr Cartwright, during his joint-managership of the Duke of

York's Theatre with Mr Dana, has not kept a firm grip of this distinction. Instead of seeking for dramatists who share the limitations of the public sufficiently to be able to do their very best and most earnest work without getting over the heads of the gallery, he seems to have fancied that the same result can be arrived at by cleverish literary men purposely slackening their wits and writing down to their notions of the popular level. At least I see no other explanation of the fact that the plays which have failed at the Duke of York's Theatre have failed because they were imbecile at precisely those points where the author obviously set himself to be popular at any price. I wish I could persuade not only managers, but all persons concerned with works of art, that a fifth-rate man doing his best will always beat a second-rate man doing less than his best. I leave the first-rate man out of the question; for it is one of the conditions of being first-rate that you cannot do less than your best even if you try.

Mr H. B. Irving, who is now, I presume, the only Mr Henry Irving on the stage, appeared in The Fool of the Family as a burglar, disguised as an elderly musical enthusiast for the purpose of obtaining a foothold in the crib he ultimately cracked. By an odd remnant of stage convention, when the moment came for operating on the safe, he changed his dress for the symbolic costume, something between that of a ratcatcher and a convict, by which the draughtsmen of the comic papers still indicate the housebreaker. Suppose Mr Willard had done this in The Silver King in 1882! Would not London have laughed at such a quaint relapse into barnstorming conventions? Yet here we are, a whole theatrical epoch later, invited to pay west end prices to witness melodrama abyssmally inferior to The Silver King, played by an Irving who signifies that he is impersonating a burglar by putting on a dress as purely conventional and remote from real life as that of a harlequin. The phenomenon suggests uneasy reflections as to the possibility of a rapid reversion to primitive types, culminating in the production of Maria Martin, or the Murder in the Red Barn, at the Lyceum, whilst amateur dramatic clubs, on the Browning Society model, will get up occasional

37

precarious performances of the unacted masterpieces of Jones, Pinero, and Grundy.

Mr Irving, by the way, is the son of his father in allowing a certain boyish freakishness of imagination to lead him to decorate his part with Mephistophelian exultations which are but obscurely, if at all, connected with the drama. Not that I protest against this. It is such a mercy to find an actor with any sign of imagination nowadays, that I should be the last person to disparage even the most eccentric manifestations of it. Where one does *not* recognize Mr Irving's parentage is in such utterances as "a wordle ookn nakshonmaybetrayus," which is really not good English, much less good Irvingese.

But the fact is, the diction of our stage is becoming appalling. Even well-known mispronunciations are now quite common. One of the most familiar traps for a speaker is the word "exemplary," once pretty safe on the stage because of a line in Bulwer Lytton's Richelieu which would not scan unless the word were pronounced correctly with the stress on the first syllable. Dramatic authors have taken a fancy to it of late; and now, Richelieu being forgotten, I hear "ex*em*plary" in all directions. "Lu*dick*rous" is another flower of speech which I lately heard from a leading lady. Now I quite agree that this, by itself, does not matter in the least. I go further: I hold that the man who regards an intelligibly spelt or prettily uttered word as "wrong" because it does not conform to the dictionary is a congenital fool. I therefore do not cite these instances as faults; but I do offer them as corroborative evidence of my general indictment against young actors, that they do not study diction. It is natural enough that the young generation should refuse any longer to part with his hard-earned guineas merely to be taught by some relic of the old school to pronounce wrongly, and to generally corrupt, vulgarize, and denaturalize themselves; but it does not follow that the only alternative to misguided study is no study. I do not see why I, a mere critic with a very superficial knowledge of phonetics, should so often find myself noting on my program slips in diction which my dislike of pedantry and personality prevents me from publishing, made by people whose profession it partly is to teach me to speak finely. I have found Danish actors of twenty-two much more highly trained in this respect than many English actors of forty. Any virtuosity we happen to get comes mostly by imitation of born artists who seek distinction of speech by instinct. Of straightforward study and practice of the alphabet—which is what the whole fine art of speech stands on—there are no signs. Thus, if you hear a young actress articulating well, you will generally soon catch her pinching her vowels—especially the English "a"—in such a fashion as to shew that she is simply imitating Mrs Patrick Campbell. If a young actor substitutes pure vowels for diphthongs, he generally also reinforces his voice by the nasal resonance that betrays the imitator of Sir Henry Irving, though he may naturally have a voice as independent of any such artifice as Mr Terriss's or Mr Bernard Gould's. The horrible genteel convention, by which very pleasant and welcome Welsh, Scotch, Irish, Canadian, and other varieties of speech disguise themselves in an unendurable mincing in which "a" becomes "é" and "o" becomes "ow," is a commonplace of middle-class snobbery, fortified by the example of Mr Hare, the only actor who has succeeded in giving an artistic character to it. I admit that nothing can be less desirable on the stage than for every one to speak exactly like everyone else, which is, of course, the logical outcome of imitation, and of the common academic systems as taught in Conservatoires and by Mr Vincent Crummles; and for that reason the public is right in thinking that ordinary talking, provided it be audible and intelligible, is preferable to "the traditions"; but to conclude that unmitigated colloquialism is essential to variety and sufficient for artistic purposes is to overlook two facts. First, that it is easy to take a group of artistic speakers whose speech, far from being alike, supplies the strongest contrasts—say, Miss Marion Terry and Mrs Patrick Campbell, Sir Henry Irving and Mr Bernard Gould, Mr Hare and Mr Vernon, Signora Duse and Madame Bernhardt—but who have, nevertheless, arrived at identical conclusions as to the elements of diction. Second, that without

39

a highly cultivated sense of beauty of speech and a trained athleticism of execution, it is absolutely impossible to perform poetic, heroic drama effectively. It is a mistake to suppose that if a company can perform Caste it can also perform Coriolanus. The disability may not matter as long as the public is delighted with Caste and tired of Coriolanus; but it becomes a serious matter for the untrained actor when the pendulum of popular taste swings to the opposite end of its arc.

I am not sure that I have not been provoked into this digression as much by Miss Lena Ashwell as by Mr H. B. Irving. Miss Ashwell may be regarded as the heroine of The Fool of the Family; for nobody else appears to have gained anything by it, whereas she unquestionably did add substantially to her reputation by her very clever and attractive performance as Kitty Trevor. The author, I am afraid, meant her to be an entirely inartistic hoyden; but she defeated that inglorious project by being a very artistic one, with plenty of feeling behind the fun, and with a brightness and grace that reminded one occasionally of Miss Ada Rehan's earlier achievements in romping farce. But I wish Miss Ashwell would remember that there are short vowels in the dictionary as well as long vowels. "Fascination" is an excellent word; but when it is pronounced with the first vowel so long that the second syllable has to be omitted to make room for it, it becomes somewhat overpowering. "Pawpialr" is charming: I would not for worlds have Miss Ashwell let it down into "popular"; only I wish I could feel sure that she does it on purpose.

Miss Gertrude Kingston was condemned to impersonate that most exasperating of all the melodramatic impossibilities—the wicked woman who remembers what she once was, much as landladies are apt to remember better days. I wish Miss Kingston a speedy engagement with some manager who may have at least an elementary idea of how to make use of her.

By the way, the mystery of Michael and his Lost Angel deepens. The withdrawal of the play on the tenth night left us all under the impression that it had disastrously failed; and this result seemed to me so curious and so deplorable that I have just seized an opportunity which presented itself of making myself acquainted with the exact figures. It would be a breach of confidence for me to give these figures; but I may be permitted to say that I found, to my great astonishment, that the smallest audience drawn produced only a few shillings under a hundred pounds; that the average for the ten nights was close upon £150; and that the business was increasing steadily during the week in which the play was withdrawn. In the face of these facts, I find it extremely difficult to believe—and experts in theatrical business will share my difficulty—that Michael and his Lost Angel was withdrawn for purely business reasons. As to the real reason, I do not know it; and I am so afraid that, with my romantic imagination, I shall begin guessing at it in spite of myself if I do not immediately break off, that—

THE TAILOR AND THE STAGE

[15 *February* 1896]

AMONG the announcements for the forthcoming season I find one concerning an entertainment of Living Pictures to be given at St George's Hall in the first weeks of May. Mr Coote and his supporters need not be alarmed: far from being an exhibition of nudities, these pictures, it is promised, will be an exhibition of dress, including the dress of the future as well as that of the present and of the past. Indeed, the pictures of the eighteenth century, of medieval Italy, of ancient Greece, and so on, are evidently only to lead up to the real point of the enterprise—the pictures of the twentieth century. The artists will be Mr Walter Crane, Mr Henry Holiday, Mrs Louise Jopling, Mr Lasenby Liberty, and Mr G. A. Storey, R.A., who come forward to justify the ways of the Healthy and Artistic Dress Union. The aims of this Society I infer from its title, having no further acquaintance with it than an occasional glimpse of its illustrated fashion journal of twentieth-century modes, called Aglaia.

I need not say what wild hopes such an enterprise raises in an unfortunate dramatic critic at a period when actors and actresses are little more than walking fashion-plates. The actor, in particular, with his carefully ironed new trousers, and his boots conscientiously blacked on the sole underneath the arch of the foot, is a curiously uncomfortable spectacle. The interest and fascination of dramatic storytelling are so intense that the most nonsensical stage arrangements, provided they are customary, or even the entire absence of scenery and historic costume, can be overcome by ever so little real drama and real acting. But in our theatres at present there is so seldom either drama or acting that I find myself compelled to study the adjuncts of the drama in order to prevent myself publicly and scandalously going to sleep at my post. I have gradually come to regard the leading man in a play as a set of applied tailor's measurements; so that, if anyone were to get up an exhibition of clothes worn by popular actors, I would undertake, without consulting the catalogue, to point out which suits were Mr Lewis Waller's, which Mr George Alexander's, which Mr Coghlan's, and so on; whereas if I were to meet these gentlemen themselves in a swimming-bath, I should probably not recognize them. This does not mean that the clothes are characteristic of the men: it means that the clothes have usurped the men's place. In moments of passion the men rebel: Mr Waller, for instance, who never escapes from the tyranny of the Maddox Street tailor (at least I have never seen him in a costume-play), always shews strong feeling on the stage by biting his lips and making a determined attempt to escape from his cloth prison at the wrists and ankles. I remember once, when he was astonishing the audience by a moment of almost passionate intensity of feeling, hearing a lady in the stall behind mine exclaim, "How wonderfully Waller is coming out!" She was perfectly right: he was coming out almost to the elbows; and the action conveyed to me irresistibly the actor's sense that if he could only come out of his tailor's tubes altogether, he could shew the audience what a real man was like—which is the essence of acting. Take another example—Mr Alexander in The Prisoner of Zenda. In the first act (not the prologue) he appears in fashionable tourist costume, with a soft hat, thus enjoying the utmost concessions the west end tailor makes to humanity even in holiday-time. But the suit effaces the man literally at every turn. The man has knees and elbows (the fact is proved in the other acts); but the suit says, "I have no knees and no elbows; and the man who gets inside me and sits down near the fire with his arms bent murders me." The trousers consent to repress the fickle flexibility of the human leg every evening for a couple of hours only on condition of re-forming themselves on the stretcher during the other twenty-two, it being understood, of course, that the wearer will always be gentleman enough to recognize the necessity of lacing his boots first and putting on his trousers afterwards. Mr Alexander has been hardened into iron by these rigorous terms. He has carried to an extraordinary degree the art of doing without his knees and elbows; and I have no doubt that the comparative coldness of his style is due to his keeping carefully away from the fire. Hence his pre-eminence among leading gentlemen. But wait for the third act of The Prisoner of Zenda, where Rassendyl appears in an undress tunic. The suit of clothes is changed into a man; the name of Alexander springs into meaning and denotes force and personality; the actor looks alive all over as well as at the fingers and lips (an indecency which it is the great object of modern stage training to avert); he drops ten years of his apparent age; his spirits rise; he gambols about; he enjoys his part; and when the curtain falls and he returns to his dressing room, he flatly refuses to resume his chains, and plays the last act boldly in his shirt-sleeves.

The more a human being is an artist by temperament, the more intolerable to him is the hampered movement and sartorial pre-occupation of the modern gentleman. My main reason for adopting literature as a profession was, that as the author is never seen by his clients, he need not dress respectably. As a stockbroker, a doctor, or a man of business, I should have had to wear starched linen and a tall hat, and to give up the use of my knees and elbows. Literature is the only genteel profession that has no livery—for even your painter meets his sitters face to face—and so I chose literature. You, friendly reader, though you buy my articles, have no idea of what I look like in the street—if you did, you would probably take in some other paper. Now if the tyranny of fashion is intolerable to the author, whose art is not one of personal display, what must it be to the actor, whose art is all personal display? As I have said, the more he is a born artist, the less he is at home in modern fashionable attire, and the more effective he is in a rational and artistic dress. Let me again illustrate from our stage. Mr Forbes Robertson is a painter as well as an actor. Mr Bernard Gould is that eminent black-and-white draughtsman, Mr J. B. Partridge; and for all I know, he may be an eminent sculptor, architect, and goldsmith under three other names. Now Mr Forbes Robertson as a modern gentleman is a deplorable spectacle; but as Romeo, in a dress designed by himself, he is handsome; and as Lancelot, in a fifteenth-century Italian costume designed by Burne-Jones, he is a St George: you hear the women in the theatre gasp with pure admiration when he appears. As to Mr Gould, I invite those who have seen him as Biron in Love's Labour's Lost, as Pierrot in De Banville's Le Baiser, as Ulrik Brendel in Rosmersholm (a mere matter of a riding-coat and top-boots), or even in the indifferent Bulgarian uniform of Sergius Saranoff in Arms and the Man, to go to the Criterion Theatre, and contemplate him as the fashionable seducer in Mr Carton's adaptation of L'Ami des Femmes. His whole aspect seems to say, "How can you expect me to seduce anybody in this confounded frock-coat and this idiotic collar and scarf? They dont give a man a chance."

I might easily multiply instances. Try to conceive what our notion of Sir Henry Irving as an actor would be if we had never seen him dressed otherwise than as a fashionable doctor. Consider why the most commonplace harlequin in a provincial panto-mime is so much more lively and expressive in his action than a west end actor-manager in a modern play. No matter where you pick your illustration, you will be driven to the same conclusion: namely, that the art of acting is half strangled by the fashionable tailor. Obviously this is not the tailor's fault. He will make you a tunic and a pair of knee-breeches or knickerbockers just as willingly as a coat and trousers, if you give him the order. Why do you not give him the order? The answer must take the shape of a profound disquisition on morals and civilization.

Now that we are nearly done with the nineteenth century, it can hurt no one's feelings to remark that it has been one in which the leading faculty has been the business faculty, and the leading ambition the attainment of unprecedented riches. Functional adaptation has worked towards capitalism rather than towards art or religion. We have kept up an air of supporting the arts by substituting respectability for the beauty of life, regularity of arrangement for the beauty of form, laundry work for beauty of color, historical interest for beauty of theme, and so on. If you take a man in whom this substitution has been completely effected by deliberate precept and social environment (as far as such dehumanization is possible), and present to him a fabric which drapes in graceful folds and is beautiful in color, he will immediately pronounce it eminently unsuitable for use as a dress material. The folds are irregular, and therefore disreputable; the color is sensuous, and therefore immoral; the general effect appeals to the individual, idiosyncratic preference, and is, therefore, eccentric and in bad taste. Only, if the color be a very bright primary one—say bright scarlet or yellow—which will shew the least speck of dust or weatherstain, and will not, like the tertiary colors, soften and actually take on a new beauty as it wears, he will admit its suitability for uniforms to be worn on State occasions. But for everyday wear absolute perfection means to him shiny black and shiny white—the absence of color with the maximum of surface polish, the minimum of drapery, and the most conclusive evidence of newness and washedness. At first his great difficulty was with his shirt, because folds and even outrageous crumplings were unavoidable if it was to be worn at all. But, at all events, a part of the shirt could be stiff, like a cuirass. So he took a piece of linen large enough to cover his chest, and at first, not realizing that it only needed original-ity and courage to immediately attain his ideal of no folds at all, arranged the folds in perfectly rectangular parallel rows, by

45

means of his great invention of box-plaiting. Down the middle, as a last concession to the traditions of the chemise, he affixed a frill, like a row of textile parsley. Thus he produced the British Islanders' shirt-front. In his delight with it, he attached sleeves and a body; starched it within an inch of its life; put it on, with a complete clergyman's suit over it; and, restless with joy, walked about, sat down, got up, and even stooped. On removing the suit, he of course discovered that the shirt was all crumpled except the front. He therefore cut a large window out of his waistcoat, through which the uncrumpled part of his master-piece could be viewed, and cut the coat away so as not to obstruct the window. And then he was in evening dress. Later on he discarded the row of parsley; the box-plaits went next; the button-holes were reduced from three to one by the more logical spirits; variegated studs gave way to the colorless diamond or even the vapid mother-of-pearl; and finally the shirt was buttoned behind, leaving the front so unbrokenly perfect that poets and artists could not behold it without longing to write a sonnet or draw a caricature on it.

Meanwhile, the hatter and the tailor had been at work. They had observed that the human body presents two aspects—the flat and the cylindrical. They accordingly applied planes and cylinders of shiny black to it; and lo! the frock-coat, the trousers, and the tall hat, correctly named "Cylinderhut" by the Germans. The bootmaker was baffled by Nature in applying this formula; so he adapted the human toes to the simple and regular form of a bishop's mitre, and so produced, with the help of Day & Martin, the fashionable boot.

There are persons who affirm that the cylinder hat and trousers are the most comfortable, convenient, useful, and natural coverings for the legs and head, and that on this ground they can never be displaced by the fads of dress reformers. Some of these persons know no better: others, I regret to say, are hardened and intentional liars, as you may see by their sporting suits the moment they escape from the scrutiny of London to the license of holiday life in the country. Respectability in dress is happily breaking down at a fairly rapid pace now. First the shirt-front was reduced to absurdity by its own act in asserting an independent existence as a dickey. Then it went into paper, and in that vulgar material outshone its original whiteness and shininess. Then it condescended to celluloid, so that the wearer might keep it up to the mark with his nailbrush whenever he washed his hands. Then certain women took to wearing it; and instantly the dormant sense of beauty in man woke up and saw that it was horribly ugly. Then science began to hint, as far as it could do so without compromising its social position, that starch and blacking are not material forms of cleanliness—that, if you come to that, they are material forms of dirt, destructive to the dead leather of our boots, and unhealthy for the live leather on our chests. Dr Jaeger made the ungentlemanly but irrefragable remark that the verdict of the nose was against the black and white ideal of purity; and on that shrewd hit he established the cult of all-wool, White bread and black boots were challenged by brown bread and brown boots. A sub-sartorial revolution went on in underclothing; and the bolder spirits are now beginning to discard what they formerly only dodged. The bicycle "caught on"; and the man of forty discovered that it was possible to pass for thirty in knickerbockers. And so, to make a long story short, we have come to the right moment for Living Pictures from the year 1925 (say) by the Healthy and Artistic Dress Union. I respectfully recommend them to the attention of our "leading gentlemen" of the stage as a possible chance for them to persuade the public that the prevalent notion that they cannot act is but an illusion produced by their tailors.

TWO PLAYS

JEDBURY JUNIOR. A light comedy in three acts. By Madeleine
Lucette Ryley. Terry's Theatre, 14 February 1896.

ON 'CHANGE. A comedy in three acts. Adapted by Eweretta
Lawrence from the German of Von Moser. (A revival.) Strand
Theatre, 15 February 1896.   [22 *February* 1896]

I WISH some manager would nerve me to my weekly task by
producing either a very good play or a very bad one. The plays
that unman me as a critic are those which are entertaining without being absorbing, and pleasant without being valuable—
which keep me amused during an idle hour without engaging
my deeper sympathies or taxing my attention—which, in short,
would be excellent value for half a crown in a summer theatre in
the Park, if only that agreeable German institution would make
haste to advance with us beyond the Olympian and Wild West
stage of development. It is in dealing with such plays that the
critic is apt to forget the immense difference between his economic relation to the theatre and that of the playgoer. A critic
not only gets a seat in the best part of the house for nothing, but
is actually paid for sitting in it. The effect of this on him is highly
complex. Whether the net result is to make him more exacting
than the ordinary playgoer, or less, seems a simple question; but
the answer varies from play to play, and from stalls to gallery.
It varies even with the age of the play and of the critic; for an
experienced critic is often as sulky over a new development of
the drama as a skilled workman over a new machine or process;
whilst a freshman is equally apt to form wild hopes of the new
thing merely because it is new: both sides investing it with imaginary faults and qualities by pure association of ideas, without
the smallest reference to the unfortunate author's text. In most
cases I should say that the critic, whatever he may say in print
for the sake of a quiet life, is less easily pleased than the rest of
the public. But with reference to the particular sort of play now
in question, I am not so sure. His verdict, if based on the fact that

he finds the piece worth seeing, may differ very materially from a verdict based on the experience of the man who has to turn out from a comfortable house in the suburbs, and make his way to the Strand with his wife, and perhaps his daughters, at a cost of half a guinea a head, plus travelling expenses, or else to wait on a cold and wet night at the doors to secure a not very advantageous or luxurious seat in the cheaper parts of the house. It seems to me that a play must have a very strong element of interest in it, or a performance a very strong element of fascination, to induce a rational person to spend the evening so expensively or uncomfortably as it must be spent at a theatre; and I have seen play after play which would have been accepted cheerfully as excellent pastime on moderate terms, shunned by the public because the terms were not moderate. The last time I paid half a guinea for a stall was to see Duse play Magda. I paid it without hesitation, though I had already seen the performance (for nothing) in my professional capacity. But if you ask me whether I would pay half a guinea to see an average London play with an average London cast, I shall have the greatest difficulty in conveying a negative sufficiently emphatic to do justice to my feelings without the use of language inconsistent with my dignity.

These reflections have been suggested to me by the two comedies produced last week, Jedbury Junior and On 'Change. Both are pleasant enough in their way; but they are not fascinating, not important: the playgoer who misses them will miss nothing but an evening's amusement. If the prices ranged from one shilling for the gallery to five shillings for the stalls, I should say that both plays were excellent value for the money. As it is, I prefer not to give my opinion from that point of view. Even if you wish to know which of the two plays is the better worth going to, I must point out to you that the prices charged are not the same, except to the stalls and gallery, which are, as usual, half a guinea (a monstrous charge) and a shilling respectively. The intermediate charges are, at Terry's, seven and sixpence, six shillings, four shillings, and two and sixpence; at the Strand, six, four, three, and two shillings. That is, the prices at Terry's are higher. You will naturally conclude that the play at Terry's is better, the cast stronger, the theatre warmer, more comfortably seated, and nearer the railway station. The facts do not bear out these inferences. On the contrary, as far as there is any difference, the play is worse, the cast weaker, the theatre colder, less comfortably seated, and farther from the railway station. It is a mistake to look for logic in such things. The fact that there comes every now and then a play which makes a fortune in spite of all drawbacks, leaves every manager obsessed with the hope of chancing on that play, and convinced that nothing can materially help him if he misses it, or hinder him if he hits on it.

Jedbury Junior is a flimsy, almost schoolgirlish, work, redeemed by the happy notion of the Fuegian marriage, which proves fertile in funny complications, and by a great number of amusing lines, for which the author, one guesses, probably supplied the opportunity rather than the actual text. She has a strong sense of fun, and ridicules everybody over forty, and most people under it, with much vivacity. Her young man is a remarkably good-hearted and affectionate young man; and her young woman, as might have been expected, has a touch of reality; but the serious passages between the other characters are, to say the least, jejune. It is impossible to expatiate on the acting, since, save the young man and young woman aforesaid, none of the parts present any difficulties upon which one dare compliment an actor of good standing. Mr Beauchamp, Mr Playfair, and Mr Farquhar are amusing, Mr Farquhar having the best of it as a butler who bowdlerizes and translates into diplomatic language the messages which his master and mistress, not being on speaking terms, charge him with in one another's presence. Mr Kerr is more determined than ever to be an antidote to Ibsen; he is frank, manly, wholesome, and English to an overpowering degree—so unaffected in his speech, too, that when he follows Miss Millett's vanishing form with his honest eyes, and says "She's gorn!" a tear of sympathy with this good-hearted Johnny blurs the vision and softens the heart. In fact, Mr Kerr has got in Jedbury Junior what every actor-manager demands from the drama-

tist: that is, an outrageous caricature of himself. At no point does
the part get beyond his familiar routine; and though I enjoy that
routine as much as anybody, I cannot reasonably be expected to
deal with it as with the creation of a new character. Miss Maude
Millett is more fortunate. For years it has been her fate to provide "comic relief" in couple with Mr Sydney Brough, or some
other fellow-victim. She, too, has a routine which I know by
heart. I am always glad to see her; and she generally makes me
laugh once or twice; but to say that I look forward to her entrance with either hope or fear, or leave the theatre after her exit
pondering on what I have seen, and resolving to be a better man
in future, would be simply to tell a breath-bereaving lie. Happily, as Dora Hedway, the most human character in this flippant,
stuck-together-anyhow little play, she gets an opportunity of
acting, and seizes it with complete success. Probably she will not
enjoy another for ten years to come; so, before she is thrust back
into comic relief, I recommend all her admirers to haste to see
her in the last act of Jedbury Junior.

'On Change, a revived play, was new to me, as far as a piece
made up of such stale material could be new. At all events, I had
not seen it before; and I was duly captivated by Mr Felix Morris's
impersonation of the Scotch professor. For an old and often-
repeated performance it is surprisingly delicate and unexagger-
ated. The working up of the quarrel at the end of the first act by
Mr Morris and so skilful an old stage hand as Mr William Farren
is an excellent piece of business, and produces the best "curtain"
in the piece. I warn Mr Morris, however, that he had better hide
his gifts carefully if he wishes to keep constantly before the public. I know no surer way of avoiding engagements on the stage
at present than to know your business. On 'Change is an exceptional play in respect of its bringing into action at least four
gentlemen who can act. Besides Mr Farren and Mr Felix Morris,
there is Mr Yorke Stephens. He, as we all know, is capital in a
part which happens to fit him like a glove—the war correspon-
dent in Held by the Enemy, Dick Rusper in The Crusaders,
Captain Bluntschli in—I forget the name of the play, but no

matter. But Joe, in On 'Change, does not fit him like a glove; on the contrary, it would be difficult to imagine a part more foreign to his characteristic style and personality than this translation into English of the conventional German, warm-hearted, hard-working, cheerful, simple, unfashionable clerk, a good son and affectionate wooer—a provincialized, Teutonified variant of the Kerresque Johnny, in short. Yet Mr Yorke Stephens, through the mere effect of inevitability produced by the smartness, address, and grace of a skilled and disciplined actor, gets through his unsuitable part, not only without having his appropriateness challenged at any moment, but with every appearance of having been expressly born to play it. Finally, Mr James Welch is in the cast, revelling in the part of the Scotch philosopher's cockney landlord with fearful thoroughness. I say finally, because Mr E. H. Kelly's much-laughed-at performance as De Haas is not acting: it is only tomfooling, which is a different matter. The part, it must be admitted, does not allow of much else; still, it is no worse than much of the stuff allotted to the others. Miss Eweretta Lawrence gives the American version of the conventional serio-comic love scene very prettily in the third act—fortunately for the play, which is rather deficient in feminine interest. Only, that dangerous business with the matches made me nervous. The weak spot in the cast is Mrs Burnett, who should be played by an elderly actress with a strong comic talent for hen-pecking. The lady who plays it at present declines to conceal the fact that she is young and pretty. She is, I take it, more anxious to avoid being cast for such parts in future than to secure the success of the play.

The first piece at the Strand, Mr Louis Parker's Man in the Street, though it is not new, should not be missed, as Mr Welch has worked up his character-sketch of the old vagabond Jabez Gover to an extraordinary pitch of completeness and intensity. At Terry's the curtain-raiser is a very ordinary sentimentality called An Old Garden, by Hill Davies, which is pulled through by Mr W. J. Robertson and Miss Mona Oram with conscientious sincerity and force.

One of the most remarkable pieces of realistic acting I have seen lately has not been on the stage, but on the concert platform, by Miss Beatrice Herford. Miss Herford, with the aid of a chair, pretends to be a lady with a child in a tramcar, a shop-girl, a dressmaker hired out by the day, and a maddeningly fidgety old lady in a train. Very ordinary entertainer's business, apparently —until you see it. Miss Herford began by amusing me, and ended by appalling me. But for her occasional jokes, and her funny and clever pantomime, I should, so to speak, have changed carriages, so faithfully did she reproduce the ways of irritating people. If Miss Herford goes on the stage, we shall not be at a loss for a successor to Mrs John Wood.

PINERO AND GRUNDY ON G. B. S.

GOSSIP. A play in four acts. By Clyde Fitch and Leo Dietrich-stein. Comedy Theatre, 22 February 1896.

THE ROMANCE OF THE SHOPWALKER. A new and original comedy. By Robert Buchanan and Charles Marlowe. Vaudeville Theatre, 26 February 1896.

THE THEATRICAL WORLD OF 1895. A reprint of Mr William Archer's criticisms of the drama during last year. With a prefatory letter by Arthur W. Pinero. London: Walter Scott. 1896. [29 *February* 1896]

I MUST retire politely before Gossip at the Comedy. An excellent play of its kind (no doubt), it is hardly the class of work I am retained to criticize. If Mr Comyns Carr were to reopen the Grosvenor Gallery with a collection of the chromolithographs given away with the Christmas numbers of our illustrated papers for the last twenty years, I should willingly go and study the exhibition as a conspectus of the history of popular art during that period. But if he were to engage a third-rate artist to produce a composite plagiarism of them all, and exhibit that as a new work of art, I should carefully stay away. Similarly, if he were to undertake a series of revivals of all the successes of the Hare-Kendal and Bancroft managements in the seventies and eighties, I should

undoubtedly profit by an attentive study of them. But to produce a hash of them, made by a couple of playwrights of no very
striking attainments, as the latest enterprise of a first-rate west
end theatre, is really a rather uninteresting thing to do. If Mrs
Langtry's force were in the least a comic force; if she had the
double-edged genius of Mrs Kendal; if she were even Miss Lottie
Venne or Miss Fanny Brough, both of whom she imitates by
snatches; were it possible to feel as curious to see her apart from
her art as it was to see the Jersey Lily of twenty years ago, I
might perhaps have found Gossip tolerable. None of these conditions being fulfilled, I was heavily oppressed, and should not
have endured to the end but for Miss Calhoun, who played admirably as Mrs Stanford. The dresses and diamonds were, to me,
dreadful. I can enjoy looking at a woman who is characteristi-
cally dressed by herself, or affectionately and beautifully dressed
by an artist; but fashionable ladies hung with the trophies of their
tradesmen are among my strongest aversions; and it seemed to
me that this was the effect deliberately aimed at in Gossip. The
parade of jewellery was especially disappointing after the stealing of Mrs Langtry's jewels. I have always felt sure that the theft
was the work of some dramatic critic determined to get rid of
that ugly colorless glitter at all costs; but what is the use of stealing Mrs Langtry's diamonds when she purchases or hires a fresh
set next day?

The authors announce on the playbill that they "have made
use of several suggestions found in a novel by Jules Claretie."
I can only say that if they had made use of several suggestions
to be found in these columns, they would not have written the
play at all. Oh, that goody-goody Amurrican husband—a Wall
Street King Arthur (Tennysonian species)! And oh, that young
wife who was about to run away from him when she was reminded of her own mother and her own chee-yild! Oh my goodness! It *was* dull.

There is one notable use to which Gossip may be put. Evidence has been accumulating for a couple of years past that however dangerous it may be to go ahead with the drama, it is still

more dangerous to attempt to escape by going back. The two policies are fairly exemplified in the production of The Benefit of the Doubt, followed by the production of Gossip at the same theatre. I hope Mr Comyns Carr, when the run of Gossip is over, will publish the returns from both plays, so that we may see whether the back track really leads to the gold-mine.

The annual reprint of Mr William Archer's dramatic criticisms —always an interesting event, and specially so now that it deals with a year in which Bernhardt and Duse contended with one another part to part—is extra-specially interesting to me this time because of its remarkable preface by Mr Pinero. At first I could not make out what Mr Pinero was driving at: page after page brought forth nothing but an amusing bogus autobiography. I call it bogus on two grounds. First, because it contains not a word about Mr Pinero himself, his personality, his views, his hopes and fears for the drama, or anything else distinctively Pinerotic. It might be the autobiography of an insurance canvasser, for all the internal evidence to the contrary. Second, the particulars that it does contain as to Mr Pinero's lodgings and landladies, his hotels, his luggage, and the topography of Edinburgh, are not, on strict examination, credible. On this point my judgment may err; but can the reader expect me to believe such stories as that of the boy who said to the eminent dramatist, "The governor dragged me up one dirty lane and down another, and pointed out this hovel and that, and had some tale to tell almost of the very cobbles in the streets, *until he just upon bored me to suicide*"? If a boy exists who has so completely mastered the secret of Mr Pinero's dialogue, I say produce him, name him. There is no such boy. He is an invention; and as the man who will invent one thing will invent another, I reject the whole autobiography as the merest wantonness of fiction.

But, I shall be asked, is it to be believed that Mr Pinero has written over twenty pages of realistic romance out of pure impishness, to enjoy a laugh in his sleeve at Mr Archer and the public? By no means: the whole autobiography is only a dramatist's device for gathering the attention of the readers of the preface so as to enable him to impart a momentous secret to the public with the fullest dramatic effect. And what is the secret? No less than that Mr Pinero does not read *my* criticisms.

I dont believe it.

Let me again submit the matter to the judgment of the reader. Mr Pinero, after declaring that for a fortnight after the production of one of his plays he reads nothing but The Mining Journal, proceeds as follows (I italicize the phrases on which my case is founded): "One of the flaws of my system is that it robs me of the privilege of reading *much brilliant writing*. For instance, I am compelled, by my system, wholly to abstain from studying those articles upon dramatic matters contributed to a well-known journal by your friend Mr G***** B****** S***—*of whom I protest I am, in general, a warm admirer*." Very well then, how does he know that my writing is brilliant? How can he be a warm admirer of an author he never reads—unless his admiration is excited solely by my personal appearance? Such an affectation would not impose on a baby. Besides, look at the collateral evidence. Consider the enormous improvement which took place in his work between The Notorious Mrs Ebbsmith, written before my dramatic articles had been in currency long enough to produce any effect, and The Benefit of the Doubt, written when I had been in the field for a whole year! What other cause can be assigned for this beneficent change that was not equally operative between The Second Mrs Tanqueray and The Notorious Mrs Ebbsmith—a period of temporary decline? None—absolutely none. And yet I am to be told that Mr Pinero reads The Mining Journal instead of The Saturday Review! Stuff! Why, Mr Pinero is one of the most conspicuous of the very, very few playwrights we have who are more interested in the drama than in mines.

To clinch the matter, I adduce the evidence of Mr Sydney Grundy, who actually declares that Mr Pinero is "marching to his doom" through immoderate indulgence in the luxury of reading criticisms. There is no mistaking the vehemence, the anguish almost, of his tone. "My dear Pinero, make no mistake. These fawning first-nighters have no following: these fulsome news-papers represent nobody's opinion outside a newspaper office. You are superior to the newspapers. Dont listen to them; but make them listen to you. *If need be, fill your ears with wax, and bind yourself to the mast; but steer your own course, not theirs.* You will lose nothing: they will soon return to your heel." This is not the language of a man accustomed to see Mr Pinero austerely passing over The Saturday Review, the World, and the Speaker, and burying himself in the columns of The Mining Journal.

There is none of Mr Pinero's coquetry about Mr Grundy, whose article (in The Theatre for March) is well worth reading, if only for its repeated and affectionate references to myself. Mr Grundy quotes me as "the crankiest of the stove-pipe fanatics." I do not precisely catch the bearing of the stove-pipe epithet. There is evidence in the article that Mr Grundy has studied my costume too carefully to suppose that I wear a stove-pipe hat. Perhaps he means that instead of consuming my own smoke in decent privacy, I fuliginously obscure the clear atmosphere of the "well-made play" with it. So I do; but what then? A man must live. If I like my own plays, and Ibsen's, and Shakespear's, and Goethe's, and Labiche's, and Moliere's better than The Late Mr Castello and Les Pattes de Mouche, why should I not say so, considering the freedom with which gentlemen of the opposite persuasion offer *their* opinions? All the same, I do not approve of the heartlessness of Mr William Archer, who has gone on the war-path against Mr Grundy, and tomahawked his arguments, scalped his figures, burnt his facts alive, and insulted their ashes with taunting demands for the production of the returns from Slaves of the Ring, Mr Castello, and so on, in order to compare them with the returns from the later Pinero plays. This is bar-barous, and only serves superfluously to establish the fact that Mr Grundy has no case—as if anyone supposed that he had. For my part, I find Mr Grundy's article lively reading, and quite as sensible as most of my own. Only, I would humbly ask Mr Grundy whether he really finds these well-made "mechanical rabbit" plays which he champions so very succulent? Does he ever go to see them, for instance, except when he writes them himself? Depend on it, he has not been inside a theatre for ten years except on his own business. If he had to go as often as I have, he would lose his verdant illusions as to the ravishing superiority of Delia Harding to The Wild Duck or As You Like It.

I was so sternly reproved for my frivolity in rather liking The Strange Adventures of Miss Brown, that I hardly dare to confess that I got on very well also with The Shopwalker. I am as well aware as anybody that these Buchanan-Marlowe plays (Marlowe is a lady, by the way) are conventional in the sense that the sympathy they appeal to flows in channels deeply worn by use, and that the romance of them is taken unaffectedly from the Alnaschar dreams of the quite ordinary man. But allow me to point out that this sort of conventionality, obvious and simple as it seems, is not a thing that can be attained without a measure of genius. Most of the plays produced in the course of the year are attempts to do just this apparently simple thing; and most of them fail, not because they aim at realizing the vulgar dream, giving expression to the vulgar feeling, and finding words for the vulgar thought, but because, in spite of their aiming, they miss the mark. It seems so like missing a haystack at ten yards that many critics, unable to believe in such a blunder, write as if the marksman had accomplished his feat, but had bored the spectators by its commonness. They are mistaken: what we are so tired of is the clumsy, stale, stupid, styleless, mannerless, hackneyed devices which we know by experience to be the sure preliminaries to the bungler's failure. Now Mr Buchanan does not miss his mark. It is true that he is so colossally lazy, so scandalously and impenitently perfunctory, that it is often astonishing how he gets even on the corner of the target; but he does get there because, having his measure of genius, it is easier to him to hit somewhere than to miss altogether. There is plenty of scamped stuff in The Shopwalker: for example, the part of Captain Dudley is nothing short of an insult to the actor, Mr Sydney Brough; and a good half of the dialogue could be turned out by a man of Mr Buchanan's literary power at the rate of three or four

58

thousand words a day. Mr Pinero or Mr Jones would shoot themselves rather than throw such copious, careless, unsifted workmanship to the public. But the story is sympathetically imagined; and nearly all the persons of the drama are human. One forgives even Captain Dudley and Lady Evelyn as one forgives the pictures of lovers on a valentine. Mr Buchanan does not count on your being a snob, and assume that you are ready to sneer at the promoted shopwalker and his old mother: he makes you laugh heartily at them, but not with that hateful, malicious laughter that dishonors and degrades yourself. Consequently there is, for once, some sense in calling a popular play wholesome. All I have to say against The Shopwalker is that there is hardly any point on which it might not have been a better play if more trouble had been taken with it; and that a little practical experience of the dramatic side of electioneering would have enabled the authors greatly to condense and intensify the scene in the last act, where the shopwalker, as parliamentary candidate, produces his mother. It is a mistake, both from the electioneering and poetic point of view, to make Tomkins merely splenetic at this point: he should appeal to the crowd as men, not denounce them as curs. However, Buchanan would not be Buchanan without at least one incontinence of this kind in the course of a play.

The acting is excellent, Mr Grossmith, with all his qualities in easy action, being capitally supported by Miss Victor, Miss Nina Boucicault, and Mr David James. Miss Palfrey improves, though not quite as fast as she might if she gave her mind to it. Miss Annie Hill is satisfactory as Dorothy Hubbard, but has not much to do. The other parts are mere routine.

I shall have to contain myself until next week on the subject of the new Lyceum play, adapted into English blank verse by Mr Davidson from M. François Coppée's Pour la Couronne, a work which is, from the literary point of view, an alexandrine wilderness, windy, barren, and platitudinous to the last degree, but which contains several moving and effective situations. The first night was enormously successful; and Mrs Patrick Campbell reigns again in splendor. But more of that anon.

THE RETURN OF MRS PAT

FOR THE CROWN. A romantic play in four acts, done into English
by John Davidson, from François Coppée's Pour la Couronne.
Lyceum Theatre, 27 February 1896.   [7 *March* 1896]

HAVE you observed, reader, how almost every critic who praises
For the Crown thinks it necessary to apologize for the fifteenth
century? Fancy sane men trying to extenuate a guarantee of
beauty! However, since that appears to be the proper thing to do,
let me be in the fashion. Yes, there is no denying it: Mr Forbes
Robertson wears a caftan instead of a frock-coat, and an exquisite
martial cap of metal and ivory instead of a masterpiece by Lin-
coln & Bennett. Mrs Patrick Campbell's dresses are not made
by Worth: no controversy can possibly arise over her sleeves:
worst of all, she does not once appear in a hat. It is true, on my
credit—four acts, and not one hat. Playgoer: be generous. Overlook this: they mean well, these people at the Lyceum. But what
can you expect from an actor who is a painter, and an actress who
is a musician?

For the Balkan Mountains and Bulgaria no apology is necessary. Honor to whom honor is due! I—I who pen these lines—
first rooted the Balkan mountains on the English stage in Arms
and the Man—I first saw the immense dramatic possibilities of
Bulgaria. And—let me confess it—I cannot help feeling a little
sore that the work of adapting La Couronne was not entrusted
to me on this account. I feel that I could have given that
heroic tale a turn which Mr Davidson, with all his inspiration,
has missed.

Somehow, I find I cannot bring myself to pass over this ridiculous apologizing for the fifteenth century with a mere ironic
laugh. What does it mean? It is not the puerile chaff which the
modern revival of artistic and religious feeling provoked earlier
in the century, when our journalists and comic-opera parodists
were too ignorant and callous to be ashamed to jeer like street
boys at the pre-Raphaelite and Wagnerian movements, until even

George Eliot, though on the materialist side herself, protested indignantly against "debasing the moral currency." All that ribaldry is obsolete: nobody now dreams of sneering at Mr Forbes Robertson as "æsthetic," or conceives that to compare him to a medieval hero-saint, in "stained glass attitudes" or otherwise, would be anything but a high compliment to him. And yet there is the unmistakeable vein of apology and deprecation, if not about the costumes and scenery, at least about the play. And here we have the secret of it. The apologetic critics are thinking, not of the golden age of the arts and crafts, but of the later horrors of historical drama in five acts and in blank verse, which no more belong to the sensuously artistic fifteenth century than to the religiously artistic fourteenth century, or the sanely, humorously artistic thirteenth, since they are in fact a characteristic product of the rhetorical, intellectual, idealistic, inquisitive, logical, scientific, commercial, essentially anti-artistic period which we count as beginning with the sixteenth century, and in which we trace, not the beautiful growth and flowering of the arts, but their consummation and devastation in the giant hands of Michael Angelo and Shakespear. Those who desire to rejoice in Shakespear must confine themselves (as they generally do) to reading his own plays. Read those which have been written since he overwhelmed English dramatic poetry with his impossible example, and you will wish that he had never been born.

In order to write a true dramatic poem, one must possess very deep human feeling. In order to write historical drama in rhetorical blank verse, one only need possess imagination—a quite different and much cheaper article. Shakespear had both in an extraordinary degree: consequently his rhetoric, monstrous as much of it is, is so quickened by flashes and turns of feeling that it is impossible to be bored by it; whilst his feeling expresses itself so spontaneously in rhetorical forms that at the climaxes of his plays rhetoric and poetry become one. And so, since his time, every poor wretch with an excitable imagination, a command of literary bombast, and metric faculty enough to march in step, has found himself able to turn any sort of thematic material, however woodenly prosaic, into rhetorical blank verse; whereupon, foolishly conceiving himself to be another Shakespear, he has so oppressed the stage with yards upon yards and hours upon hours of barren imagery, that at last the announcement of a new historical play in verse at a London theatre produces an involuntary start of terror among the critics, followed by reassuring explanations that although it *is* a fifteenth-century business (more or less), it is really not so bad after all.

François Coppée, as a Frenchman, has not caught the rhetorical itch in its full Shakespearean virulence; but unfortunately the milder form in which it afflicts him is duller than the English variety by just as much as Racine and Corneille are weaker than our immortal William. Therefore Mr Davidson, as a countryman of Shakespear's—or, at any rate, of Macbeth's—has felt bound to prepare La Couronne for the English stage by intensifying the sublimity of its balderdash to an extent which no audience unaccustomed to Shakespear would stand without amazement and laughter. Accordingly Miss Winifred Emery, having to convey to us that she is somewhat bored, is condemned to do so by shrieking for the Balkan Mountains to move, and the Day of Judgment to dawn, with nothing to sustain her in this vortex of academic nonsense except the silly popular delusion that there is something fine in it all—a delusion which I will not insult her intelligence by assuming her to share. I need say no more about this aspect of the play beyond mentioning that wherever Mr Davidson has attempted to outdo M. Coppée in rhetorical folly, he has easily succeeded. I admit that the heightened effect proves, on the whole, that when you set out to be nonsensical, the more nonsensical you are the better. But fifty million lines of such stuff will not extract from me an admission that the writer is a dramatist, much less a poet. The utmost I will concede is that since poets so great as Shakespear and Shelley did not escape the infection, we must forgive Mr Davidson for it, though only, I hope, on the distinct understanding that it is not to occur again.

Unfortunately for the liveliness of the play, M. Coppée's power of imagining ready-made heroic situations and characters is not fortified by any power of developing them. Bazilide and Michael Brancomir never get beyond the point at which they are first dumped on the stage: they keep saying the same things about themselves and one another over and over again until at last the spectator feels that the play would be greatly improved if most of it were presented by accomplished pantomimists in dumb show. The second act—the Lady Macbeth act—is especially wearisome in this way. A Turkish spy forces the hand of Bazilide by the masterly argument that if Michael Brancomir does not betray his country somebody else will—probably the scullion. Bazilide passes on the argument to Michael, improving the scullion into a horseboy. But poor Michael is quite unable to get any forwarder with his conventional compunction, whilst Bazilide is equally at a loss for any idea except the horseboy, on whom she falls back again and again, the whole conversation being strung up to concert pitch of absurdity by the monstrously tall talk in which it is carried on. The pair prance as if they were bounding over the Alps; but they do not advance an inch. One has only to think for a moment of Lady Macbeth tempting Macbeth, or Iago tempting Othello, to realize how comparatively stupid the poet is, and how, of all methods of marking time, the most futile is to mark it in blank verse. Even in the striking scene of the parricide, there is hardly a human note struck, except in the preliminary chat between the sentinel and the shepherd, which is a welcome relief after Bazilide's fustian. When the catastrophe approaches, father and son do not rise for a moment into any human relation with one another. The more terribly the emergency presses, the more literary do they become, taking it by turns to deliver tearing apostrophes to heaven, hell, honor, history, hope, memory, Christianity, the fatherland, the past and the future; each waiting with great politeness until the other has finished, the audience meanwhile watching patiently for the fight and the finish. In short, except as a display of rhetoric for the sake of rhetoric—a form of entertainment which is chiefly interesting as the only known means by which an author or speaker can make the public respect him for unmercifully boring it—the play has no value apart from the force of the main situation and the charm of the pretty love scenes between Militza and Constantine.

The acting, though full of matter for the critic, is mostly but poor sport for the lay spectator. Miss Winifred Emery was not well advised to accept the part of Bazilide. The original Bazilide of Coppée is a passably credible Bernhardtian wicked woman of the stage, corseted into alexandrines, but not bombasted and hyperbolicized out of all humanity, like the pen-and-ink monster Mr Davidson has produced in the ferment of his imagination. Nothing but a specific artistic talent, and a most tactful virtuosity in the artificial declamation and heroic bearing of the rhetorical school, could enable an actress to get through such a part with credit. Now Miss Emery's talent is a specifically prosaic one: we have repeatedly seen that the more closely her parts touch the actual life and society of our day in the classes which she has under her own daily observation, the better she acts. In The Benefit of the Doubt she almost persuaded us that she was the best actress on our stage. Remove the venue even so small a distance towards the imaginative region as the plays of the late W. G. Wills, and she is comparatively colorless. Shift it completely to the Sahara of rhetorical blank verse or the heights of genuine dramatic poetry, and she holds her own merely as a pretty woman and a clever professional. For Bazilide she has not even the right sort of prettiness: she is no "docile rhythmic serpent of the East." Her habit of speech is positively subversive of the poetry of tone and measure. When she says "Nothing must tarnish the greater glory of Michael's love for me," the words "greater glory" came out with a fashionable smartness at which it is hardly possible not to smile. All that can be said for her Bazilide is that by dint of going at her business with great spirit, and with a cleverness that only stops short of perceiving that she had better not have gone at it at all, she gets safely through, thanks to her great popularity, her good looks, and a resolute application of her vigorous stage talent to a bold experiment in ranting, on the pretty safe chance of the public rising at it as Partridge rose at the King in Hamlet. Which the public obediently does, like the silly lamb it is in its moments of pretension to fine connoisseurship.

And Mrs Patrick Campbell, what of her? Ah, the change from that mournful first night of the slain Michael and the Lost Angel, when we were all singing, both on the stage and off:

> But what are vernal joys to me?
> Where thou art not, no Spring can be.

What a ballad could have been written then with the title Come back from Dorchester; and what terrible heart twistings we suffered when we knew that she would not come unless we gave her Henry Arthur Jones's head on a charger! Well, we gave it to her; and on the first night of For the Crown we agreed, before she had been three seconds on the stage, that her return was cheap at the price: nay, we would have given her Shakespear's head as a makeweight if she had given the faintest pout of dissatisfaction. You will tell me, no doubt, that Mrs Patrick Campbell cannot act. Who said she could?—who wants her to act?—who cares twopence whether she possesses that or any other second-rate accomplishment? On the highest plane one does not act, one *is*. Go and see her move, stand, speak, look, kneel—go and breathe the magic atmosphere that is created by the grace of all these deeds; and then talk to me about acting, forsooth! No, Mrs Campbell's Militza is an embodied poem; and if it is much more a lyric poem than a dramatic one, why, so much the worse for dramatic poetry! This time, too, the poetry was not without a little tenderness as well as much beauty of movement and tone. The old vituperative note was not heard; and there was an access of artistic earnestness and power. Possibly the vituperative mood had exhausted itself on the devoted author of Michael.

Mr Forbes Robertson was torn by a struggle between the riotous high spirits he was evidently enjoying in his own person, and the remorse and horror which racked him as Constantine Brancomir. However, art is never the worse for a happy inspiration; and though in filling the part of Constantine he was really filling a brainless void, he filled it like an artist. Miss Sarah Brooke played a small part well; and Mr Dalton, as the elder Brancomir, outfaced the nothingness of his part with sufficient assurance to impress the Partridges almost as successfully as Miss Emery did. It was all that he could do under the circumstances.

The play is worth seeing for its mounting alone by those who, like myself, care very little for the spouting of Marlovian mighty lines. Everything, from the captured standards of the Turks to Signor Lucchesi's equestrian statue in the style of Verrocchio, shows the choice of the artist, not the fulfilment of an order by a tradesman. The first scene, Mr Walter Hann's Citadel in the Balkans, with its most unrhetorical, delicately beautiful mountains stretching to the horizon in a sea of snowy peaks, is so good that one asks with some indignation whether some means cannot be invented of doing away with the ridiculous "sky borders" which deface the firmament. The stage management in this first act, by the way, is excellent. Later on it is perhaps a trifle unimaginative; and Mr Forbes Robertson has not yet mastered the art of arranging the Lyceum stage so as to disguise its excessive spaciousness when interiors are to be represented. For instance, in the second act, since there is neither a Court procession to enter nor a ballet to be danced, the room, in view of the biting climate and Bazilide's light draperies, might be made a trifle snugger with advantage to the illusion.

In short, then, everything—except perhaps the play—is worth seeing. The spoilt children of the public have certainly strained their privilege hard by their treatment of Michael and his Lost Angel; but still, since Michael was succeeding in spite of its having completely beaten the company, whereas all the forces concerned have their share in the success of For the Crown—since, above all, we can now see Mrs Patrick Campbell every evening if we will, the change in the Lyceum bill will be forgiven. No doubt Mr Jones has lost a thousand or two; but in every other respect he has gained; and, after all, what is the loss of a thousand pounds to a successful dramatic author? Merely a stimulant to increased production, the first fruits of which we shall presently receive at the hands of Mr Willard. And so let us be jocund, and book our places at the Lyceum without delay.

ON NOTHING IN PARTICULAR AND THE
THEATRE IN GENERAL

[14 *March* 1896]

BEING at a loss for something to write about, I look through the tickets in my drawer, hoping to find by chance some forgotten first night to help me out of my difficulty. Among others I turn up an odd-looking green ticket with no less than four counterfoils, for a performance that is to last four nights—or rather four summer afternoons and evenings in July next. On the first evening the play will begin at five o'clock; and the performance will not be divided into acts. On the second and third evenings, the first act is timed for four o'clock, the second for six, the third for eight. On the fourth evening, the first act will begin at four, but the second and third not until half-past six and half-past eight. My seat each evening will cost me a pound; and, being an economical person, I shall perhaps keep the cost of my cabs, trains, and so forth, down to fifteen or sixteen pounds; so that I shall get safely out of this piece of playgoing for a twenty-pound note. Need I say that I cannot afford it? And yet what am I to do? The theatre is the best and most famous in the world—no, it is not Drury Lane: it is called the Stage Festival Playhouse of Bayreuth. It is the only theatre where you can wander from a pine forest into your stall, and wander out at the end of the act into the terebinthine air again, leaving the theatre to renew its freshness so that you can see the play out without a headache. He who has not been there knows nothing about theatres, no matter how often he may have been stuffed into a fabulously ground-rented cockpit in the Strand, and regaled with the delights of the British drama.

Now the aggravating thing about this is that the Stage Festival Playhouse might just as well be in Middlesex or Surrey. We could build it for ourselves better and cheaper than the Bayreuthers built it for Wagner. Within a shilling railway ride from Charing Cross we have heaths, commons, hills and forests, as lovely as the Fichtelgebirge. Our orchestral and scenic resources far surpass those of the Bühnenfestspielhaus; our wealth is to Bayreuth's as Lombard Street's to a China orange; and even our restaurants are not altogether inferior. When once our enthusiasm is aroused—say by a race meeting or the Crystal Palace fireworks—we go afield readily in pursuit of amusement and edification. On fine Bank Holidays you may see, from the Vale of Health to the Lea Bridge Road, how thoroughly congenial to human nature the Wagnerian combination of country holiday with sightseeing is; whilst on wet ones, in the Underground trains leading to Madame Tussaud's, Olympia, and Earl's Court, we may see what black oppressions of inconvenience the British public will face for the sake of entertainments in no way more lively than Der Ring des Nibelungen. Why then must I, next July, face those two weary journeys of a night and a day, with half a day thrown in, by sea and land, to see what I might as well see here at my ease if only English theatrical enterprise could rouse itself from its dull routine of boom, bankruptcy, and boredom to give us something that we really want, whether we know it or not?

I see it stated that the new theatre which Mr Beerbohm Tree is building on the site of Her Majesty's is to be modelled on the Bayreuth Wagner Theatre. There is something exasperating in the cool, bluff innocence which reports such things as if they were possible. The very first requirement for a theatre modelled on Wagner's is practically unlimited ground space. The Bayreuth Festival Playhouse pays no rent. The space occupied by its scene docks alone would bring in several thousands a year in the Haymarket. In it there are no galleries; and the stalls, much more commodious than those in some of our London theatres, number thirteen hundred odd, fifty-six to the row in the widest part. Imagine the ground-rent of floor-space enough to accommodate thirteen hundred people within a minute's walk of Piccadilly Circus, not to mention the row of boxes at the back for kings and people of that sort, and room enough on the stage for the scenery of Der Ring and the panorama in Parsifal, with dressing-rooms

68

for principals, and hiding-places for choruses, courts, and armies when they are not on the stage! Even at Covent Garden, with its tiers upon tiers of boxes and galleries, a subsidy has to be subscribed to make both ends meet. The notion that we are going to have anything like the Bühnenfestspielhaus in the Haymarket is one which London may put out of its silly head (on some matters it *is* a silly head) once and for ever. No doubt some improvement will be made. It took our impresarios quarter of a century to find out Lohengrin; and it seems just possible, as we live in an increasingly progressive age, that our architects, with so comparatively enlightened and enterprising a manager as Mr Tree to stimulate them, may celebrate the twentieth anniversary of the Wagner Theatre by discovering its existence; but to suppose that the Festspielhaus can be reproduced in the heart of the theatrical west end is about as sensible as to expect to get a villa with grounds and a conservatory on the river between Waterloo and Charing Cross for the same rent as on the Downs just outside Guildford.

Then, it may be asked, why not build your theatre somewhere else? Why not on Hampstead Heath, in Battersea Park, on Richmond Hill, in Epping Forest, on Blackheath, Wimbledon Common, Hackney Downs, or the like, obtaining the use of the land from the County Council, or Corporation, or whatever the authority may be, on conditions designed to secure an equivalent public benefit from the existence of the theatre? The answer is conclusive. The theatres of the metropolis must be strictly centralized for the convenience of two all-important classes: to wit, the critics, who never pay for their seats, and the plutocracy and aristocracy of the west end, who never go to the theatre at all, having more effectual methods of boring themselves in one another's houses, with the contingent advantage of the marriage market for their daughters thrown in. The rest of London either has as much, or more, trouble in getting to the centre than to any point in the circumference, or else would very willingly go farther and fare better in the way of lower prices and greater comfort.

It is clear to me that we shall never become a playgoing people until we discard our fixed idea that it is the business of the people to come to the theatre, and substitute for it the idea that it is the business of the theatre to come to the people. Let me whisper a question which must not be overheard by those who regard the theatre as a dissolute wayside house on the road to ruin. Suppose we had no churches or chapels in London except St James's, Westminster Abbey, St Margaret's, St Martin's, St Mary-le-Strand, St Clement Danes, the Temple Church, and St Paul's, how often would an average inhabitant of Hammersmith, Kilburn, Hampstead, Highgate, Holloway, Stoke Newington, Bow, Blackheath, Peckham, Dulwich, Brixton, Clapham, Wandsworth, Battersea, or Richmond go to church? Probably about as often as he now goes to the pantomime. And how many, after discovering experimentally how easy it is to stay at home, would ever go to church at all? We know the answer so well that we multiply churches and chapels all over the suburbs, and are demolishing them in the central districts instead of building fresh ones. If you move into a new house or flat in London, you have hardly done nailing up your pictures when the clergyman comes to book you (if I may be permitted the expression) for his church next Sunday, and, if necessary, to argue and exhort you into a lively sense of the benefits of going there regularly and the infamy of staying away. And how much cleaner, wholesomer, roomier, cheaper than theatres these churches and chapels are! How much fresher a genealogy read out from the book of Numbers is than the latest rehash of Froufrou or A Scrap of Paper! How much sweeter the strains of Goss's O taste and see than the seventy-five thousandth repetition by a trumpery little band of Ambroise Thomas's Raymond overture, or Mr German's pretty but not absolutely inexhaustible Henry VIII dances! I wish I could instil some true religion into the minds of the theatrical profession. Then, ceasing to regard the Church as an institution for which they have the greatest respect, and whose good opinion they are anxious above all things to conciliate (both respect and conciliation taking the practical form of carefully staying away from the services), they would begin to regard it seriously as their most formidable rival, not only in business, but in the attachment, the esteem, the veneration of the masses. I rejoice to see Mr Wilson Barrett "tumbling to" this with prodigious commercial success. It is by identifying its religion with its art that Bayreuth draws people to its theatre as Mecca draws its pilgrims. Thousands travel from San Francisco or St Petersburg to Bayreuth to see Parsifal or The Ring. What sane person would go from Eaton Square to Camberwell to see Gossip? Whenever the Church loses supporters, it is not in the least because The Origin of Species has superseded the book of Genesis, but solely because, from one cause or another—usually irreligion and incapacity in the priesthood—people find that they are neither temporarily happier nor permanently better for attending its services. And the reason the theatre does not gain supporters just now, but seems, on the contrary, to be losing the few that it had, is that people do not find themselves any happier or better for going to it: in fact, there are plenty of more profitable and less expensive ways of spending an evening, even without resorting to the Church, at local Polytechnics, concerts, entertainments, and societies for the cultivation of hobbies of all kinds, not to mention the music-halls. Half a dozen visits in the year serve all the purposes of those respectable literate citizens who are as anxious to see whatever is good in the theatre as to subscribe to Mudie's or trudge round the Royal Academy and New Gallery every year, winter and summer. Let me turn to the index of Mr William Archer's Theatrical World of 1895, and try to pick out fifty-two new plays that would have justified such a citizen in going once a week to the theatre, and so qualifying as a regular playgoer to the same extent as he is a regular churchgoer. With about twenty-five west end theatres in full action, giving between four and five thousand representations during the year, I can hardly pick out thirty which I can describe as making reasonably endurable pastime; whilst if you ask me how many of them were of sufficient artistic value to justify me in pretending that it matters a straw to any Londoner whether he saw them or not, I simply dare not answer you. All I will say is that from most of them the public had nothing to learn, and the performers less; so that we were not even improving the skill of our actors—quite the reverse, in fact. Some futile person will here interrupt me by asking whether I am such a fool as to suppose that the public goes to the theatre to learn. I crush that walker in darkness by a bald Yes. Playgoing is at bottom as utilitarian as washing; and it is precisely because the managers have persisted in catering for the voluptuary and the sluggard that the theatre is now so discredited. The voluptuary will no more support the theatre than the glutton will pay to be allowed to stare through the shop window of an eating-house: the sluggard finds easier and cheaper enjoyment in second-rate novels than in sixth-rate plays. The theatre is for active workers and alert spirits. If it were generally understood that fare as grimly serious as Ibsen's Brand could be depended on always at our west end houses, they would always be crammed; and the same people would come again and again.

Bad as things are, Mr Archer says that "the actual record of last year is highly inspiriting ... the condition of the theatre as a whole is distinctly healthier than at any time since the decline of the Patent Houses ... in all departments save one ('the Legitimate') the general tendency is upwards ... there is progress on every hand," etc. It is true that these encouraging remarks are qualified by devastating "buts" and "althoughs," followed by sentences in which every clause poleaxes some hugely boasted triumph of the past season, until the critic's congratulations culminate at last in such clarion notes of hope, joy, and exultation as: "Even spectacular melodrama seems (or is this an illusion?) a shade less imbecile than it used to be." No doubt Mr Archer is right: we are getting better. In the same way, if the death-rate of London had stood at ninety for many years past, we should congratulate ourselves much more on its reduction to eighty-five than we are at all likely to do when we reduce it to eight. But Mr Archer hastens to make it clear that the improvement he hails is only an improvement in the quality of such drama as is commercially practicable on the system now prevailing, and by no means an opening of the doors to work of a different and higher class. And he says not a word as to whether even this improvement is proceeding as fast as the general progress of mankind. If the world is advancing at the rate of sixty minutes to the hour, and the theatre at the rate of sixty minutes to the week, the two will soon be as completely out of sight of one another as if the theatre were absolutely retrogressing. His view as to whether there is such a relative retrogression may be inferred from his opinion that "we have reached, or very nearly, the limit of possible progress under existing conditions; and the cessation of advance is the signal for retreat." He therefore proposes the introduction of a new factor in the substance of "a repertory theatre, where unbroken runs shall be forbidden by the articles of association." Of that, more next week.

MUNICIPAL THEATRES

[21 *March* 1896]

LAST week I was lured to a matinée at the Comedy Theatre. I say lured, not in disparagement of the harmless performance, which consisted of one of Miss Beatrice Herford's monologues; a couple of Mrs Hugh Bell's drawing room pieces, trivial, but amusing enough on their scale; and a one-act piece of hardly greater pretension, but of much more serious merit, by Mrs Clifford, played by Mr Acton Bond and Mrs Waring. But it was by the merest accident that I saw any of these entertainments. The stalls were filled for the most part by quite the most disagreeable collection of women I have ever seen. They all wore huge towering hats, piled up, for the more effectual obstruction of the view, with every conceivable futility, vulgarity, and brutality (in the dead-bird line) that a pushing shopkeeper can force on the head of a woman in whom conscience, intelligence, character, conviction, sympathy, and every other attribute of an active and awakened nature are represented solely by a dull fear of not being in the fashion. The person who would have prevented me from seeing the stage if I had not fortunately occupied a projecting corner seat, actually had two seagull's wings in her hat, stained crimson

73

at the insertion, so as to make them appear as if freshly torn from the living bird. I wonder whether, if a Sioux or Huron Indian, with feather head-dress and array of scalps complete, were to present himself with a stall-ticket, he would be permitted to sit out the performance; or is the privilege of not only obstructing the view, but making all your commonly humane neighbors feel sick every time they look at you, confined strictly to women? Surely it is bad enough to see egret plumage waving all over the place, and reminding you at every quiver of the slaughter of great numbers of exquisitely pretty birds in order to make a few dozen trashy shop-window hats, without also having to endure imitation blood-stains on dismembered limbs.

I mention these matters, though they are exceedingly disgusting, simply to warn people who go to matinées what they are likely to get in return for the price of their stall; but the subject carries me a step further, to the consideration of a remedy. I do not propose an actual Reign of Terror; but would it not be advisable to erect a guillotine in Trafalgar Square, and give the magistracy summary powers to order afternoon police raids on vulgarly fashionable women at the theatres and concert-rooms? The prisoners could be brought straight to the police-court, and thence, on conviction, to the Square to have their hats guillotined off, after which they should be brought back to the theatre and forcibly replaced in their stalls until the fall of the curtain.

I may add, as a general observation, that a woman who uses the same hat for a garden party and for a matinée does not know how to dress herself.

The subject of women's hats is so intimately connected with churchgoing that I am reminded by it of my unfinished article last week. In it, you will perhaps remember, I got as far as Mr William Archer's recommendation of "a repertory theatre, where unbroken runs shall be forbidden by the articles of association," as a remedy for the present commercially precarious and artistically quite miserable condition of our drama. Hereupon let me point out that wherever the decentralization of the theatre has begun—in such cases, for instance, as that of Mr Mulholland's successful enterprise at Camberwell, where the Métropole Theatre is not a house catering, like the Surrey or the old Marylebone, for a special and somewhat primitive audience, but addresses itself to the same class of playgoer as the west end houses—long runs are as effectually forbidden by the fact that a fortnight is sufficient to allow everyone in the area served by the theatre to see the play as they could be by the most stringent articles of association. Consequently, from the point of view of the public, decentralization is the remedy for the long-run system. But from the point of view of the actor and his art it is no remedy at all, because it is precisely in the decentralized theatres and in the provinces, where long runs are unknown, that the entertainment is provided by touring companies who "go out with a play" and perform it in one town or London suburb after another for periods of time compared to which the London runs of Our Boys or Charley's Aunt are but as the lifetime of a mayfly. By this time it must be quite easy to find people—people called actors—who have spent the ten years which should have constituted their apprenticeship in playing a single part in The Silver King, or Dorothy, or some Gilbert-Sullivan opera. In such a school Edmund Kean himself would have acquired no more of his art than is involved in the professional manner of a doctor or a dentist—far less, in fact, since a successful doctor has to be a tolerably accomplished comedian if he is to succeed in general practice. Hence, I take it, Mr Archer's qualification of the desiderated theatre as a "repertory theatre" as well as one in which long runs are forbidden. For a repertory theatre is no mere inn yard for travelling companies: it must have a stock company to perform its repertory. I need not here reiterate my warnings against the reaction to faith in the old-fashioned stock company, or my confutation of the notion that it turned out resourceful and accomplished actors, able to sip every dramatic flower and change every dramatic hour, dancers, singers, fencers, swordsmen, elocutionists, and so forth. Nobody has better reason than I have to feel the shortcomings of our present supply of actors, who begin as amateurs and end as gentlemen.

They all seem to me to belong, not to art, but to our railway system, the serious actors being typical first-class passengers, and the comedians typical third-class ones, second class being abolished as on the Midland. They make no more distinction between one part and another than a locomotive does between the routes from Ostend to Vienna and from King's Cross to Crouch End. Their colorlessness, their tameness, their half-dozen assorted gestures and inflexions everlastingly repeated, their eternal clamor for really artistic work and their ignominious collapse when they are taken at their word by Ibsen or anyone else: all this would infuriate me as an author if I were not a critic, and, if I were not an author either, sadden me as a citizen alive to the enormous power of the theatre as an instrument of culture. But when the worst that can be said of our actors has been repeated and rubbed in to the limit of human endurance, the fact remains that we have more actors and better actors than ever we had under the old stock-company system. Let me therefore confine myself for the moment to the question of providing more theatres for our actors to perform in.

We want, not only, as Mr Archer says, *a* repertory theatre, with long runs barred, but so many of them that there shall be no part of London where a citizen may not be able to turn out any evening, and, without more trouble in the way of dressing than he would take for a political or religious meeting, go to a theatre in his neighborhood and enjoy himself there for a reasonable price in a comfortable seat. I do not propose that these local theatres should do away with the central theatres altogether, any more than I suggest that St Paul's and Westminster Abbey should be closed on the ground that all churchgoers can find sufficient local accommodation; but I certainly do mean that the local theatres should extinguish all competition except that of central theatres giving pre-eminently fine performances under pre-eminently handsome conditions by pre-eminently gifted performers. I leave Mr Archer to work out the plan of his repertory theatre as a model central house, a sort of English Théâtre Français—the ideal Français, not the real one. What interests me is the establishment of local theatres, without which we can never become a nation of playgoers.

The first thing to be cleared up is whether there is any reason for abandoning so important an institution as the theatre to private speculation. Private enterprise is immoral, irresponsible, full of the gambling spirit, always ready to sacrifice the public welfare to the magnitude of its dividends, honeycombed with corruption of all sorts, and insufferably boastful of the few virtues which the law has succeeded in forcing on it. A theatrical syndicate often represents private enterprise in its meanest depths. If it had to choose between making ten per cent out of Shakespear and Goldsmith, and thirty per cent out of an entertainment calculated to double the police and hospital rates in a town, it would go for the thirty per cent without hesitation. Public enterprise has been conducted in the past mostly by men hardened by a lifetime spent in private enterprise, and has consequently caught some of its vices; but public enterprise is responsible to public opinion, is practically unable to use the law of libel to muzzle the Press, has no secret service money to bribe with, and cannot entrench itself against the votes of the respectable public behind the votes of its own shareholders.

On the whole, except in cases where theatrical private enterprise is the artistic enterprise of some individual actor or artistic entrepreneur of high character, it presents that frightful social phenomenon, a great social force for good or evil, one which, like alcohol, is most lucrative at its cheapest and worst, abandoned to exploitation by purely commercial speculators. Nowadays there is no more necessity or excuse for this than for the backward condition of those parishes which have no public libraries and baths, or those towns which have no museums or picture galleries. In our town halls all sorts of entertainments, from oratorios and dramatic performances to the drearier chin music and farce of politics, are given almost nightly, the dramatic performances being managed by means of the makeshift called a fit-up. Now if a vestry or municipal corporation keeps a concert-room, I do not see why it should not keep a theatre. And if, as in Birmingham for instance, it provides the organ, and makes the gas in its own retorts, I do not see why it should not provide the entertainment. At Birmingham they have gone as far as a municipal public-house: in Genoa, to look a little farther afield, the municipality keeps a magnificent church, the only Italian church in which I ever found cleanliness as well as splendor, with smart, disciplined, respectable custodians, and a sacerdotal staff which would not disgrace an English cathedral. Depend upon it, we shall soon find some vestry or municipality building a town hall capable of being used as a theatre (the stage figuring in the accounts as a "platform" and the scene-dock as a "municipal office"). It will be let out as usual to travelling companies. Presently a gasman will be laid on permanently; then a carpenter or two; then a call-boy, disguised as "messenger"; then a detrimental nephew of the Mayor's will be allowed to conceal the functions of a walking gentleman under the specious title of night-patrol man; then an attractive lady typist with a Shakespearean repertory will be added to the municipal staff at a "moral minimum" wage (there are Juliets and Paulines in this country—and not very old ones either—who would jump at a permanency of thirty shillings a week almost as eagerly as a German prima donna); until at last the terms quoted to starring managers will include everything except the star himself and his portrait posters. Finally, to prevent the theatre eating its head off at the expense of the rates when a week has not been booked by some manager, the staff and company will be ordered to put up Othello or Cheer, Boys, Cheer! And then the thing will be done. Why not? The only objection that can be urged is that it is impossible. That is a negligible objection in England, because nobody ever troubles to oppose the impossible. Ten years ago I used to tell people in London that they would one day have a public authority, representing the whole metropolis, spending thousands a year in maintaining an army of skilled musicians to give open-air instrumental concerts all the summer in our parks. That gained me a large part of my reputation as an unpractical visionary. Today the accomplished fact is a commonplace of London life; and if we are startled presently by the appointment of a popular tenor as town-crier for London (in which capacity he will be regarded with complete toleration by the Local Government Board), we shall know what it means.

At all events, one thing is certain. Dramatic art is not going to die of commercialism in England. If it comes to that, commercialism is much more likely to die of dramatic art. In department after department of life private enterprise has begged to be protected from the competition of public enterprise for the sake of its own *beaux yeux*; and in no one of these cases has it been spared when it was obviously making a hopeless mess of a business vitally important to the welfare of the community. If the speculators will not give us decent theatres, where our children can be educated on rather more than a farthing's-worth of Shakespear to an intolerable deal of Morocco Bound and stale Froufrou, why, we shall sooner or later provide them for ourselves. I have no objection in the world. Has anyone, except the speculators themselves?

BOILED HEROINE

TRUE BLUE. A new and original drama of the Royal Navy. In five acts. By Leonard Outram and Stuart Gordon, Lieut. R.N. Olympic Theatre, 19 March 1896.   [28 *March* 1896]

I AM often told by people who never go to the theatre that they like melodramas, because they are so funny. Those who do go know better than that. A melodrama must either succeed as a melodrama or else fail with the uttermost ignominies of tedium. But I am fain to admit that True Blue is an exception to this rule. It is funnier by a good deal than H.M.S. Pinafore in the absurd parts, and not bad, as melodramas go, in the presentable parts. The authorship has evidently been divided among many hands. In some of the epithets which Mrs Raleigh, as the lady matador, hurls at the villain, it is impossible not to recognize the vivid style of Mr Raleigh. One of the unnamed authors—I do not know which—is clearly an idiot; for it is not conceivable that the unspeakable fatuities of the plot can have proceeded

79

from the same brain as the part of Strachan, or the dialogue, a good deal of which is animated and businesslike. Probably the idiot was the original begetter of the drama. As I conjecture, he submitted his play to Mr Leonard Outram, who, as an experienced actor, at once fell under the spell which unredeemed literary and dramatic idiocy never fails to throw over his profession. He called in Lieutenant Stuart Gordon to look after the naval realism, and supply technically correct equivalents for the Avast Heavings, and Abaft the Binnacles, and Splicing the Main Braces which we may presume the original manuscript to have contained. The Lieutenant, not being an experienced actor, no doubt suggested that if his naval realism could be supplemented by a gleam or two of common sense, it would be all the better; and I can imagine Sir Augustus Harris, on being approached on the subject of finance, not only supporting the naval officer's view with some vehemence, but taking the dialogue in hand to a certain extent himself, with his popular collaborator, Mr Raleigh, to lend a hand when time ran short. If this hypothesis be correct, we get four authors besides the nameless idiot; and it is in no small degree remarkable that the play has succeeded because the collaborators, in a sort of inspired desperation, played up to the idiot instead of trying to reclaim him. Take for example the main situation of the piece. A British cruiser is anchored at Gibraltar. Its deck is used as a sort of dramatic exchange where villains and villainesses, heroes and heroines, stroll in, like bolts out of the blue, to hatch plots and make love. First there is the lady matador who loves the captain and hates the heroine whom the captain loves. Then there is the heroine, who also loves the captain. And there is the heroine's maid, who loves the comic sailor, who loves the bottle. Suddenly the cruiser is ordered to up anchor and sweep England's enemies from the seas. The women resolve not to desert the men they love in the hour of danger. The matadoress, a comparatively experienced and sensible woman, slips quietly into the pantry adjoining the captain's cabin. The maid gets into one of those settee music boxes which are, it appears, common objects on the decks of cruisers, and is presently carried

into the captain's cabin. The heroine, taught by love to divine
a surer hiding-place, gets into one of the ship's boilers. Here the
hand of the idiot is apparent, striking out a situation which would
never have occurred to Shakespear. Once fairly at sea, the matadoress gives way to an inveterate habit of smoking, and is smelt
out by the captain. She throws her arms boldly about him, and
declares that he is hers for ever. Enter, inopportunely, the navi-
gating officer. He is scandalized, but retires. When he thinks it
safe to return, it is only to find the maid emerging from the
settee to dispute possession of the captain, on behalf of the
heroine, with the matadoress. Hereupon he describes the ship
as the captain's harem, and is placed under arrest. Then comes
the great dramatic opportunity of the matadoress. Becoming acquainted, Heaven knows how, with the hiding-place of the heroine, she takes the stage alone, and draws a thrilling picture of her
rival's impending doom. She describes her in the clammy darkness and dank cold of that boiler, listening to the wild beats of
her own heart. Then the sensation of wet feet, the water rising
to her ankles, her knees, her waist, her neck, until only by standing on tiptoe, with frantic upturned face, can she breathe. One
mercy alone seems vouchsafed to her: the water has lost its
deadly chill. Nay, it is getting distinctly warm, even hot—hotter
—*scalding*! Immortal Powers, it is BOILING; and what a moment
ago was a beautiful English girl, in the first exquisite budding of
her beautiful womanhood, is now but a boilerful of soup, and
in another moment will be a condenserful of low-pressure steam.
I must congratulate Mrs Raleigh on the courage with which she
hurled this terrible word-picture at a house half white with its
purgation by pity and terror, and half red with a voiceless, apo-
plectic laughter. Need I describe the following scene in the stoke-
hold ("stokehole," it appears, is a solecism)—how the order
comes to fill the boiler; how the comic sailor, in shutting the
manhole thereof, catches sight of the white finger of the captain's
young lady; how the matadoress in disguise comes in, and has
all but turned on the boiling water when the comic sailor disables
the tap by a mighty blow from a sledge-hammer; how he rushes

away to tell the captain of his discovery; how in his absence the fires are lighted and the cold water turned on; and how at the last moment the captain dashes in, shouting "Draw the fires from No. 7" (the heroine is in No. 7), rushes up the ladder to the manhole, and drags out the heroine safe and sound, without a smudge on her face or a crumple in her pretty white frock, amid the delirious cheers of an audience which contemplates the descending curtain as men who have eaten of the insane root that takes the reason prisoner. Many more terrors does that melodrama contain, including the public drowning of the matadoress like a rat in a trap, but nothing quite so novel as the boiling scene. The last act degenerates into mere ordinary blood and thunder, only relieved by the touching acting of Mr Rignold on becoming suddenly penetrated, for no mortal reason that anybody can discover, with a sense of his own unworthiness and the nobility of his donkey of a captain, who, though a sufficiently handsome and pleasant fellow, displays just ability enough to justify a steamboat company in trusting him, under the guidance of an intelligent boy, with the sale of tickets for a Thames steamer. Mr Rignold, however, is not the man to allow himself to be bereaved of a bit of acting by the absence of any motive for it. He has the only real part in the play: and he makes the most of it to the end.

Nearly thirty actors and actresses, most of them capable and vigorous people with more or less distinct stage talents, are provided with salaries by this melodrama. They have for the most part about as much to do as the hundreds of painted spectators in the first scene (which I forgot to mention, as it is only a bullfight). Mr Bucklaw, as the gallant, but brainless, captain, shewed that he only needs to smarten himself a little—mostly in the way of enunciating his consonants—to become popular in such parts. Miss Laura Graves was irresistible as the parboiled heroine, being powerfully aided by the fact that the authors of the dialogue have thoroughly mastered the great Shakespearean secret of always making the woman woo the man. In actual life there is no point upon which individuals vary more widely than in the effect of publicity on the demonstrativeness of their affections. Some people would rather die than offer or receive the slightest endearment with anyone looking on. Others are stimulated to exceptional ardor by the presence of an audience; and it is a tragic fact that these diverse temperaments are rather apt to attract one another. The shy, conscious man whose impulsive and warm-hearted wife *will* caress him before a roomful of people, and the fastidious reticent woman whose husband's attitude is openly and blubberingly amorous, are familiar figures in our civilization. But I cannot recall on the stage any *ingénue* quite so reckless under the sway of the tenderer emotions as the one played by Miss Laura Graves. On all public occasions she positively showers kisses on the objects of her attachment. One wonders what a French audience would think of her. It is only when she is alone with the captain in his cabin that she subsides into something like the customary reserve of the bright and beautiful English girls of whom she is offered as an authentic type. The maid is hardly behind her mistress in respect of her indifference to pub-licity; but she does not take the initiative—is, in fact, more kissed against than kissing—the effect being so much worse that nobody less clever than Miss Kate Phillips could make the part popular. As it is, I congratulate the part on Miss Phillips, without in any way congratulating Miss Phillips on the part.

One of the humors of the piece is that the three stowaway ladies never enter twice in the same costume. They change as freely as if Worth had a branch establishment on board. The fact that this gross impossibility does not interfere in the least with the illusion (such as it is) of the drama is an illustration of the fact that melodramatic stage illusion is not an illusion of real life, but an illusion of the embodiment of our romantic imagin-ings. If melodramatists would only grasp this fact, they would save themselves a good deal of trouble and their audiences a good deal of boredom. Half the explanations and contrivances with which they burden their pieces are superfluous attempts to persuade the audience to accept, as reasonably brought about, situations which it is perfectly ready to accept without any bringing about whatever. The second-rate dramatist always begins at the beginning of his play; the first-rate one begins in the middle; and the genius—Ibsen, for instance—begins at the end. Nothing is odder about True Blue than the way in which the same authors who heroically disregard the commonest physical possibilities in the matter of boilers and millinery, timidly and superstitiously waste half the first and second acts in useless explanations of the villain's designs. The thousands of fiery Spaniards waiting for the bull to appear in the ring are repeatedly supposed to sit in respectful silence for five minutes at a stretch whilst the first and second villains stroll into the arena to discuss at great length the political situation which has led to the presence of a British cruiser at Gibraltar (as if that were the most improbable place for it in the world), and which renders it desirable, from their own point of view, that the cruiser should be sunk. Even if these explanations were intelligible or plausible, they would only waste time: as it is, they are stupid.

In looking over one or two criticisms of True Blue I have been astonished to find the writers complaining that there is too much realism and too little melodrama in it. When a man who has just been regaled on boiled heroine asks for more, it is only good manners to congratulate him on his appetite; but it is also well to point out that he has not the public on his side. The really entertaining part of True Blue is Lieutenant Stuart Gordon's part. The cooking of Alice Marjoribanks is only funny as a bogus monstrosity at a fair is funny; but the weighing of the anchor is both interesting and exciting. It is true that the interest is not strictly dramatic: it is the sort of interest that makes people visit a man-of-war at Portsmouth; but then this is the very sort of interest to which True Blue is addressed. The fact that I did not catch half the expository dialogue in the first act did not disappoint me in the least—quite the contrary; but I deeply resented the gruff unintelligibility of the orders by which the anchor-weighing process was directed, as I really wanted to know about that. What True Blue wants is more of the fresh naval routine, and less of the stale melodramatic routine. Why

84

not allow the captain to descry the Venezuelan fleet on the horizon, and give us the process of preparing for action? Why not display in the third act a more interesting section of the ship shewing us both above and between decks? Why allow the catastrophe to be brought about by an impossible valet lamely rubbing out the pencil-marks on the captain's chart with a piece of india-rubber, instead of by a torpedo, or a hundred-ton pro-jectile from the enemy, or—if the maximum of probability is preferable—a collision with some other British cruiser? I am convinced, with all respect to the contrary opinion of some of my colleagues, that in this play Lieutenant Gordon worked on the right lines, and his melodramatist collaborators on the wrong ones. The play is emphatically not the thing at the Olympic; and that is precisely why True Blue is better worth seeing than most exhibitions of its class.

MARY ANDERSON

A Few Memories. By Mary Anderson (Madame de Navarro). London: Osgood, McIlvaine & Co. 1896. [4 *April* 1896]

This book is an actress's confession: consequently I should not, under ordinary circumstances, dream of believing a word of it. Nevertheless I do believe it, because I cannot find the actress in it any more than I was ever able to find her in the Mary Anderson who danced down to the Lyceum footlights like "a wave o' the sea" nearly ten years ago. What I do find is a strong-minded, clever, intelligent, self-reliant, and self-respectful girl whose hobby was Shakespear. The statement that Mary Anderson was no actress is one which I am prepared to make, but not to defend. If I meet an American tourist who is greatly impressed with the works of Raphael, Kaulbach, Delaroche, and Barry, and I, with Titian and Velasquez in my mind, tell him that not one of his four heroes was a real painter, I am no doubt putting my case absurdly; but I am not talking nonsense for all that: indeed to the adept seer of pictures I am only formulating a commonplace in an irritatingly ill-considered way. But in this world if you do not say a thing in an irritating way, you may just as well not say it at all, since nobody will trouble themselves about anything that does not trouble them. The attention given to a criticism is in direct proportion to its indigestibility; and I therefore say boldly that Mary Anderson was no actress. In no page of these Memories can you find any trace of the actress's temperament. Mary Anderson is essentially a woman of principle, which the actress essentially is not: the notion that all bravery, loyalty, and self-respect depend on a lawless and fearless following of the affectionate impulses—which is the characteristic morality of the artist, especially the woman artist of the stage—is, to her, simple immorality. The actress lives only to give herself away so that she may gain the love of the whole world: Mary Anderson, asking what it shall profit her to gain the whole world if she loses her own soul, retires or rather recoils from the stage before her apprenticeship is over, because she cannot gratify her love of Shakespear and rhetoric without giving herself away to the public nightly to be stared at. To her this grudging of herself is a virtue —an element of strength of character: it vanquishes her stage-craze finally because she does not see that a woman with the fit genius can do nothing better for the world than make this sacrifice to it. The full justification of such a sacrifice—the power to become thereby the mother of the world's noblest sympathies and deepest feelings—cannot convince her: it is perceived by her reason as a duty, an excuse, and (when performed and done with) a consolation; but it does not glow at her heart as a passion and a fulfilment. The individualist in her triumphs in the end: the inner mandate which she finally obeys is "Individual, perfect thyself," which finally triumphs over all other mandates—over "Artist, perfect thy work," and "Woman, help thy kind." Here is her whole confession on the subject:

"While on my way to England I could not help reviewing the eight years I had just finished. The retrospect brought as much pain as pleasure. The chief good my work had accomplished, I felt, was the assurance, verbally and by letter, from many young men and women, that the examples of such characters as Parthenia, Ion, and Evadne, in particular, had helped them in their daily lives and strengthened them in moments of despondency and temptation. Their gratitude to me, as the humble exponent of these *rôles*, was my most valued applause; for it proved that, in a measure, I had fulfilled the vocation, so long ago dreamed of, in undertaking a dramatic career. My efforts had, as a rule, been successful; but the strain of constant travel, the absence of home comforts in the ever-changing hotels, the responsibility of rehearsals, support, stage-management, and, above all, the extreme publicity of the life, had already begun to be distasteful to me. The disappointments connected with the art itself—the painting one's pictures with one's own person, in the full gaze of the public, the dependence upon inartistic people (often compelled to use the theatre as a trade) for carrying out the most cherished conceptions, and the constant crumbling of ideals—made me, young as I was, long to leave the stage for the peace and privacy of domestic life. I had a greater desire than ever to work, but away from the direct eye of the public. The life of a poet, composer, writer, or painter seemed ideal; for they could express their innermost thoughts through the impersonal mediums of canvas, music, literature, and still be protected by that privacy which is so dear to most women."

Here you have the whole position: a cold sense of duty steadily weakening instead of warming from its first record in her autobiography as the mere priggishness of a stage-struck schoolgirl to her retirement, and a conception of musicians and poets as exceptionally private persons minding their own innermost business in a vacuum, instead of strenuously throwing themselves into the most yearning and vital intercourse with humanity. Here is a passage which will drive home, as no comment of mine could, the absolute *deadness* of Mary Anderson's conception of artistic beauty: "I remember a visit to the studio of one of the most prominent French sculptors in Paris. After seeing everything in both of the huge ateliers, Lord Lytton, a singularly able critic in all matters artistic, suggested a visit to the Morgue as a means of driving from our minds the hideous creations we had

87

seen. We gladly assented; and, indeed, the three or four figures we saw there were far more beautiful, with the calm majesty of death upon them, than any of the representations of life we had seen in the studio."

The really compelling mandate which sent Madame de Navarro forth on her career seems to have been "Mary: be not thyself, but somebody out of Shakespear," conditioned only by an inexorable resolution to be first or nowhere. When she was an unknown country girl of sixteen she managed to induce John McCullough to visit her family. On hearing her spout her favorite bits of Shakespear, he had the enormous goodnature to offer to allow her to try her hand on the stage as Lady Anne in Richard III. "I answered," this "humble exponent" tells us (with a full sense of the humor of her audacity), "that I would rather not play second fiddle, even to him." It was magnificent; and she lived up to it and went through with it. The position she wanted to begin with (in her teens) was that of Mrs Siddons. It is useless to gasp at such presumption; for she got what she demanded. She knew that it was childish to cry for the moon; so she simply said, with quiet dignity, "Be good enough to take that moon down from its nail and hand it to me." Which was accordingly done. The world which once sent Mrs Siddons back to the provinces as a failure prostrated itself like a doormat to kiss the feet of Our Mary.

It may be said that this success was nothing more than the vogue of a very pretty woman; but Mary Anderson was neither the only pretty woman who wanted to be Mrs Siddons nor the prettiest. The live statue of Galatea was a most graceful ornament, no doubt; but it was a statue for all that; and the public neither cares nor dares to fall in love with statues. No: Our Mary was not a beauty merely: she was an ideal. We made a type of her, just as we made a type of Mr Gladstone; and though the type was the work of our imagination, and Miss Anderson was no more our ideal Mary than Mr Gladstone is our ideal Grand Old Man, yet it was a certain force and integrity of character in themselves that led to their being selected for idealization. There is plenty of other evidence of this force of character in Madame de Navarro's book. She could work; she could endure; she had a way and a will of her own; she could plan and execute enterprises; she could make friends and hold her own among the ablest people of her day; she was sensible and respectable in business and conduct (an extraordinarily rare thing both on and off the stage); she was normal, popular, and intelligible in her methods and ambition, and, being young, she exercised her qualities without the oppressive and sometimes dangerous knowledge of their power which comes with years and with the discovery of the comparative infirmity of the rest of the world. A strong, proud, positive character of this kind, enhanced by a fine person, lends itself to declamation and rhetoric, but not to sympathetic acting. Its jealous reserve, its reluctance to wear its heart on its sleeve, its very superiorities to the passions and frailties, the humilities, confessions, and renunciations of the truly poetic drama, which has for its material the instinctive human creature rather than the moralist and reasoner, disqualify it for the stage, except when the business in hand is rhetorical blank verse in five acts. "Seldom during my stage life," says Madame de Navarro, "have I ever been able to say of any performance, 'That is my best work.' In all my years before the public, I have only once been satisfied with my acting of Bianca, once in Ion, never in Perdita, and only once in Hermione." With this must be taken many other passages in her book, shewing her strong preference of rhetorical and intellectual parts to sympathetic ones, even when both were by Shakespear; her enthusiasm for stage antiquaries like Talfourd and Taylor; and her antipathy to the modern dramatists whose Heddas and Noras are making short work of the declamatory statue heroines. Her final criticism on herself, of course, is her retirement from the stage before she had reached the prime of life, or attained that rich and spirited middle period of artistic development which succeeds the efforts of the ambitious apprentice. The reason she gives is significant enough. "Many and great inducements," she says, "have since been frequently offered me to act again; but

Il en coûte trop cher pour briller dans le monde.
Combien je vais aimer ma retraite profonde!
Pour vivre heureux, vivons cachés."

Note how she assumes, this girl who thinks she has been an artist, that the object of going on the stage is to sparkle in the world, and that the object of life is happiness! After all, despite her character and force, one sees that Our Mary has never grown up—that Galatea has never been awakened. I cannot help wondering what would happen if she were. The other day, in a discussion as to the best way of casting Ibsen's Little Eyolf, a question arose as to who should play the part of Asta, failing the co-operation of some tried exponent of Ibsen. I said, "Why not Mary Anderson?" I could not persuade anyone that I was serious. And yet, why not? Madame de Navarro has declaimed, spouted, statuesqued, Shakespeared, and all the rest of it, to the height of her girlish ambition. She has also for seven years "lived hidden." Why should she not now try real acting, if only as a novelty? May not the publication of this book be taken as a sign that the charms that sages have seen in the face of seclusion are palling? It is true that Madame de Navarro says—and carries conviction when she says—"I am content to be forgotten, except by such friends as I hope will always keep a place for me in their hearts [a rather large exception, considering that these friends include the playgoing public of England and America]. But it seems to me reasonable to believe that my experience may be of some service to those who have, or think they have, an aptitude for acting. I have written these pages more for young girls, who may have the same ambitions that I had, than for anyone else; to shew them that all that glitters is not gold; and thus to do a little towards making them realize how serious an undertaking it is to adopt a life so full of hardships, humiliations, and dangers." This explains, and very honorably explains, a great part of the book; but where do those charming portraits come in? What moral are the young girls to draw from the profile drawing by F. D. Millet, the sketch in oils by Mr Watts, the adorable photograph of Mary at sixteen, Mr Boughton's Pauline portrait picture, the half-length in Albanian costume, and the 1895 photograph, the most womanly and beautiful of them all? I flatly do not believe that this portrait is exhibited to warn young girls against the hardships and dangers of the stage: I believe it is there solely to make us go down on our knees and beg Our Mary to come back to us. Which I accordingly do, without reservation. I will never admit that the girl could act unless the woman makes me change my opinion.

The book contains many an interesting passage on which I have not space to expatiate. I may note hurriedly, but with much gratification, that Madame de Navarro's experience on several points supports views which I have often expressed in these columns. She precisely confirms all that I have urged against the old stationary stock companies; and she asks, as I have asked, why women do not try their hands at theatrical management. Her instructions how to baffle an actor-manager who gets you with your back to the footlights and talks down the stage at you should be studied by the whole company at the ——Heavens! I all but let the name slip. The records of her very American searches after relics of Shakespear and Dickens are quaint, and suggest, I regret to say, an almost inconceivable audacity of imposture on the part of those Britons who follow the industry of impersonating the originals of Dickens's characters and pointing out the houses mentioned in his novels. When she played Rosalind at Stratford-on-Avon, "the stage was decorated with blossoms from Shakespear's garden; the flowers used by Rosalind and Celia, as well as the turnip gnawed by Audrey, had been plucked near Anne Hathaway's cottage; the deer carried across the stage in the hunting chorus had been shot in Charlcot Park for the occasion by one of the Lucys." Bless her innocence!

I close the book with its subject unexhausted, just as the author did. The life of the girl rhetorician is only the first volume. The second volume should be the life of a true dramatic artist. If Madame de Navarro will only live that volume, I, the critic, will gladly write it in these pages.

NIETZSCHE IN ENGLISH

NIETZSCHE CONTRA WAGNER, &c. Vol. I of the collected works
of Friedrich Nietzsche. Translated by Thomas Common.
London: Henry & Co. 1896.

A MOTHER OF THREE. A new and original farce in three acts. By
Clo Graves. Comedy Theatre, 8 April 1896. [11 *April* 1896]

IT is with a most opportune consideration for my Easter holiday
that Messrs Henry & Co. have just issued the first volume of
their translation of the works of Friedrich Nietzsche. And such
a volume, too! containing everything that he wrote just before
he reached the point at which Germany made up its mind that he
was mad, and shut him up, both figuratively and actually. Whilst
I am still at large I may as well explain that Nietzsche is a philosopher—that is to say, something unintelligible to an Englishman. To make my readers realize what a philosopher is, I can
only say that *I* am a philosopher. If you ask incredulously, "How,
then, are your articles so interesting?" I reply that there is nothing so interesting as philosophy, provided its materials are not
spurious. For instance, take my own materials—humanity and
the fine arts. Any studious, timorously ambitious bookworm can
run away from the world with a few shelvesful of history, essays,
descriptions, and criticisms, and, having pieced an illusory humanity and art out of the effects produced by his library on his
imagination, build some silly systematization of his worthless
ideas over the abyss of his own nescience. Such a philosopher is
as dull and dry as you please: it is he who brings his profession
into disrepute, especially when he talks much about art, and so
persuades people to read him. Without having looked at more
than fifty pictures in his life, or made up his mind on the smallest
point about one of the fifty, he will audaciously take it upon himself to explain the development of painting from Zeuxis and
Apelles to Raphael and Michael Angelo. As to the way he will go
on about music, of which he always has an awe-stricken conceit,
it spoils my temper to think of it, especially when one remembers

that musical composition is taught (a monstrous pretension) in this country by people who *read* scores, and never by any chance listen to performances. Now, the right way to go to work——strange as it may appear—is to look at pictures until you have acquired the power of seeing them. If you look at several thousand good pictures every year, and form some sort of practical judgment about every one of them—were it only that it is not worth troubling over—then at the end of five years or so you will, if you have a wise eye, be able to see what is actually in a picture, and not what you think is in it. Similarly, if you listen critically to music every day for a number of years, you will, if you have a wise ear, acquire the power of hearing music. And so on with all the arts. When we come to humanity it is still the same: only by intercourse with men and women can we learn anything about it. This involves an active life, not a contemplative one; for unless you do something in the world, you can have no real business to transact with men; and unless you love and are loved, you can have no intimate relations with them. And you must transact business, wirepull politics, discuss religion, give and receive hate, love, and friendship with all sorts of people before you can acquire the sense of humanity. If you are to acquire the sense sufficiently to be a philosopher, you must do all these things unconditionally. You must not say that you will be a gentleman and limit your intercourse to this class or that class; or that you will be a virtuous person and generalize about the affections from a single instance—unless, indeed, you have the rare happiness to stumble at first upon an all-enlightening instance. You must have no convictions, because, as Nietzsche puts it, "convictions are prisons." Thus, I blush to add, you cannot be a philosopher and a good man, though you may be a philosopher and a great one. You will say, perhaps, that if this be so, there should be no philosophers; and perhaps you are right; but though I make you this handsome concession, I do not defer to you to the extent of ceasing to exist. If you insist on the hangman, whose pursuits are far from elevating, you may very well tolerate the philosopher, even if philosophy involve philandering; or, to put it another way, if, in spite of your hangman, you tolerate murder within the sphere of war, it may be necessary to tolerate comparatively venial irregularities within the sphere of philosophy. It is the price of progress; and, after all, it is the philosopher, and not you, who will burn for it.

These are shocking sentiments, I know; but I assure you you will think them mere Sunday School commonplaces when you have read a little of Nietzsche. Nietzsche is worse than shocking, he is simply awful: his epigrams are written with phosphorus on brimstone. The only excuse for reading them is that before long you must be prepared either to talk about Nietzsche or else retire from society, especially from aristocratically minded society (not the same thing, by the way, as aristocratic society), since Nietzsche is the champion of privilege, of power, and of inequality. Famous as Nietzsche has become—he has had a great *succès de scandale* to advertise his penetrating wit—I never heard of him until a few years ago, when, on the occasion of my contributing to the literature of philosophy a minute treatise entitled The Quintessence of Ibsenism, I was asked whether I had not been inspired by a book called Out at the other side of Good and Evil, by Nietzsche. The title seemed to me promising; and in fact Nietzsche's criticism of morality and idealism is essentially that demonstrated in my book as at the bottom of Ibsen's plays. His pungency; his power of putting the merest platitudes of his position in rousing, startling paradoxes; his way of getting underneath moral precepts which are so unquestionable to us that common decency seems to compel unhesitating assent to them, and upsetting them with a scornful laugh: all this is easy to a witty man who has once well learnt Schopenhauer's lesson, that the intellect by itself is a dead piece of brain machinery, and our ethical and moral systems merely the pierced cards you stick into it to make it play a certain tune. So far I am on common ground with Nietzsche. But not for a moment will I suffer anyone to compare me to him as a critic. Never was there a deafer, blinder, socially and politically inepter academician. He has fancies concerning different periods of history, idealizing the Romans and

94

the Renascence, and deducing from his idealization no end of excellences in their works. When have I ever been guilty of such professorial folly? I simply go and look at their works, and after that you may talk to me until you go black in the face about their being such wonderful fellows: I know by my senses that they were as bad artists, and as arrant intellect-mongers, as need be. And what can you say to a man who, after pitting his philosophy against Wagner's with refreshing ingenuity and force, proceeds to hold up as the masterpiece of modern dramatic music, blazing with the merits which the Wagnerian music dramas lack—guess what! Don Giovanni, perhaps, or Orfeo, or Fidelio? Not at all: Carmen, no less. Yes, as I live by bread, as I made that bread for many a year by listening to music, Georges Bizet's Carmen. After this one is not surprised to find Nietzsche blundering over politics and social organization and administration in a way that would be impossible to a man who had ever served on a genuine working committee long enough—say ten minutes—to find out how very little attention the exigencies of practical action can be made to pay to our theories when we have to get things done, one way or another. To him modern Democracy, Pauline Christianity, Socialism, and so on are deliberate plots hatched by malignant philosophers to frustrate the evolution of the human race and mass the stupidity and brute force of the many weak against the beneficial tyranny of the few strong. This is not even a point of view: it is an absolutely fictitious hypothesis: it would not be worth reading were it not that there is almost as much evidence for it as if it were true, and that it leads Nietzsche to produce some new and very striking and suggestive combinations of ideas. In short, his sallies, petulant and impossible as some of them are, are the work of a rare spirit and are pregnant with its vitality. It is notable that Nietzsche does not write in chapters or treatises: he writes leading articles, leaderettes, occasional notes, and epigrams. He recognizes that humanity, having tasted the art of the journalist, will no longer suffer men to inflict books on it. And he simplifies matters, quite in the manner of the leading article writer, by ignoring things as they are, and

dealing with things as it is easiest, with our prejudices and training, to think they are, except that he supplies the training and
instils the prejudices himself as he goes along, instead of picking
up those that lie about the street as one does in writing leaders
for the daily press.

There are two reasons why I can say no more than this about
Nietzsche. The first is that I am lying on a hillside in the sun,
basking, not working. The second is that I must reserve some
space for Miss Clo Graves's Mother of Three at the Comedy,
which has plucked me up from that hillside by the roots.

Miss Graves has somewhat obscured my justification for introducing Nietzsche in a column devoted to the drama. That justification, of course, is that though plays have neither political
constitutions nor established churches, they must all, if they are
to be anything more than the merest tissue of stage effects, have
a philosophy, even if it be no more than an unconscious expression of the author's temperament. Your great dramatist philo-
sophizes quite openly: his lines become famous as aphorisms,
and serve in the intercourse of philosophers as words serve in the
intercourse of ordinary mortals. All the philosophers who are
really alive nowadays maintain intimate relations with the fine
arts: Schopenhauer and Nietzsche belong as inevitably to the
critic's library as Goethe and Wagner. But I am bound to say
that there is not much philosophy in Miss Clo Graves's play.
However, there is plenty of fun in it, and in that fun there lurks
occasionally a certain sense of the humor of indecency which
drives me to conclude that Miss Clo Graves is an Irish lady. The
Irish have a natural delicacy which gives them a very keen sense
of indelicacy; and a good deal of the humors of A Mother of
Three betrays the countrywoman of Sheridan and Swift rather
than of Mr Pinero. To this I can make no effective objection,
since we maintain a Censor to prevent questions of sex and parentage being treated properly and seriously on the stage, and to
license their improper and flippant treatment, which is at least
more tolerable than no treatment of them at all. Miss Graves,
struck, no doubt, by the success of Charley's Aunt and The

Strange Adventures of Miss Brown, in which the main joke is the dressing up of a man as a woman, has tried the effect of dressing up a woman as a man. The effect was rather unexpected. Miss Fanny Brough, whose comic force in parts belonging to her own sex no one can deny, no sooner changed her skirt for a pair of shepherd's plaid trousers and a frock coat than she suddenly became quite genuinely tragic. I have never seen the peculiar tragic feeling of impending catastrophe more unmistakeably produced than in the second act, where Miss Brough, provoking roar after roar of not very refined laughter by the delivery of lines which she drove home, apparently in spite of herself, with the deadliest cleverness, seemed to be torn by a cumulative agony of rage and shame. This had so nearly passed the limit of her endurance when the curtain fell, that when it rose again for a moment in response to the applause, she seemed to have nothing of her self-possession left, except a precarious remnant of the mere habit of it. I can only compare the effect to that of Salvini's closet scene in Hamlet. That an artist capable of producing it should have been driven to do so in the wrong place by her revolt against such a heartless misuse of her powers as the thrusting of her into what can only be described, at best, as a not very decorous piece of buffoonery, is pitiful enough; but the incident will not have been altogether an unhappy one if it opens the eyes of our dramatists to the extent to which they have been wasting on mere farce a talent which evidently has a rare intensity of emotional force behind it. Perhaps I misunderstood Miss Brough, who may have been giving us a serious artistic study of Mrs Murgatroyd's feelings, uninfluenced by any repugnance of her own to her part; but there can be no mistake as to the effect, which might even have upset the piece if the lines had been less funny.

The play has, as its chief merit, a sustained jocularity which keeps the audience laughing pretty continuously. A good deal of the stage business is frank burlesque; and the acts end, in a rather old-fashioned way, not at any period in the action, but at some climax of absurdity from which no other extrication is possible. But the play is by no means brainless; and it is astonishing how much this small mercy counts for in the theatre.

Miss Rose Leclercq, Miss Beringer, Mr Cyril Maude, and Mr Felix Morris are in the cast—more to its advantage than their own. The curtain-raiser is a piece called The Guinea Stamp, by Mr Cyril Hallward. It consists principally of cant, and is badly spoken and indifferently acted.

TWO EASTER PIECES

THE SIN OF ST HULDA. A new romantic drama. By G. Stuart Ogilvie. Shaftesbury Theatre, 9 April 1896.

BIARRITZ. A musical farce. By Jerome K. Jerome. Lyrics by Adrian Ross. Music by F. Osmond Carr. Prince of Wales Theatre, 11 April 1896. [18 *April* 1896]

OUR managers owe so much to Mr Stuart Ogilvie that they can do no less than occasionally produce, presumably at his own expense, dramas of his which I feel they would hardly accept from me. But it is not altogether a misfortune that these works are produced to please Mr Ogilvie rather than to please the public; since no manager, however cynical, would attribute to Mr Ogilvie or any other individual fellow-creature the depravity and silliness of taste which everybody ascribes as a matter of course to all their fellow-creatures collectively. Nevertheless Mr Ogilvie's plays are to some extent the worse for his culture and his independence. They have the defect of being second-hand: that is to say, they have the unreality, and consequently the tediousness, of the images which the imagination produces when, instead of being solidly fed on experience, it is merely excited by the contemplation of other works of art. Nobody can sit out The Sin of St Hulda without seeing that Mr Ogilvie has read dramas and romances, looked at pictures, and listened to operas. But it is equally clear that he has never met a real St Hulda in his life. He may here ask me sarcastically whether *I* have ever met one—whether they grow on every bush for dramatists to study. I reply, unabashed, "In London, yes." The nearest Salvation Army barrack or London Mission will supply half a dozen saints of infinitely greater sanctity and heroism than the waxwork angel whom Miss Kate Rorke impersonates at the Shaftesbury. The education movement, the hospital nursing movement, and all the movements for the realization of religion in social reform have been largely the work of women of heroic devotion and sometimes of extraordinary eloquence, many of them alive and accessible to anybody who sincerely wishes to understand themselves and their work. They present to the dramatist's study temperaments rich in the passionate qualities, and personal histories rich in the struggles and braveries, which are the material of tragedy; whilst their characters positively sparkle with the incongruities and ironies and contradictions which are the life of comedy. Among our dramatists, Mr Henry Arthur Jones alone seems capable of realizing the existence of these masses of dramatic material lying ready to his hand. Mr Pinero, in The Notorious Mrs Ebbsmith, hardly got beyond certain irresolute recollections of newspaper notices of "platform women"; and it is clear that Mr Ogilvie does not even read the newspapers because they are not written in blank verse. He holds up a blurred mirror to the librettos of Meyerbeer's "historical" operas, and would like, one guesses, to make the stage affect the audience as the pictures of Delaroche and Gérome have affected him. This method—the method of bringing a reaping machine to glean a crop from a field after the harvest—is barren: great writers—Sir Walter Scott, for instance—may have amused themselves with it sometimes; but its results are counted among their exercises or follies, not among their masterpieces. If Mr Ogilvie finds that he is only affected by works of art, he may at once give up all hope of producing them; for this is the characteristic stigma (I thank thee, Max, for teaching me that word) of the born amateur. If, on the other hand, he is affected by real life, then the sooner he sets about representing it at first hand in his dramas the better. For I think there is not much of it in The Sin of St Hulda. I say I think, because to a good deal of the play I did not listen. I cannot defend this negligence, or deny that it was my business—my paid business—to listen to every word; but I could by no means achieve it. The blank verse flowed in at one ear and out at the other without producing any sort of activity between the two. I collapsed in this way more especially when St Hulda was on the stage. St Hulda is a combination of Delaroche's Christian Martyr with the Woman with a Past. She is herself incommoded by the incongruity, and wants to confess, but will not come to the point because she has to save her secret up for the last act—a miserly and evasive policy, exasperating from the dramatic point of view. She proves, I am afraid, that Mr Ogilvie has a chivalrous imagination, which is the sort of imagination that never produces a real woman. Not that the men are much more real; but they presume less on their unreality, and are consequently less tedious. They all begin with a considerable air of becoming important presently —so considerable, in fact, that it was quite late in the evening before I finally despaired of them. Prince Otho in particular was a rare impostor in this way. In spite of his rather Tappertitian beginning by making a haughty noble who had formerly insulted him publicly clean his boots, he kept up appearances long after I had given up Heinrich, Knipperdolling, and Manteuffel (a walking gentleman who entered as if he were going to eclipse Louis XI and Richard III) as men of straw. In this he was powerfully abetted by his impersonator, Mr Cartwright, who seems to possess stage temperament and susceptibility to an extraordinary degree without any backing to them. He sometimes makes clever—even delicate—strokes by instinct; and his staginess is not altogether unoriginal; but he seems unable to connect any of the things he can do with any definite conception of character. Mr Kemble almost made a part out of the Burgomaster: as it was, he certainly made a picture of him. Mr Lewis Waller, as Heinrich, apparently shared my opinion of St Hulda; for he was as cool a lover as ever I saw, taking the lady's death with a Christian resignation which belied the lamenting lines he had to utter. Here, as in the second act of A Woman's Reason, he seemed quite disabled, when the moment came for a display of pitiable abandonment, by his own dignity and good sense. But in the prouder passages he played with unexpected force, and in the climax to the third act rose fully to the situation, and struck in his defiance of Otho up to the hilt. Nobody would have recognized in this bold and handsome young medieval knight the sentimental leading man struggling with his tailor, with whom Mr Waller's admirers have hitherto been familiar.

Miss Kate Rorke did what all experienced and competent actresses do when they have a great many blank verse lines to deliver, and no part. She fell back on her style. It was all very intelligent, and very musical, and very plastic; and it had a certain technical interest, just as Mme Patti practising her scales would have had. But there was a great deal too much of it; and I have rarely experienced a more refreshing relief than when, on the company being called on the stage to receive applause at the end, Miss Rorke smiled quite naturally, and beckoned to Mr Ogilvie to come forward. That little touch of sincerity gave away all the rest of her performance, revealing its utter formality in a flash.

The play would, I am afraid, be rather dull if it were not for a certain operatic fire which serves Mr Ogilvie for solid Shakespearean power. Heinrich standing fascinated by the vision of St Hulda at the end of Act I, Otho's Mephistophelean laugh at the end of Act II, St Hulda's denial at the end of Act III, and the apotheosis at the end of Act IV are all operatic, and all as effective in that way as they can be without music. The sword combat, in which Mr Cartwright inadvertently nearly clove Mr Waller in twain, and the death of the heroine, are in the same taste. The costumiers have made the most of the swaggering hats and plumes, puffs and slashes, square-toed shoes and two-handed swords, which we know from Holbein and Dürer; but the result is handsome and "historical" rather than artistic. The fact that Miss Rorke's saintly dresses are too Victorian to be interesting, and that three of the four scenes are German interiors, the open-air one being dark, crowded, and very artificially lighted for the sake of Miss Rorke's halo, produces a certain heaviness of effect. A dramatist should never forget that plays want plenty of fresh air. Half the charm of For the Crown, the success of which has probably helped to smooth the way for St Hulda, lies in its liberal supply of mountain ozone.

I have rarely seen an audience so unanimous as that which crowded to witness the first representation of Biarritz at the Prince of Wales Theatre. It was unanimous in hope at the beginning, unanimous in doubt in the middle, and unanimous in derision at the end. Biarritz is sure to run triumphantly for several years, since nothing but the substitution of "special features" for every five minutes of the original work, and their frequent renewal, involving the conversion of the whole into a variety entertainment, could possibly keep it in existence for a fortnight. What Mr Jerome K. Jerome was thinking of when he wrote it is hard to imagine; but he has written to the papers promising to explain everything when the worst is over. As to Mr Lowenfeld, he appears to have been exercising his judgment, with the usual result. The only promising idea in the piece from the Prince of Wales Theatre point of view, is the placing of the scene in a hotel. This gives openings for those sallies of schoolboyish blackguardism which are supposed to throw a spell of fascinating wickedness round the "musical farces" which serve as a setting to the jewel of Mr Arthur Roberts's talent. Thus an old gentleman, having, like Mr Pickwick on a celebrated occasion, lost his room and forgotten its number, wanders about in his dressing gown asking everybody for his wife; and when he is at last taken upstairs by a chambermaid, a knowing laugh cackles up from the young gentlemen who think they know what large Continental hotels and their chambermaids are—never having been in one. When every obvious and uninteresting variation on this is exhausted, Mr Roberts comes to the rescue with a song, in which he describes how he met in Piccadilly a woman who lived in St John's Wood as somebody's mistress; how he accosted her; what he gave her for supper; and how he went to St John's Wood with her. The story was much less interesting than an ordinary police case; but when Mr Roberts had sung it, the audience seemed proud of him, and he seemed proud of himself. He also made mirth by his manner of beginning his conversations with women by the remark, "Where have I seen you before?" which is understood to be the formula by which gentlemen in the Empire Theatre promenade get over the embarrassment of addressing ladies to whom they have not been formally introduced. I confess I found this desperately dull. Witty things can be said by witty people about prostitution, as about any other subject; but prostitution is not a merry subject in itself—rather the reverse. For the rest, Mr Roberts gabbled, and dropped his aitches, and got from one of his favorite points to another anyhow, not thinking his audience worth the trouble of maintaining any style or taking any care. Naturally, a comedian who has no great respect for himself has none for the public who encourage him. However, I have no right to preach at Mr Roberts: all I am entitled to say is that I am tired of his mannerisms and that his Leicester Square pleasantries bore and offend me.

If "Faith, creating what it feigned" (a Shelleyan motto prefixed by Mr Ogilvie to St Hulda) broke down in the case of a favorite like Mr Roberts, who has talent enough to fall back on acting as a means of livelihood when the public begins to tire of his present occupation, it need hardly be said that his colleagues were not more fortunate. I appreciate the brightness and determination with which Miss Kitty Loftus asserts herself as "a jolly little folly" (so Mr Ross expresses it), with uncommon gifts as a dancer, singer, and speaker; and as soon as I am fortunate enough to find her dancing a single step, singing a single note, or speaking a single line, in a really uncommon way, I shall admit her pretensions and renounce my present heresy, which is, that Miss Kitty Loftus is a vivacious young lady who works very hard at being gay and pretty without knowing exactly how artists manage such things. Miss Phyllis Broughton dances her old dance, smiles her old smile, and sauces her old sauciness with her old success as if they and she had been invented yesterday. Miss Sadie Jerome, in attempting to repeat the success of her Lalage Potts song, only betrays the fact that she has gained nothing by her appearance in Gentleman Joe but a relapse into amateurishness. Miss Millie Hylton maintains a certain degree of artistic form, playing a trivial part prettily enough. Some of the other ladies on the stage have no artistic business there at all. Why are there so many mannerless girls, graceless girls, silly girls, impudent girls, and girls condemned to hopeless ugliness by having to wear trousers with jackets cut to fit waists like corset advertisements—a stupidity that would make Psyche herself unpresentable? I object to all these austerities: I am voluptuary enough to like nice girls, interesting girls, well-dressed and well-grouped girls; and I conceive the duties of a manager as including the selection and engagement of such girls and no others. Two minutes of Biarritz would reconcile a Trappist to his monastery for life.

The best part of the entertainment is Mr Osmond Carr's music —mere stereo, no doubt, much of it, but smart, appropriate stereo. A few of the numbers are pretty and musically witty. And the music has been thoroughly well got up by Mr Herbert Bunning, who handles the band excellently.

PUNCH AND JUDY AGAIN

THE ROGUE'S COMEDY. A play in three acts. By Henry Arthur Jones. Garrick Theatre, 21 April 1896.   [25 *April* 1896]

A SAFE rule for the dramatist is, "When in doubt, revive Punch and Judy." Mr Henry Arthur Jones is not in doubt; but he is in dudgeon—not peevish personal dudgeon, but artistic, philosophic dudgeon, inevitable after the unnatural death of Michael and his Lost Angel. Accordingly, he has fallen back on Punch and Judy, the eternal rogue's comedy, tempting the business dramatist by its assured popularity, and fascinating the artist dramatist by its unlimited depth, which yet involves no obligation to fully fathom it or else fail. Success is safe at any depth, from an inch downwards. At the street corner, with a deplorable Judy, an infant thrown out of the window, a dog Toby, and a few assorted types of law and order culminating in a hangman and a devil, the great issues of the comedy can be ribaldly touched to the music of pipes and drum. At the other end of the range, Mozart's Don Giovanni, the world's masterpiece in stage art, is only Punch on a higher plane. Every brace of vagabonds can master and perform the one; the greatest artists in the world can, at their best, only bungle through the other. Between the two lies all philosophic comedy, high and low, with its Faustuses, its Robert Macaires, its Affable Hawks, its Jeremy Diddlers, its common Joeys with red-hot poker and sausages, its Pierrots, and, since last Tuesday night, its Mr Bailey Prothero. The first question about him, then, is as to which of his ancestors in the great family of Punch's reincarnations he most resembles. Not that rare bird the Mozartian Don assuredly. It is true that Bailey drinks four glasses of champagne, and "bucks up," as he expresses it, after them; but he cannot sing a pæan to the joy of life like Finch' han dal vino, nor need our actors so miserably fail in catching his ecstasy as to drive anyone to find a new mode of utterance for its wicked rapture through the mechanism of the most brilliant of instruments, as Liszt was driven in the Don's case. Bailey does not cut a figure in the high comedy region: his place is in melodramatic farce. This suggests Robert Macaire; and there is certainly a family resemblance; but as Robert was an entire and perfect scoundrel, and we cannot nowadays bear to damn anyone, Bailey has been made a good husband and father. As a rascal redeemed by sentiment, he is more like that amiable young relative of the family, the Chevalier des Grieux, only older, coarser, and without Manon Lescaut. Instead of Manon, he has a lawful wife, so far like Mrs Jerry Cruncher in A Tale of Two Cities, that her habit of "flopping"—that is, kneeling down in prayer—jars on her husband. I do not think much of Mrs Prothero. Her humanity is sacrificed to write up the actor-manager's part—a sacrifice of the eternal to the temporal. In the first act we see her enjoying an income of £80 a year and dressing like Mrs Langtry on it, her dramatic function being to act as her husband's confederate in his fortune-telling business. Not until the second act does she develop a tender conscience; and even then she makes no difficulty about shutting it up tight at her husband's urgent request, herein departing from the example of Mrs Cruncher, who braved boots and pokers rather than refrain from praying steadfastly against the success of Mr Cruncher's illicit pursuits as a resurrection-man. When, in the third act, Judy Prothero allows Bailey to assure their son that of his mother, at least, he need never be ashamed, it is impossible not to revolt at the recollection of her active complicity in the duperies of the first act. It is all very well for Mr Jones to set her to catch sympathy for Mr Willard; but the plain truth is that she is just as bad as Bailey—worse, in fact, because she sets up religious pretensions to be morally superior to him whilst living on the profits of his swindling.

The characterization of the figures which surround Bailey Prothero does not go very deep. Of course Mr Jones, with his fertile imagination and humorous observation, could no more miss individualizing a figure here and there than Dickens could. The most entertaining result of his powers in this way is Mr Robert Cushing, who plays Bertrand to Prothero's Macaire so faithfully that when his unfortunate habit of purloining the spoons comes into play, the scene needs nothing but a creaking snuff-box in Mr Willard's hands to take us back to the Auberge des Adrets at once. But the characterization is capital underneath the farce, and very funny. The wretch is so feeble that even his efforts to swear do not get beyond a fat, flat, twaddle-toned "Oh my goodness gracious!" The abject folly of his perfectly sound plea of "total loss of self-respect," and the helpless way in which he succumbs to every opportunity of doing wrong, even with the certainty of ignominious detection staring him in the face, not only make highly ticklesome buffoonery, but hit off in a few strokes the leading lines of a hopelessly rickety and rotten moral constitution. Cushing is the best character in the play; and though he is only on the stage for a few minutes, I am not sure that Mr Standing, who plays him to a miracle, is not luckier than Mr Willard himself in his part. Another personage who is purely comic in his dramatic function, but yet individualized as a character type, is the silly-billy Lord Dovergreen, a little burlesqued by Mr Sydney Brough, but not spoiled. Lord Bicester is also a vivid thumbnail sketch; and there is life in Miss Proye and Lambert the footman. These people not only say funny things, but say them with a genuine character modification—not a mere trick of phrase or manner. For all that, the play is not one of Mr Jones's best. That part of the dialogue which is mere social chatter is not nearly so witty as the small talk in The Masqueraders; and as to the high comedy of Rebellious Susan, it is quite out of sight. Some of the characters are downright bad: for instance, Lord John Bucklow is the hackneyed old stage roué— the "man of pleasure become a man of pain," as Charles Reade put it—with the hackneyed manner and make-up. Mr David James, with his simperings, and his dammees, and his whistlings of the intervals of the common chord (as if that were a possible nervous trick), certainly acts him as badly as possible; but the part invites his abuse of it. Lady Clarabut, again, is nothing but a night's work for Lady Monckton; and the two lovers decorously carry on the story without stepping forward into any sort of individuality. In short, the leading characters are not characters at all, but only supports for Bailey Prothero. In a play by Mr Grundy, or any other votary of the "well made" or mechanical rabbit play, I should not complain of this, since everybody knows that if a mechanical rabbit is to move, it must have wheels for entrails; but one expects living members from Mr Jones. At all events, one pays him the compliment of noticing the appearance of automata among his characters as a thing not altogether to be expected. As to the character for which this sacrifice has been made, I confess I should like, before judging it finally, to see it played by a genuine comedian—say Mr Wyndham or Mr Hare. Mr Willard is a good actor, but not of that kind. He begins with comic "character acting" laid on in hearty and by no means delicate strokes; and when the vein changes, he plunges, without the slightest gradation, head over heels into melodrama. His grip throughout is far too strenuous to admit of dainty handling: he grinds out his words at a clerically low pitch with a voice that has changes but no inflexions, wedging his face into a mask that can be instantly rearranged for mirth or melancholy, but which has no shades, and can therefore tell of moods and shocks, but not of processes or fluctuations. The part presents certain well-marked main aspects—the rogue at work, the rogue triumphant, the rogue alarmed, the rogue reckless, the father wounded, the father tender, and the husband goodnatured. These being patent and unmistakeable, Mr Willard seized on them vigorously enough; but as each one recurred he treated it exactly as he had treated it before, with a single facial expression and a single tone; so that his performance resolved itself into a repetition of some half-dozen effects, and would have become monotonous but for the activity with which the author kept the story going. In fact, it did become monotonous, especially in the matter of voice, wherever the author's pace slackened. Nevertheless, it kept the audience in good humor by its geniality and sustained vigor; and in the final scene it had pathetic strength—the final exit, with the shake-hands with the son and the "Buck up, old girl" to the wife, was admirable; but of the subtle, continuous, exquisitely nuanced acting, apparently infinite in variety, which becomes classical in high comedy—such work as we have seen in Duse's Mirando-lina, Coquelin's Duval, Hare's Baron Croodle, Charles Mathews's Mercadet, and Jefferson's farcical heroes—there was not a trace. It is true that the play itself, as I began by saying, is melodramatic farce rather than high comedy; but all the classical examples I have cited are examples of high comedians playing in farces. I should add that the character of Bailey Prothero is completely redeemed from the falseness and crudity of melodrama by many admirable touches, notably the absence of conventional exaggeration in the fatherly emotion, which is presented for exactly what it is worth by the author with an acute nicety that is also stealthily humorous. Fortunately, this is one of the points to which Mr Willard's performance does justice.

Miss Olliffe, who played Mrs Prothero, was new to the critics, though I had had the luck to discover her at the Avenue during the illness of Miss Alma Stanley some time ago. She deepened the favorable impression I received on that occasion, and will, I have no doubt, soon be a familiar and indispensable figure in our London casts. The end of that will be, I suppose, that she will give up acting, and have all her parts written expressly for her. Indeed, of the play as a whole I cannot say that it altogether escaped that rawness and uneasiness of presentation from which Mr Jones's recent plays have suffered so frightfully, the truth being that the moment our actors are taken out of the routine parts which are merely the latest dramatizations, or rather stagings, of their own personal peculiarities—the moment, in short, they are called upon to impersonate new characters instead of being presented with old characters that impersonate them—they lose their style, and even their ease and assurance; so that Mr Jones's originality is positively made a means of worrying the audience into a longing to get back to that familiar little world in which Mr Sydney Brough makes love to Miss Maud Millett under the parental eyes of Miss Rose Leclercq and Mr Cyril Maude, whilst some nice leading lady and gentleman give object lessons in fashionable dressing and polite courtship and marriage to the graduates of suburban society. This is the real explanation, I believe, of the fact that for some time past every play with any sort of originality in it has provoked three or four weak-souled first-nighters in the gallery to utter piteous howls on the appearance of the author at the fall of the curtain. Mr Jones, having, not unnaturally, no sort of taste for deliberate and premeditated incivility, declined to make the customary appearance on Tuesday night. It took twenty-five minutes to convince the audience that he was in earnest. They cheered and called and applauded until they were physically exhausted; then stopped to recover, and returned to the charge again and again; then, as their numbers dwindled, intoned a long, melancholy note like the organ giving the diapason to the orchestra before an oratorio performance; then hooted dismally; and finally sang "We wont go home till morning," the strains of which, like Haydn's Farewell Symphony, died away as the performers stole away one by one and left the theatre empty. And then I went home too.

I am greatly obliged to whoever sent me a belated ticket for an afternoon performance at the Court Theatre on Wednesday; but I may perhaps be allowed to observe that the Saturday Review does not keep a staff of critics, like boy messengers, waiting on the premises to be dispatched to performances at a moment's notice. I did manage to arrive in time for the last act of something; but as the playbills were all gone before I arrived, I know not what, or by whom, it was. Suffice it that the effort to make any sense of it almost unhinged my reason. I think it must have been a burlesque of The Corsican Brothers; but I am not sure. At all events there was Mr Yorke Stephens, and Mr Yorke Stephens's ghost. Also a Mahatma. Perhaps I was mad, and only imagined it. Perhaps Mr Yorke Stephens was mad. Possibly the author was mad. I really do not understand the affair.

THE IMMORTAL WILLIAM

The Shakespear Anniversary Celebration at the Métropole Theatre, Camberwell, 23 April 1896.   [2 *May* 1896]

WITHIN reason, I am always prepared to do honor to Shakespear. Annual celebrations are all very well in theory, and are almost as popular with the people who dont take any part in them, and dont intend to, as Annual Parliaments are with the people who never vote and never electioneer; but outside that large circle they are too much of a good thing. I have long ceased to celebrate my own birthday; and I do not see why I should celebrate Shakespear's. There can be no objection in the world to Mr Benson, or Mr Greet, or anyone else in the Shakespearean business taking the fullest advantage of an anniversary to give that business a fillip; but whoever expects me to put myself every 23 April in an attitude at all differing from my attitude on the 23 October is doomed to disappointment. I went to Camberwell on the afternoon of last Thursday week because, on the whole, I thought it my business to be there; but when the Irving Dramatic Club wanted me to resume work the moment I got back to the west end by going to Cymbeline at St George's Hall, I struck. Shakespear is for an afternoon, but not for all time. Under ordinary circumstances I should have done the other thing—that is, gone to see the amateurs in the evening instead of the professionals in the afternoon; but it happened on this occasion that the professional cast was the fresher, younger, and more interesting of the two; so I went to Camberwell. Let me not, however, exaggerate my own virtue by leaving it to be inferred that I got there in time. The hour appointed was half-past two; and though I spared neither energy nor expense in my journey, making no less than three separate embarkations in train, bus, and tram, at a total cost of fourpence, it was three o'clock before the Métropole was sighted. This had two grave consequences. First, Camberwell had rallied round the Bard so multitudinously that the offer of untold gold could procure me nothing better than a mere skylight of a box, from which my view of the legitimate drama was considerably foreshortened. Second, I was late for Miss Dorothy Dene's Juliet. This I greatly regretted; for I have not seen Miss Dorothy Dene since the now almost remote days when Mr Henry Arthur Jones was making his reputation by writing melodramas for Mr Wilson Barrett at the Princess's. Why? Here was a young lady who had, not the painted show of beauty which is so common on the stage, and so tedious, but that honest reality of it which is useful to painters. Her speech shewed unusual signs of artistic cultivation; she had plastic grace; she took herself and her profession seriously; and her appearances in leading parts were not unpopular. The mystery is, what became of her? Did she fall into the abyss of opulent matrimony? Did the studio violently reclaim its adored model? Did she demand impossible terms? Or were the managers obdurate in their belief that there is only one safe sort of actress—the woman who is all susceptibility and no brains? Far be it from me to deny that every deviation from this type involves a certain risk of unpopularity—of a demand on the part of the actress, or rather the woman, that in the intercourse between her and the public the wooing and the worth shall not all be on one side. Further still be it from me to forget the fact that in cases of positive genius for the stage no question as to the dignity of the actress's occupation can arise. For instance, Duse is clearly a most laborious artist hard at work, and not a pretty woman making an exhibition of herself. But the appearance of a

Duse is as rare on the stage as that of a woman who absolutely cannot act at all. Most of the routine of our leading theatrical work in London is done by ladies who are not altogether artists and not altogether exhibitions, but who eke out a little art with more or less personal attractiveness. Probably the reason our managers prefer the brainless-susceptible woman is that she is a ready-made actress as far as she can act at all; and small blame to them, since we have no apprenticeship system to secure to a manager the services of an actress whom he trains, and no system of training to replace the apprenticeship system. But I get so tired of the brainless-susceptible heroine that even an American lecturer would sometimes be a relief to the eternal sympathetic leading lady, who is called sweetly womanly because, having nothing but her sex to insist on, she insists on that continually. And yet, since women of the other sort get no engagements, it ends in her being the only one who gets sufficient stage practice to be trusted with important parts, whence it comes that the important parts never are important. We want more women of the clever, positive type on the stage (also men). We also want more objectively beautiful women on the stage; for your brainless-susceptible one is often your beautyless-susceptible: she may appeal to your sentimentality; but a sculptor or a painter would not look twice at her from his dry business point of view; and her graces of carriage and movement are of the cheapest. Her hold on the stage is largely a result of the stage's hold on her through her disadvantage of being fit for nothing else; so that economic necessity does for her what irresistible vocation does for an actress of genius—gives her, that is, the unconditional singleness of aim and pertinacity which move mountains in the long run. The clever, positive woman, on the other hand, has alternative activities: she has ability and character enough to make her living in other professions, or to discharge social and domestic duties as the wife of a Philistine citizen in a responsible, capable, respectable way. Granted that she may have only the makings of a second-rate actress in her, she would probably make second-rate acting much more important than a good deal of what passes as first-rate acting at present; and her influence on the drama would be highly beneficial owing to her demand for real parts in which to put forth her brains and skill against the rivals who rely on sex and sympathy in every kind of part. It takes all sorts to make a stage, just as it takes all sorts to make a world; and we do not get all sorts at present. We get the geniuses and the *hystériques*; but the intermediate talents, however promising, are driven back from a profession in which brains and self-respect have no chance against emotional facility and neurotic sexuality. The latter are invaluable, the former quite useless, in an empty part which is nothing but the merest cue to the imagination of the audience; but confront the facile, neurotic, empty-headed actress with a part which demands not only sympathy but intelligence and trained nervous energy; not only "womanly" softnesses and graces but plastic, picturesque, vigorous action; nay, ask her to deliver a ten-line speech—not a hysterical explosion, but a speech with thought as well as feeling in it—and you will soon find how a dramatic author is hampered at present by the limited compass of the instruments at his disposal. There are always clever, educated, ambitious young women ready to try their fortune on the stage; but how are they to get the necessary experience to make skilled artists of them? It takes years of practice to develop the power of emotional expression; for most educated women have been trained to fight against emotional expression because it is a mode of self-betrayal. Now self-betrayal, magnified to suit the optics of the theatre, is the whole art of acting; and the strong, continent woman, unless she is descended from generations of actors, is certain to be beaten at first on the stage by the hysterical, incontinent one, or even by the stupid, prosaic hereditary actress who, within certain limits, acts as a duck swims. Under present conditions this handicap is sufficient to baffle the clever recruit drawn from the newly emancipated women of the middle class in her quest for engagements, thus depriving her of the practice necessary to train her, and so defeating her attempt to gain a footing on the stage. The theatre is unable to keep and drill able-bodied and able-minded recruits; and the result is that the class of work which would in any other profession be perfectly within the competence of the rank and file, has to be entrusted to the leaders. And even the leaders are often more remarkable for what is called social charm than for any rarer artistic qualification.

On the whole, perhaps it is as well that I did not see Miss Dorothy Dene; for it is not conceivable that disuse has matured her powers, or years increased her natural suitability to the part of Juliet. Just at present I am more anxious about Miss Dorothea Baird, whom I did see, as Rosalind. Rosalind is to the actress what Hamlet is to the actor—a part in which, reasonable present-ability being granted, failure is hardly possible. It is easier than Trilby up to a certain point, though it will of course hold much more acting. Miss Baird plays it intelligently and nicely; and this, to such a very pretty Ganymede, is enough to secure success. How far the niceness and intelligence of the pretty young lady will develop into the passion and intuition of the artist, or whether the prettiness will develop into the "handsome is as handsome does" fascination which holds the stage for many years against Time, remains to be seen. All that can be said at present is that Miss Baird's Rosalind is bright and pleasant, with sufficient natural charm to secure indulgence for all its shortcomings. Of these the most serious is Miss Baird's delivery of the lines. Everybody by this time knows how a modern high-schoolmistress talks —how she repudiates the precision, the stateliness, the awe-inspiring oracularity of the old-fashioned schoolmistress who knew nothing, and cloaks her mathematics with a pretty little voice, a pretty little manner, and all sorts of self-conscious calineries and unassumingnesses. "Poor little me! what do *I* know about conic sections?" is the effect she aims at. Miss Baird's Rosalind has clearly been to the high school and modelled herself upon her pet mistress, if not actually taught there herself. But that dainty, pleading, narrow-lipped little torrent of gabble will not do for Shakespear. It is so unintelligible across the footlights that even I, who know As You Like It almost as well as I know Beethoven's Pastoral Symphony, could not always catch what she was saying. This being so, it may safely be taken that Camberwell did not catch more than a very small conic section of it. For even an expert cannot make sense of Elizabethan blank verse at a first hearing when it is delivered at the rate of 200 words a minute and upwards. Besides, its lyrical flow, if such a tiny ladylike patter can be credited with so broad a quality, is not that of Shakespear's verse. The effect is like a canary trying to sing Handel.

Mr H. B. Irving is in the full flood of that Shakespearean enthusiasm which exalts the Bard so far above common sense that any prosaic suiting of the action to the word and the word to the action seems to be a degradation of his genius to what Nicholas Rowe called "a mere light of reason." Mr Irving gave us the closet scene from Hamlet. He entered, surcharged with Fate, and instead of Hamlet's sharp, dry, "Now, mother: whats the matter?" followed by his reply to her affected "Thou hast thy father much offended," with the purposely blunt "Mother: *you* have my father much offended," gave us a most tragic edition of the conversation, with the yous altered to thous, and an agitated slip or two to enhance the effect. When he lifted the arras and found that he had killed Polonius instead of the King, he betrayed not the smallest surprise, but said, in a superior tone, "Thou wretched, rash, intruding fool, farewell!" much as if he were dismissing a deservedly and quite intentionally flogged schoolboy. He was resolved to make an effect by seizing the Queen and throwing her down on the floor; and the moment he selected was in the middle of the following passage:

> At your age
> The heyday in the blood is tame: it's humble,
> And waits upon the judgment; and what judgment
> Would step from this to this?

The Queen was floored after the phrase "and waits upon the judgment," shewing that at Mr Irving's age the heyday in the blood does not wait upon the judgment, but has its fling (literally) regardless of reason. The only dramatic profit from this proceeding was the point given to the Ghost's "But see! amazement on thy mother sits." Nevertheless, the performance, nonsensical

as it was, was not ridiculous. Mr Irving is not altogether unsuccessful in his attempts to be tragic and to make effects; and if
he could only bring his tragedy and his effects into some intelligent relation to the drama in hand, he would find himself highly
complimented in the Saturday Review. To be abstractly and
irrelevantly tragic; to brandish a sword; to discourse in blank
verse; to stagger and fall and hurl frail heroines away, is just as
absurd in Hamlet, if done at the wrong moment, as it would be in
Box and Cox. There are people so unfit for the stage that they
could not do these things even at the right moment without making the audience laugh. That is not Mr Irving's case. When he
learns what to do and when to do it, he will not be at a loss as to
how to do it. More than that it is impossible to grant him at
present. The scenes from As You Like It included nothing of
Jaques except the few scraps of dialogue between the pessimist
and Orlando; and no exception can be taken to the way in which
these were handled by Mr Irving. He dressed and looked the part
well.

The best bit of work was Mr Bernard Gould's Orlando; the
worst, Mr Ben Greet's Touchstone. Mr Greet put himself out of
the question before he had been two minutes on the stage by the
profound stroke of picking one of Orlando's sonnets from a tree,
and reading from it the impromptu burlesque:

> If a hart do lack a hind,
> Let him seek out Rosalind, etc.

This was a new reading with a vengeance. He was not much more
successful as executant than as Shakespearean student. He completely missed the piled-up climax of the speech to William, and
was, in short, as bad a Touchstone as a critic could desire to see.
It is no disgrace to an actor to be unable to play Touchstone; but
why, under these circumstances, and being a manager, he should
cast himself for it, passes my understanding. Mr Rawson Buckley
played Oliver very well, but persisted, as usual, in dressing himself smartly, and then describing himself as "a wretched ragged
man, o'ergrown with hair." Mr Gould managed his part, especi-

ally the difficulties of the sham courtship with Ganymede, better than I can remember having seen it managed before; and some of his lines were finely spoken; but he was not Orlando. Orlando's intelligence is the intelligence of the heart: he always comes out best as an amiable, strong, manly, handsome, shrewd-enough-to-take-care-of-himself, but safely stupid and totally unobservant young man. Now, Mr Gould plays with his head; his intelligence is always on the alert; and he is so observant that in spite of his many valuable stage qualities he almost disqualifies himself as an actor by his draughtsman's habit of watching himself and everyone else so keenly and interestedly that he is more apt to forget his part than to forget himself in it. The born actor looks in: Mr Gould looks on. He acts like a good critic, and probably represses his tendencies—if he has any—to the maudlin self-sympathy, the insane egotism, the bottomless folly, the hysterical imaginative mendacity which—with the help of alcohol—make acting easy to some men who are for all other purposes the most hopeless wastrels. However, I do not object: I recognize the fact that the ascendency of the sentimental amorphous actor means the ascendency of the sentimental amorphous drama, and that the critical actor, like Mr Gould, is indispensable to a drama with any brains in it. Still, the critical actor need not be also a draughtsman actor. I once elaborately explained to Mr Gould a part of which I was myself the author. He paid me the closest attention; retired to ponder my utterances; and presently returned with a perfectly accurate and highly characteristic drawing of me, which I shall probably never live down. And if I had been Shakespear explaining Orlando, it would have been just the same.

THE FARCICAL COMEDY OUTBREAK

THE NEW BABY. A deception in three acts. Adapted by Arthur
Bourchier from Der Rabensvater, by H. F. Fischer and J.
Jarno. Royalty Theatre, 28 April 1896.

MONSIEUR DE PARIS. A play in one act. By Alicia Ramsey and
Rudolph de Cordova. Royalty Theatre.

A NIGHT OUT. Farcical comedy in three acts. By Georges Feydeau and Maurice Desvallières. English version. Vaudeville
Theatre, 29 April 1896.   [9 *May* 1896]

ONE of the strongest objections to the institution of monogamy
is the existence of its offspring, the conventional farcical comedy.
The old warning, "Beware how you kiss when you do not love,"
ought to be paraphrased on the playbills of all our lighter theatres
as "Beware how you laugh when you do not enjoy." To laugh
without sympathy is a ruinous abuse of a noble function; and the
degradation of any race may be measured by the degree of their
addiction to it. In its subtler forms it is dying very hard: for instance, we find people who would not join in the laughter of a
crowd of peasants at the village idiot, or tolerate the public
flogging or pillorying of a criminal, booking seats to shout with
laughter at a farcical comedy, which is, at bottom, the same thing
—namely, the deliberate indulgence of that horrible, derisive joy
in humiliation and suffering which is the beastliest element in
human nature. I make these portentous observations not by way
of breaking a butterfly on a wheel, but in order to bring out with
violent emphasis the distinction between the high and the base
comedy of errors—between Pink Dominos and Twelfth Night;
or, to illustrate from another art, between the caricatures of Leech
or Gavarni and those which mark the last intolerable stages of the
degradation of Ally Sloper (who in his original Ross-Duval days
was not without his merits). To produce high art in the theatre,
the author must create persons whose fortunes we can follow as
those of a friend or enemy: to produce base laughter, it is only
necessary to turn human beings on to the stage as rats are turned

into a pit, that they may be worried for the entertainment of the spectators. Such entertainment is much poorer fun than most playgoers suspect. The critic, trained to analyse all his artistic sensations, soon gets cured of the public's delusion that everything that makes it laugh amuses it. You cannot impose on him by the mere galvanism of the theatre; for all its manifestations, from the brute laughter produced by an indecency or a bout of horseplay, to the tricks, familiar to old actors, by which worthless explosions of applause can be elicited with mechanical certainty at the end of a speech or on an exit, become so transparent to him that, instead of sharing the enthusiasm they excite, he measures merit by their absence. For example, one of the admirable points in Mrs Patrick Campbell's performance in For the Crown is the way in which, after her recitation of the butterfly poem, she avoids the round of clapping which any third-rate actress could get for it—however execrably it might be delivered—by simply finishing it with a swagger and waiting for the audience to make a fool of itself. I have no doubt that many old stagers regard this as the ineptitude of a novice letting a sure point go "for nothing" or "without a hand." But everybody remembers the recitation; everybody is struck by it; everybody is conscious of a spell which would be broken by any vulgar attempt to "bring down the house": the commercial result being that people go to see Mrs Campbell, whereas they stay at home when there is nothing to be enjoyed at the theatre except the galvanic tricks of the trade. If it could once be borne in upon the mental darkness of most of our public performers that the artists who draw best are not those who are fondest of making the noisy and hysterical section of the audience interrupt the play—that, in fact, applause in the middle of an act is not only discreditable on most occasions to both actor and audience but bad business as well—we should get vastly better work at the theatres.

I shall now, perhaps, be understood (if not, no matter) when I class the laughter produced by conventional farcical comedy as purely galvanic, and the inference drawn by the audience that since they are laughing they must be amused or edified or pleased, as a delusion. They are really being more or less worried and exhausted and upset by ill-natured cachinnation; and the proof is that they generally leave the theatre tired and out of humor with themselves and the world. Lest I should err here on the side of over-much righteousness, let me hasten to admit that a little galvanism may be harmless and even beneficial in its effect on the lungs and liver; but three acts of it is too much. I first learnt the weariness of it from Pink Dominos, although that play had an excellent third act; and I have been wearied in the same way by every new version. For we have had it again and again under various titles. Act I, John Smith's home; Act II, the rowdy restaurant or casino at which John Smith, in the course of his clandestine spree, meets all the members of his household, including the schoolboy and the parlormaid; Act III, his house next morning, with the inevitable aftermath of the complications of the night before: who that has any theatrical experience does not know it all by heart? And now here it is again, with a fresh coat of paint on it, and as rotten as ever underneath.

But farcical comedy, like any other stage entertainment, may become artistically valuable, and even delightful, through fine execution. Pink Dominos is memorable, not for itself, but for the performances of Wyndham and Clarke. One remembers the charm of Miss Eastlake before she took up the heavy and violent work of supporting Mr Wilson Barrett in tragic melodrama; and this generation, contemplating Sir Augustus Harris with awe, little suspects how lighthearted he was as Harry Greenlanes. Since then, Mr Hawtrey, Mr Penley, and Miss Lottie Venne have managed to keep up the notion that farcical comedies are intrinsically amusing with considerable success. But the moment an attempt is made to run this sort of dramatic work on its own merits, its fundamental barrenness and baseness assert themselves and become intolerable. Therefore I shall make no pretence of discussing as drama the two specimens just produced at the Royalty and Vaudeville. Suffice it that the Royalty piece, The New Baby, is, from that point of view, so far beneath contempt that it never once rises to the point of even suggesting the disgust which its story would rouse in anyone who took it seriously; whilst A Night Out, at the Vaudeville, though a masterpiece of ingenuity and urbanity in comparison to the other, is essentially the same as previous nights out, from that in Pink Dominos downwards, and reproduces the stage arrangements of the second act of Forbidden Fruit pretty faithfully. But it is noteworthy that although The New Baby includes incest in its bewilderments, and one of the central incidents of A Night Out is the sudden retirement of a gentleman from a supper party on a pretext which Smollett might, and probably would, have employed, they are comparatively free from that detestable, furtive lubricity which was the rule twenty years ago. Farcical comedy used to have the manners of a pimp. It is now progressing upward towards the morals of Tom Jones.

The question then being one of acting, we had better start by making certain allowances: first, for the absence from the cast of those light comedians who have been specially successful in this class of entertainment, and, second, for the homeliness of our English attempts to volatilize ourselves sufficiently to breathe that fantastic atmosphere of moral irresponsibility in which alone the hero of farcical comedy, like Pierrot or Harlequin, can realize himself fully. On the understanding that these difficulties have not been surmounted, one may say that A Night Out is not in the main badly acted. Mr Giddens's humor, brought into play with apparent recklessness, but really with most skilful discretion, is irresistible. Mr Sugden's Paillard could not be improved without overdoing the part; and Mr Wyes has at last succeeded in presenting the peculiar monstrosity he has invented for stage purposes with something like a real artistic command of it. Mrs Edmund Phelps's performance as Madame Pinglet (frankly pronounced Pingly) is clever; but there are two points in which it might be improved. The business of grovelling on the floor in the third act is shockingly ugly; and the grimace by which she expresses extreme discomfiture is, owing to the turning up of the corners of the mouth, in effect a smile, not unlike that of Bailey Prothero in The Rogue's Comedy. Miss Fannie Ward is a determined young lady with plenty of assurance, and gumption enough to simulate the not very subtle emotions of her part plausibly enough; but she is hardly an artist. Miss Pattie Browne, the inevitable maid who seduces the inevitable schoolboy, is merely that impossible superstition, the stolidly bouncing English stage chambermaid. In this, and in such details as the crudity with which the second waiter keeps senselessly shouting Madame Paillard's name with an obvious consciousness of the mischief he is doing, not to mention the unnecessary noisiness of some of the scenes, one sees the chief fault of the production—puerility of stage management. Mr Seymour Hicks has given way to his sense of fun, forgetting that a stage manager should have no sense of anything except fine art.

But if the management is immature at the Vaudeville, what is it at the Royalty? Alas! it is hardly to be described. Here is Mr Bourchier, a born actor—the likeliest successor, so far, to Mr Wyndham in light comedy—with a theatre of his own and an excellent company, the centre of which is well knit together by private as well as artistic ties, and with a handsome capital in personal popularity and good wishes to reinforce his cash balance, positively playing with his chances like an undergraduate. I protested mildly against the way in which The Chili Widow was romped through. No doubt it was jolly; but it was not artistic management, and it was hardly acting. But The New Baby is worse. Mr Bourchier has not only cast himself for an elderly part which he is physically unfit for—a part which might be played appropriately by James Lewis—but he treats it as a pure lark from beginning to end, rattling along anyhow as if nothing mattered so long as his good humor and high spirits infected the audience sufficiently to keep them smiling. In desperation I ask Mr Bourchier, does he really think he is keeping himself up to his work at the Royalty? Would any other manager stand from him the happy-go-lucky playing he stands from himself with apparent complacency? Would any other author allow him to do so much less than his best at the very moment when he should be concentrating his intensest energy on the consolidation of his position? Does he expect me to pay him any higher compliment than to admit that his performance is at least good enough for the play he has selected? There are two well-acted parts in The New Baby, and only two. Miss Alice Mansfield, a very clever actress, does for the piece what Mr Giddens does for its rival at the Vaudeville; and Mr W. G. Elliott plays the fiery Spaniard as conscientiously and excellently as Mr Bourchier himself would perhaps play it if he were the actor and Mr Elliott the manager. Mr Blakeley almost succeeds by his well-known grimaces and attitudes in persuading the audience that he has a real part. But the play is too foolish to have much chance even of a success of folly.

The strongest part of the Royalty performance is a one-act drama, of exceptional merit as such things go, entitled Monsieur de Paris, in which Miss Violet Vanbrugh, instead of trifling with her talent as she did in The Chili Widow, plays a purely romantic part with striking effect. The sanguinary ending of the play is as mechanical, obvious, and unimaginative as a Chicago pig-sticking; and Miss Vanbrugh, by overrating its value, attempts—what no thoroughly expert actress would attempt—a sustained and unvaried crescendo of forcible expression which only betrays the fact that it is her imagination and not her feeling that is at work; but the performance proves a great deal as to her remarkable qualifications for more serious work on the stage. May I add without offence that in the finest diction "crime," "quick," "true," and "heaven" are not vehemently dissyllabic?

I never go to celebrations and never write about them. What is more, I never eat supper. But I went to the Hotel Cecil yesterday week to shake hands with Mr Wyndham, and never succeeded in getting within a dozen yards of him. It was an amazing spectacle. There we were in our thousands—players and authors and critics —geniuses and beauties—lost sheep strayed from the Philistine fold of respectability—the disgraces of our own families—the delight of everybody else's families—the mighty *cabotinage* of London in all its fascination, and all its unlimited capacity for flattery, champagne, and asparagus. Nine out of every ten guests were players by profession; and fully one out of every two hundred and fifty could really act—first among these, beyond all challenge,

Wyndham himself, whose health was proposed by that tragic comedian the Lord Chief Justice. I say nothing of the peers and politicians and other interlopers: a crowd of them can be seen anywhere. I missed Sir Henry Irving and Miss Ellen Terry: they, like Mr John Hare, were in America. I also missed Ibsen, greatly to my surprise. But it was a wonderful occasion, for all that—excellently managed and worked up, no doubt, but none the less owing the extremity of its huge success to its genuineness as a demonstration of admiration and regard for Mr Wyndham.

HENRY IV

HENRY IV. Part I. Haymarket Theatre, 8 May 1896.

[16 *May* 1896]

THIS is a miserably incompetent world. The average doctor is a walking compound of natural ignorance and acquired witchcraft, who kills your favorite child, wrecks your wife's health, and orders you into habits of nervous dram-drinking before you have the courage to send him about his business, and take your chance like a gentleman. The average lawyer is a nincompoop, who contradicts your perfectly sound impressions on notorious points of law, involves you in litigation when your case is hopeless, compromises when your success is certain, and cannot even make your will without securing the utter defeat of your intentions if anyone takes the trouble to dispute them. And so on, down to the bootmaker whose boots you have to make your tortured feet fit, and the tailor who clothes you as if you were a cast-iron hot-water apparatus. You imagine that these people have professions; and you find that what they have is only, in the correct old word, their "mystery"—a humbug, like all mysteries. And yet, how we help to keep up the humbug! I know men of quite exceptional intelligence—men so sceptical that they have freed their minds from all philosophic and religious dogma, who nevertheless read the Lancet and the British Medical Journal from end to end every week as devoutly as any superstitious washerwoman ever read Zadkiel or Old Moore, and not only believe it all, but long tremblingly for the next symptom that will give them an excuse for calling in the medicine man to mistake typhoid fever for influenza or paint their tonsils with caustic when their kidneys are out of order. Every week they have some joyful tidings for me. Another disease has been traced to its germ; an infallible destroyer of that germ has been discovered; the disease has been annihilated. What wonderful triumphs has not science enjoyed in my time! Smallpox has been made totally impossible; hydrophobia has vanished; epilepsy has yielded to the simplest of operations; the pangs of angina pectoris have been relieved as if by magic; consumption is a dream of the past; and now there is to be no more diphtheria. Instead of vainly seeking, as of old, for a universal remedy, we are the proud discoverers of a dozen, and can change with the fashion from one to another. Mercury, salicylic acid, iodide and bromide of potassium, hashed thyroid, antipyrine, with lymphs innumerable: there they are, making us all safe and happy until we are unfortunate enough to fall down in a fit, or get bitten by a mad dog, or fall sick with an ugly rash and a bad pain in our backs, when we promptly place ourselves in the hands of the very gentleman who wrote to The Times to pledge his honor and reputation, founded on a pyramid of vivisected rabbits, that such things could never happen again. Depend upon it, if Macbeth had killed Macduff, he would have gone back to the Witches next day to ask their advice as to the best way of dealing with Malcolm.

It is the same with all the professions. I have other friends who are law-mad—who believe that lawyers are wise, judges high-minded and impartial, juries infallible, and codes on the brink of perfection. The military-mad and the clergy-mad stalk at large throughout the kingdom. Men believe in the professions as they believe in ghosts, because they want to believe in them. Fact-blindness—the most common sort of blindness—and the resolute lying of respectable men, keep up the illusion. No mortal, however hard-headed, can feel very safe in his attempts to sift the gold of fact and efficiency out of the huge rubbish heap of professionalism.

My own weakness is neither medicine, nor law, nor tailoring, nor any of the respectable departments of bogusdom. It is the theatre. The mystery-man who takes me in is not the doctor nor the lawyer, but the actor. In this column I have prated again and again of the mission of the theatre, the art of the actor, of his labor, his skill, his knowledge, his importance as a civilizing agent, his function as a spiritual doctor. Surely I have been in this the most ridiculous of all dupes. But before you lay me down in derision, never to read my articles again, hear my excuse. There is one sort of human accomplishment that cannot be dismissed as a figment of the spectator's imagination. The skill with which a man does that which he has done every day for twenty years is no illusion. When the operative at his mule in the cotton-mill pieces the broken yarn, when Paderewski at his Erard grand plays a sonata, he is not hypnotizing you, or inviting you to make-believe. He is actually doing things that would be miracles if done by an untrained man. Or take him who, with no eye to cotton cloth or the interpretation of Beethoven, does difficult things for the sake of their difficulty, simply as marvels: for instance, the acrobat. You cannot deny the reality of his feats. His complete physical self-possession, his ambidextrous grace, his power of making several deliberate movements in the space of a pang of terror—as when, for example, he will coolly alter the disposition of his body at a given moment, whilst he is falling headlong through the air: all these accomplishments of his really exist, and are by no means the product of the imagination of an innocent clergyman, sitting in the auditorium with his nose buried in a volume of Shakespear, and ready to take the word of the newspapers next day for what is happening on the stage. Now, am I to be greatly blamed for having supposed that the actor was a genuinely skilled artist like the acrobat, only adding to the skilled mastery of his powers of movement a mastery of his powers of speech, with an ear for verse, a sense of character, a cultivated faculty of observation and mimicry, and such higher qualities as Nature might throw into the bargain? There were great examples to mislead me: Kean was a harlequin as well as a Hamlet; Duse's Camille is positively enthralling as an exhibition of the gymnastics of perfect suppleness and grace; and I have seen Salvini come out before the curtain to accept a trophy from an admirer in a stage box with more art and more fascination —the whole thing being carried out in strict accordance with certain rules of his art—than an ordinary skirt dancer could get into the clumsy imposture she calls dancing after two years' hard practice. Further, it has been a matter of common observation in my generation that the burlesque of the Byron-Farnie-Reece-Burnand period did not, as it turned out, prove a bad training for the people who played in it. Nobody will contend, I imagine, that the training was intellectual: the secret lay in the music, the dancing, the marching, the fantastic walks round, the boundless scope for physical agility, the premium which the very barrenness and vulgarity of the entertainment placed on personal feats and on mimicry. Even that terrible stage calamity the stock actor of the old régime learnt something more from the Christmas pantomime than he would have known without it.

I plead, then, that acting is potentially an artistic profession, and that by training and practice a person can qualify himself or herself to come to a manager or author and say, "Within the limits imposed by my age and sex, I can do all the ordinary work of the stage with perfect certainty. I know my vowels and consonants as a phonetic expert, and can speak so as to arrest the attention of the audience whenever I open my mouth, forcibly, delicately, roughly, smoothly, prettily, harshly, authoritatively, submissively, but always artistically, just as you want it. I can sit, stand, fall, get up, walk, dance, and otherwise use my body with the complete command of it that marks the physical artist." An actor might know all this, and yet, for want of the power to interpret an author's text and invent the appropriate physical expression for it, never, without coaching, get beyond Rosencrantz or Seyton. It is, therefore, only the minimum qualification of a skilled stage hand; and if an actor is not that, then he is merely a stage-struck unskilled laborer or handy man, and his "conceptions" of Ibsen or Shakespear are mere impertinences. I naturally concluded that the minimum was in force, and acting a real profession. Alas! that only proves that my desire and hope got the better of my observation—my imagination of my experience.

However, I am cured now. It is all a delusion: there is no profession, no art, no skill about the business at all. We have no actors: we have only authors, and not many of them. When Mendelssohn composed Son and Stranger for an amateur performance, he found that the bass could only sing one note. So he wrote the bass part all on that one note; and when it came to the fateful night, the bass failed even at that. Our authors do as Mendelssohn did. They find that the actors have only one note, or perhaps, if they are very clever, half a dozen. So their parts are confined to these notes, often with the same result as in Mendelssohn's case. If you doubt me, go and see Henry IV at the Haymarket. It is as good work as our stage can do; but the man who says that it is skilled work has neither eyes nor ears; the man who mistakes it for intelligent work has no brains; the man who finds it even good fun may be capable of Christy Minstrelsy but not of Shakespear. Everything that charm of style, rich humor, and vivid natural characterization can do for a play are badly wanted by Henry IV, which has neither the romantic beauty of Shakespear's earlier plays nor the tragic greatness of the later ones. One can hardly forgive Shakespear quite for the worldly phase in which he tried to thrust such a Jingo hero as his Harry V down our throats. The combination of conventional propriety and brute masterfulness in his public capacity with a low-lived blackguardism in his private tastes is not a pleasant one. No doubt he is true to nature as a picture of what is by no means uncommon in English society, an able young Philistine inheriting high position and authority, which he holds on to and goes through with by keeping a tight grip on his conventional and legal advantages, but who would have been quite in his place if he had been born a gamekeeper or a farmer. We do not in the first part of Henry IV see Harry sending Mrs Quickly and Doll Tearsheet to the whipping-post, or handing over Falstaff to the Lord Chief Justice with a sanctimonious lecture; but he repeatedly makes it clear that he will turn on them later on, and that his self-indulgent good-fellowship with them is consciously and deliberately treacherous. His popularity, therefore, is like that of a prizefighter: nobody feels for him as for Romeo or Hamlet. Hotspur, too, though he is stimulating as ginger cordial is stimulating, is hardly better than his horse; and King Boling-broke, preoccupied with his crown exactly as a miser is pre-occupied with his money, is equally useless as a refuge for our affections, which are thus thrown back undivided on Falstaff, the most human person in the play, but none the less a besotted and disgusting old wretch. And there is neither any subtlety nor (for Shakespear) much poetry in the presentation of all these characters. They are labelled and described and insisted upon with the roughest directness; and their reality and their humor can alone save them from the unpopularity of their unlovableness and the tedium of their obviousness. Fortunately, they offer capital opportunities for interesting acting. Bolingbroke's long discourse to his son on the means by which he struck the imagina-tion and enlisted the snobbery of the English people gives the actor a chance comparable to the crafty early scenes in Richelieu. Prince Hal's humor is seasoned with sportsmanlike cruelty and the insolence of conscious mastery and contempt to the point of occasionally making one shudder. Hotspur is full of energy; and Falstaff is, of course, an unrivalled part for the right sort of comedian. Well acted, then, the play is a good one in spite of there not being a single tear in it. Ill acted—O heavens!

Of the four leading parts, the easiest—Hotspur—becomes pre-eminent at the Haymarket, not so much by Mr Lewis Waller's superiority to the rest as by their inferiority to him. Some of the things he did were astonishing in an actor of his rank. At the end of each of his first vehement speeches, he strode right down the stage and across to the prompt side of the proscenium on the frankest barnstorming principles, repeating this absurd "cross"—a well-known convention of the booth for catching applause—three times, step for step, without a pretence of any dramatic motive. In the camp scene before the battle of Shrewsbury, he did just what I blamed Miss Violet Vanbrugh for trying to do in Monsieur de Paris: that is, to carry through a long crescendo of excitement by main force after beginning fortissimo. Would it be too far-fetched to recommend Mr Waller to study how Mozart, in rushing an operatic movement to a spirited conclusion, knew how to make it, when apparently already at its utmost, seem to bound forward by a sudden pianissimo and lightsome change of step, the speed and force of the execution being actually reduced instead of intensified by the change? Such skilled, resourceful husbandry is the secret of all effects of this kind; and it is in the entire absence of such husbandry that Mr Waller shewed how our miserable theatre has left him still a novice for the purposes of a part which he is fully equipped by nature to play with most brilliant success, and which he did play very strikingly considering he was not in the least sure how to set about it, and hardly dared to stop blazing away at full pitch for an instant lest the part should drop flat on the boards. Mr Mollison presented us with an assortment of effects, and tones, and poses which had no reference, as far as I could discover, to the part of Bolingbroke at any single point. I did not catch a glimpse of the character from one end of his performance to the other, and so must conclude that Shakespear has failed to convey his intention to him. Mr Gillmore's way of playing Hal was as bad as the traditional way of playing Sheridan. He rattled and swaggered and roystered, and followed every sentence with a forced explosion of mirthless laughter, evidently believing that, as Prince Hall was reputed to be a humorous character, it was his business to laugh at him. Like most of his colleagues, he became more tolerable in the plain sailing of the battle scene, where the parts lose their individuality in the general warlike excitement, and an energetic display of the commonest sort of emotion suffices. Mr Tree only wants one thing to make him an excellent Falstaff, and that is to get born over again as unlike himself as possible. No doubt, in the course of a month or two, when he begins to pick up a few of the lines of the part, he will improve on his first effort; but he will never be even a moderately good Falstaff. The basket-work figure, as expressionless as that of a Jack in the Green; the face, with the pathetic wandering eye of Captain Swift belying such suggestion of character as the lifeless mask of paint and hair can give; the voice, coarsened, vulgarized, and falsified without being enriched or colored; the hopeless efforts of the romantic imaginative actor, touching only in unhappy parts, to play the comedian by dint of mechanical horseplay: all that is hopeless, irremediable. Mr Tree might as well try to play Juliet; and if he were wise he would hand over his part and his breadbasket to Mr Lionel Brough, whose Bardolph has the true comic force which Mr Tree never attains for a moment.

Two ideas have been borrowed from the last London revival of Henry V by Mr Coleman at the Queen's Theatre in Long Acre. One is the motionless battle tableau, which is only Mr Coleman's Agincourt over again, and which might just as well be cut out of cardboard. The other is the casting of Miss Kate Phillips for Mrs Quickly. As Mrs Quickly is plainly a slovenly, greasy, Gampish old creature, and Miss Phillips is unalterably trim, smart, and bright, a worse choice could not have been made. One would like to have seen Miss Mansfield in the part. Mrs Tree, as Lady Percy, did what I have never seen her do before: that is, played her part stupidly. The laws of nature seem to be suspended when Shakespear is in question. A Lady Percy who is sentimentally affectionate, who recites her remonstrance with Percy in the vein of Clarence's dream in Richard III, and who comes on the stage to share the applause elicited by the combats in the battle of Shrewsbury, only makes me rub my eyes and wonder whether I am dreaming.

Besides Mr Lionel Brough and Mr Lewis Waller, there were three performers who came off with credit. Mr Holman Clark played Glendower like a reasonable man who could read a Shakespearean play and understand it—a most exceptional achievement in his profession, as it appears. Mr D. J. Williams, who played William in As You Like It the other day at the Métropole, and played him well, was a Smike-like and effective Francis; and

Miss Marion Evans was a most musical Lady Mortimer, both in her Welsh song and Welsh speech.

The chief merit of the production is that the play has been accepted from Shakespear mainly as he wrote it. There are cuts, of course, the worst of them being the sacrifice of the nocturnal innyard scene, a mutilation which takes the reality and country midnight freshness from the Gadshill robbery, and reduces it to a vapid interlude of horseplay. But the object of these cuts is to save time: there is no alteration or hotch-potch, and consequently no suspicion of any attempt to demonstrate the superiority of the manager's taste and judgment to Shakespear's, in the Daly fashion. This ought to pass as a matter of course; but as things are at present it must be acknowledged as highly honorable to Mr Tree. However, it is not my cue just now to pay Mr Tree compliments. His *tours de force* in the art of make-up do not impose on me: any man can get into a wicker barrel and pretend to be Falstaff, or put on a false nose and call himself Svengali. Such tricks may very well be left to the music-halls: they are altogether unworthy of an artist of Mr Tree's pretensions. When he returns to the serious pursuit of his art by playing a part into which he can sincerely enter without disguise or mechanical denaturalization, may I be there to see! Until then let him guard the Haymarket doors against me; for I like him best when he is most himself.

RESURRECTION PIE

Jo. A drama in three acts, adapted from Charles Dickens's Bleak House. By J. P. Burnett. (A Revival.) Theatre Royal, Drury Lane, 14 May 1896.

THE MATCHMAKER. A new comedy in four acts. By Clo Graves and Gertrude Kingston. Shaftesbury Theatre, 9 May 1896.

ROSEMARY. A new play in four acts. By Louis N. Parker and Murray Carson. Criterion Theatre, 16 May 1896.

[23 *May* 1896]

THERE is a strain of resurrectionism in all of us, I suppose. In the most eligible places we get suddenly smitten with a hankering to take another look at some dull district where we were born; or in the British Museum Library we turn from the treasures of literature and abuse the services of the staff to get out some trumpery story-book that we read in the nursery; or we suddenly lapse, between the acts of a Wagnerian performance, into a longing curiosity to hear I Puritani or Don Pasquale once more. Fortunately most of these whims cost too much to be carried very far. We can afford to make a sentimental journey, or to hunt up an old book, but not to produce an old opera or an old play. There is only one man among us who is an exception to this rule. That man is Sir Augustus Harris. And what a resurrectionist he is! When my theme was music, I used egotistically to suspect him of a fiendish fancy for tormenting me personally; for in the very middle of a phase of advanced operatic activity, with Die Meistersinger figuring in the repertory with a comparatively venerable air beside a group of the most modern Italian and French works, he would suddenly stretch out his imperial hand; drag some appalling tenor from I know not what limbo of street-piano padrones, penny-icemen, and broken choristers; set the wretch to bleat Ah si, ben mio, and roar Di quella pira just once; and then snatch him for ever from the ken of a coldly astonished London season, leaving no trace of his adventure except my own infuriated protests and an inscrutable smile on the countenance of the impresario. That smile may have meant sentimental memories of auld lang syne, or it may have meant such derision as a wise man allows himself when he has given a witty lesson to a foolish generation: I never could tell; but before I had recovered my temper and settled down to Die Meistersinger and the rest, there would come along an obsolete seventeen-stone prima donna who could sing O mio Fernando, and get through regular old-fashioned arias with florid cabalettas at the ends of them. Immediately La Favorita would be dug up to rattle its skeleton for a night on the shuddering boards; and again I would go home, boiling with rage, to rack my brains for every extremity of sarcastic or indignant remonstrance. And again the impresario would smile inscrutably. Finally, having done my worst, I abandoned the criticism of music and devoted myself to the drama. Yet here again I met the resurrectionist impresario as resurrectionist manager; and again I am unable, for the life of me, to guess whether he is a sentimentalist turning to *ses premières amours*, or a preceptor giving those of us who find fault lightly with his modern achievements a stern object lesson in the strides he has had to make to get away from a ridiculous and overrated past.

At some remote date which I have not precisely ascertained—somewhere between the drying of the Flood and the advent of Ibsen—Bleak House shared the fate of most of Dickens's novels in being "adapted to the stage." The absurdity of the process is hardly to be described, so atrociously had these masterpieces to be degraded to bring them within the competence of the theatre; but the thing was done somehow; and the Artful Dodger, Smike, Micawber, Peggotty, and Jo were born again as "famous impersonations." I am less versed in these matters than some of our older critics; but it has been my fate at one time or another to witness performances founded on Pickwick, Oliver Twist, Dombey and Son, and David Copperfield. The fame of other adaptations of Dickens reached me, notably that of Bleak House, with Miss Jennie Lee as the crossing-sweeper; but I never saw Jo until the other night, when Sir Augustus revived it at Drury Lane, just as he might have revived Semiramide at Covent Garden. The revival is under the direction of the author of the adaptation, Mr J. P. Burnett, who has evidently conducted it with the strictest fidelity to its traditions; so that we can now see for a few nights what stage work was like in the days when Dickens, the greatest English master of pathetic and humorous character presentation our century has produced, did *not* write for the theatre. And truly the spectacle is an astonishing one, though I well remember when its most grotesque features were in the height of the melodramatic fashion. What will the stage sentimentalities on which I drop the tear of sensibility today seem like a quarter of a century hence, I wonder!

One facility offered to the stage by Dickens is a description of the persons of the drama so vivid and precise that no actor with the faintest sense of character could mistake the sort of figure he has to present, even without the drawings of Browne and Barnard to help him out. Yet each attempt only proves that most of our actors either have no character sense or else have never read Dickens. The Drury Lane revival has plenty of examples of this. One would suppose that Mr Snagsby, with his nervous cough, his diffidence, his timid delicacy, and his minimizing formula of "not to put too fine a point on it," could hardly be confused with a broadly comic cheesemonger out of a harlequinade, nor the oily Chadband in any extremity of misunderstanding be presented as a loose-limbed acrobat of the Vokes-Girard type. Imagine the poor pathetically ridiculous Guster not only condemned to mere knockabout buffoonery, but actually made to fall down in a *comic* epileptic fit on the stage! Bucket has his psychology considerably complicated by the fact that the author has rolled him up with Mr Jarndyce and the Cook's Court policeman; so that there are three characters in one person, a trinitarian expedient which presents an absolutely insoluble problem to the actor. As to Mr Guppy, he is not within a thousand miles of being himself. What Jobling-Weevle, and Smallweed, and Miss Flite, and George and the rest would have been like if they had been included in the adaptation can only be guessed with a qualm. Literary criticism was more apt to remonstrate with Dickens for caricature than to mistrust his touch as too subtle, and his outlines as too elusive, for the man in the street to appreciate. On the stage, one perceives, Dickens was impossible because he was infinitely too poetic, too profound, too serious, too natural in his presentment of things—in a word, too dramatic for the theatre of his day. Not that I shall allow anyone to persuade me that Jo was ever anything more than third-rate work at any period of our stage history; but it must have been much more highly esteemed when it was first perpetrated than it is now, even by an audience invited at "cheap summer prices," and so carelessly catered for, that in the scene in which Guppy explains to Esther Summerson that what she takes for smoke is a London fog, we are treated to the most

135

brilliantly sunshiny front cloth the scene-dock of Drury Lane affords.

All that can be said for Miss Jennie Lee's Jo nowadays is that if the part had been left between herself and Dickens, something credible and genuinely moving might have come of it. But Mr Burnett has carefully laid out his lines and stage business for the crudest and falsest stage pathos and stage facetiousness. Jo is one moment a cheeky street arab, and, the next, is directly expressing, to slow music, not the darkened ideas of Jo, but Mr Burnett's version of the compassionate horror roused in the social and political consciousness of Dickens by the case of Jo and his fellow-outcasts. Dickens himself is not wholly guiltless of this: in the novel one or two of Jo's speeches are at bottom conscious social criticisms; but it is not the business of the dramatist to develop a couple of undramatic slips in a novel into a main feature of the leading part in a play. Lady Dedlock, no longer bored, but fearfully and tragically serious in her crinoline and flounces (wild anachronisms, surely, if the play is to be dated by the costumes of Tulkinghorn, Bucket, and Snagsby), is quite worth seeing, especially on her visit to the graveyard, where she combines a now ludicrously old-fashioned sort of distressed heroine business with a good deal of the Ghost in Hamlet, old style. How Miss Alma Stanley has contrived to recover the trick of a vanished stage mode so cleverly, and to keep her countenance meanwhile, I know not. But she does it with wonderful success; and I hope she will never do it again. Mrs Rouncewell, excellently played by Miss Fanny Robertson, is called Mrs Rouncell in the playbill; and the number of newspaper notices in which this blunder is reproduced may be taken as the number of critics who have never read Bleak House.

Perhaps, now I come to think of it, the Jo enterprise is not Sir Augustus Harris's at all, but only Mr Burnett's. Whether or no, I prefer La Favorita.

The untimely end of The Matchmaker at the Shaftesbury rather weakens any interest that may attach to my opinion of it. In its combination of cynicism as to the society represented by the fashionable marriage market, and sentiment as to pet individuals, with a humorousness that is nothing if not naughty, it is thoroughly characteristic of the phase of social development represented by the two ladies—a London actress and a London journalist respectively—to whose pens we owe it. This is as much as to say that The Matchmaker was as sincere as its authors could make it without dropping the usual affectation of taking life farcically; and as they have some bright dramatic talent between them, the play, though tacked together anyhow, and built on the sandiest of foundations, might, in a summer theatre at reasonable prices, have done very well, though of course at the Shaftesbury in May, with all the comfortable seats costing half-a-guinea or six or seven shillings, no great success was possible. Two scenes, the pathetic one in the first act between Miss Lena Ashwell and Mr Lewis Waller, and the comic one in the third between Mr Waller and Miss Beatrice Ferrar, will be remembered when some more successful plays are forgotten. It was particularly interesting to see how sympathetically Mr Waller responded to the note of genuine pathos in the first scene, although in A Woman's Reason and The Sin of St Hulda he hardly succeeded in even pretending to respond to the conventional demands of the pretentious but unreal despair piled up for him in these works. The effect was completed by the playing of Miss Ashwell, the touching quality of whose acting, both in comedy and sentiment, is now finding the cultivated artistic expression it lacked in former seasons.

As to Rosemary, at the Criterion, there is very little to be said; for though it is a pleasant piece of storytelling, it does not really supply a motive for the very remarkable display of acting which Mr Wyndham imposes on it, and to which it owes its success. His performance may almost be called acting in the abstract, like those mock dialogues in which a couple of amateur comedians amuse a drawing room by simply bandying the letters of the alphabet to and fro with varying expressions. It is quite possible to be most powerfully affected by an emotional demonstration of which the cause is hidden: indeed, I have known a case in which an actress, off the stage, gave such poignant expression to her feelings that a visitor came to the conclusion that she had lost her favorite child, whereas the actual provocation, as it turned out, was the exhibition of somebody else's name on a poster in letters an inch longer than hers. If a foreigner were to enter the Criterion half way through the third act of Rosemary, he would be greatly struck by Mr Wyndham's acting; but if he were asked to guess the nature of Sir Jasper Thorndyke's grief, he would certainly suggest something much more serious than the disappointment of a man of forty at being unable to marry a pretty young girl, quite a stranger to him, on whose wedding he had just stumbled. The truth is that the play has one pervading defect. It is engaging, humane, fanciful, well written, refined, humorous according to a somewhat literary conception of humor, and full of happy reminiscent touches and a pardonable Dickens worship; but it is continuously silly; and in the hands of actors who were no better than their parts it would, I suspect, act very vapidly indeed. In the last act—a nonogenarian monologue—the lines, though no doubt very nice and sympathetic, are dramatically aimless; and although I am quite aware that we shall never get the drama out of its present rut until we learn to dispense on occasion with dramatic aim in this sense, and allow feeling to flow without perpetually working up to points and situations, yet that sort of freedom must be conquered, not begged—a feat that can hardly be achieved in an openly and shamelessly old-fashioned play like Rosemary. However, I will not pretend that I found it tedious; indeed, Mr Wyndham entertained me better than I expected, considering that the art of senile make-up, in which Mr Hare wasted half his career, is to me the most transparent and futile of impostures. For the rest, there are half a dozen pleasant and popular artists in half a dozen pleasant and popular—but always silly—parts; and the management is admirable, as it always is at the Criterion.

G. B. S. ON CLEMENT SCOTT

FROM THE BELLS TO KING ARTHUR. A critical record of the first-
night productions at the Lyceum Theatre from 1871 to 1895.
By Clement Scott. (London: John Macqueen. 1896.)

SHAW v. SHAKESPEAR AND OTHERS. Article by W. A. (Mr William
Archer) in the current number of The World.

[30 *May* 1896]

MR CLEMENT SCOTT is not the first of the great dramatic critics;
but he is the first of the great dramatic reporters. Other men may
have hurried from the theatre to the newspaper to prepare, red
hot, a notice of the night's performance for the morning's paper;
but nobody did it before him with the knowledge that the notice
was awaited by a vast body of readers conscious of his personality and anxious to hear his opinion, and that the editor must
respect it, and the sub-editor reserve space for it, as the most important feature of the paper. This strong position Mr Scott has
made for himself. His opportunity has of course been made by
circumstances—by the growth of mammoth newspapers like
the Daily Telegraph, the multiplication of theatres, and the
spread of interest in them; but it has not been made for Mr Scott
more than for his competitors; and the fact that he alone has
seized it and made the most of it in a metropolis where every
adult is eager to do his work for nothing but the honor and glory
and the invitations to first nights, proves, you may depend on it,
that his qualifications for the work are altogether extraordinary.

The main secret of Mr Scott's popularity is that he is above
all a sympathetic critic. His susceptibility to the direct expression of human feeling is so strong that he can write with positive
passion about an exhibition of it which elicits from his colleagues
only some stale, weary compliment in the last sentence of a conventional report, or, at best, some clever circumlocutory discussion of the philosophy of the piece. Whoever has been through
the experience of discussing criticism with a thorough, perfect,
and entire Ass, has been told that criticism should above all

139

things be free from personal feeling. The excellence of Mr Scott's criticisms lies in their integrity as expressions of the warmest personal feeling and nothing else. They are alive: their admiration is sincere and moving: their resentment is angry and genuine. He may be sometimes maudlin on the one hand, sometimes unjust, unreasonable, violent, and even ridiculous on the other; but he has never lost an inch of ground by that, any more than other critics have ever gained an inch by a cautious, cold, fastidious avoidance of the qualities of which such faults are the excesses. Our actors and actresses feel the thorough humanity of his relation to them; and they commonly say—except in those gusts of fury at some unfavorable notice in which they announce that they make it a rule never to read criticisms at all—that they would rather be "slated" by Mr Scott than praised by colder hands. By colder hands they generally mean Mr William Archer, who has made himself as eminent as Mr Scott, and complementary and antidotal to him, at the opposite pole of contemporary dramatic criticism. The public believes in Mr Scott because he interprets the plays by feeling *with* the actor or author—generally more, perhaps, with the actor than the author—and giving his feeling unrestrained expression in his notices. An average young University graduate would hang himself sooner than wear his heart on his sleeve before the world as Mr Scott does. And that is just why the average young University graduate never interests anyone in his critical remarks. He has been trained to do nothing that could possibly involve error, failure, self-assertion, or ridicule; and the results of this genteelly negative policy are about as valuable as those which might be expected by a person who should enter for a swimming race with a determination to do nothing that could possibly expose him to the risk of getting wet. Mr Scott, in spite of his public school education, is happily not that sort of person. He understands the value of Lassalle's dictum that "History forgives mistakes and failures, but not want of conviction."

Now for Mr Scott's shortcomings. The most amiable of them is a desire to give pleasure and gain affectionate goodwill. This, in the absence of any provocation to the contrary, guarantees to everybody, from Sir Henry Irving down to the most friendless novice thirsting for a little encouragement, a flattering word or two in the Daily Telegraph. No doubt he is very often helpful with judicious encouragement; but he is occasionally shameless in his gratuitous kindliness. This might not do any harm if he could always be depended on to be annoyed by bad work; but unfortunately this is not the case. His extraordinary susceptibility is, as I advisedly described it, a susceptibility to the direct expression of human feeling, and to that alone. Interpose any medium between him and the moving, uttering, visible human creature, and he is insulated at once. It may be the medium of music; it may be painting; it may even be the reflective thought inspired by passion instead of the direct instinctive cry of the passion itself: no matter: the moment the substitution is effected Mr Scott loses his distinction; writes like any Philistine citizen of ordinary artistic tastes; and is crowed over by every whipper-snapper in his profession whose eyes and ears and powers of abstract thinking have been trained a little by practice on the outside of the arts, and by an academic course of philosophy. In this collection of his Lyceum criticisms we find him brought face to face with the remarkable development of the pictorial side of stage art effected by Mr Comyns Carr when he succeeded in bringing the genius of Burne-Jones, the greatest decorative artist of his time, to bear on the production of King Arthur. Mr Scott, instead of being delighted with the result, was simply incommoded and disturbed by the change in the accustomed arrangements. He complained that King Arthur wore black armor instead of looking like Mr Henry Neville dressed in a roasting-jack and a flaxen wig; and he was scandalized at the knights having their hair cut. "Where," he asks, "is the fair hair, where the robes, where the drapery, where the air of dignity and distinction, in this tight-fitting, black tin armor? An actor of the highest distinction has to work desperately hard to counteract the impression for which he is not in the least responsible. It was decided —we know not for what reason—that all the principal actors in this play should wear their own hair, Bond Street cut. Never was there a play where assumed hair seemed to be more imperative."

Again, when Mr Scott touches on the subject of music, he distinguishes between "melody" and "classical music," and is so deeply depressed by sonata form that even the slow movement from Raff's Im Walde symphony struck him as an unpardonably dismal business when Herr Armbruster played it at the Lyceum on the first night of Michael. He also complains because Gounod's music is not used in the Lyceum Faust. Painting and music seem to affect his imagination as ruins affected the imagination of Sir Walter Scott—that is, by setting him thinking of something else. His criticism of all stage effects, scenic or personal, which appeal to the cultivated intelligence of the eye and ear, instead of to the heart, is quite commonplace.

When I say that Mr Scott is also unable to recognize a feeling when it is presented to him in the form of a thought—unless of course that thought has been so long associated with it that the distinction between them has vanished, and the utterance of the thought has become the natural expression of the feeling—I touch the disability which has brought him into conflict with the later developments of the drama. Like all energetic spirits, he was a pioneer at first, fighting for the return to nature in Robertson's plays against the stagey stuff which he found in possession of the theatre. Since that time the unresting march of evolution has brought us past Robertson. Our feeling has developed and put new thoughts into our heads; and our brains have developed and interpreted our feelings to us more critically. Ideas which were formerly only conceived by men of genius like Ibsen, or intensely energetic spirits like Nietzsche, are freely used by dramatists like Sudermann, and are beginning to creep into quite ordinary plays, just as I can remember the pet discords of Schumann and Wagner beginning to creep into the music-hall after a period of fashionable novelty in the drawing room. When Ibsen's Ghosts forced the old ideas to take up the challenge of the new, Mr Scott was the only critic whose attack on Ibsen was really memorable. In the ranks which he led there was plenty of elderly peevishness and envious disparagement, virtuous indignation and vicious scurrility, with the usual quantity of time-serving caution among the more considerate; but Mr Scott alone, looking neither forward nor backward, gave utterance to his horror like a man wounded to the quick in his religion, his affections, his enthusiasms—in the deepest part of him. I greatly doubt whether to this day he has any adequate conception of the way in which he pitched into us who were on the other side during those moments when he was persuaded that we were filthy-minded traffickers in mere abomination. But he came off with the advantage of the doughty fighter who lays on with conviction: he had not only the excitement of the combat and the satisfaction of making his quarterstaff ring on the heads of his adversaries, but he sowed no harvest of malice, rather establishing on us the claim of an old opponent, always a strong claim in a free country. The incident was the more curious because I am persuaded that if the feeling that is at the bottom of Ghosts were presented dramatically as a simple and direct plea for the right of a man of affectionate, easy, convivial temperament to live a congenial life, instead of skulking into the kitchen after the house-maid, and stealing a morsel of pleasure in the byways of drink and disease when his conscientiously conventional wife and her spiritual adviser were not looking, Mr Scott would be one of its most merciful critics. But Mr Scott is not a thinker: whatever question you raise with him you must raise as a question of conduct, which is a matter of feeling, and not of creed, which is a matter of intellectual order. The notion that when conduct conflicts with creed, the question as to which of the two is in the wrong is an open one—that it is not alone humanity that is constantly on its trial, but the ethical, political, and religious systems that claim implicit obedience from humanity—that a deliberate violation of these systems may be, not a weakness to be pitied and pardoned, but an assertion of human worth to be championed and carried to victory in the teeth of all constitutions, churches, principles, and ideals whatsoever: this, which explains all that is peculiar in the attitude of the modern movement, especially in dramatic poetry, has no meaning for Mr Scott. He will not, when the time comes, be an enemy of the drama which tacitly assumes it: his sympathy will secure him against that; but the drama which asserts and argues it—which is polemical rather than instinctive in its poignancy—will never be tolerated by him.

I need not say that a volume of criticisms dealing with Lyceum productions exclusively does not cover those newly opened regions in which the steadiness of Mr Scott's footing is doubtful. The book is full of old drawings by Mr Barnard, which, however, are surpassed in delicacy, charm, and fidelity by the newer ones from the hand of Mr Partridge (Mr Bernard Gould), and photographic portraits, among which I miss that of Mr Scott himself. Perhaps the few notes I have made above on my fellow-critic may help to supply the deficiency. For form's sake, I will add just this ghost of a criticism on a passage in the book. When Olivia was revived at the Lyceum, Mr Scott was so much touched by the point at which the Vicar, trying to lecture Olivia for her wickedness, breaks down and clasps her in his arms (who does not remember Miss Terry's head dropping as she took the attitude of the reproved child?), that he records with enthusiasm the astonishment and delight of the house, adding, "As regards acting, it was a moment of true inspiration, a masterpiece of invention." But now, in cold blood, Mr Scott will agree with me, I think, that the invention is clearly the author's, and that the original Vicar produced the same effect. Indeed, to my mind, he produced it better than Sir Henry Irving, whose embrace I thought too loverlike. Mr Hermann Vezin, a less passionate actor, was for that very reason a more old-fashionedly fatherly Dr Primrose than his eminent successor.

Mr Archer's article in the World is an elaborate demonstration that my opinion of Henry IV at the Haymarket is not a criticism, but a purely theoretic deduction from my race, my diet, my politics—in short, my nature and environment. And he argues that it is a monstrous injustice that Mr Beerbohm Tree should be made to suffer for my nature and environment. What outrageous nonsense! Besides, Mr Tree is infinitely obliged to me; for all

London, it appears, is flocking to the Haymarket to see whether Henry IV is really so bad as I think it.

THE NEW MAGDA AND THE NEW CYPRIENNE

MAGDA. A play in four acts. Translated by Louis N. Parker from Hermann Sudermann's Home. Lyceum Theatre, 3 June 1896.

THE QUEEN'S PROCTOR. A comedy in three acts. Adapted by Herman Merivale from Divorçons, by Victorien Sardou and E. de Najac. Royalty Theatre, 2 June 1896. [6 *June* 1896]

IN all the arts there is a distinction between the mere physical artistic faculty, consisting of a very fine sense of color, form, tone, rhythmic movement, and so on, and that supreme sense of humanity which alone can raise the art work created by the physical artistic faculties into a convincing presentment of life. Take the art of acting, for instance. The physically gifted actor can fill in a conventional artistic outline with great charm. He—or she (I really mean she, as will appear presently)—can move exquisitely within the prescribed orbit of a dance, can ring out the measure of a line of blank verse to a hair's-breadth, can devise a dress well and wear it beautifully, can, in short, carry out with infinite fascination the design of any dramatic work that aims at sensuous and romantic beauty alone. But present this same fascinating actress with a work to the execution of which the sense of humanity is the only clue, in which there is no verse to guide the voice and no dance to guide the body, in which every line must appear ponderously dull and insignificant unless its truth as the utterance of a deeply moved human soul can be made apparent, in which the epicurean admiration of her as an exquisite apparition, heightened, of course, by sex attraction, can be but a trifling element in the deep sympathy with her as a fellow-creature which is produced by a great dramatist's revelation of ourselves to our own consciousness through her part, and then you may very possibly see your bewitching artist making a quite childish failure on the very boards where a little while before she was disputing the crown of her profession with the greatest actresses in the world.

If you doubt me, then do you, if you have had the good fortune to see Mrs Patrick Campbell play Militza in For the Crown like an embodied picture or poem of the decorative romantic type, now go and see her play Magda. And go soon; for the play will not run long: human nature will not endure such a spectacle for many weeks. That is not the fault of the play, which does not fail until she kills it. At the end of the first act, before Magda appears, the applause has a rising flood in it which shews that the house is caught by the promise of the drama. Ten minutes after Mrs Campbell's entry it is all over: thenceforward the applause, though complimentary and copious, is from the lips outward. The first-night audience had for the most part seen Bernhardt and Duse in the part, and knew what could be done with it. Nobody, I presume, was so foolishly unreasonable as to expect anything approaching the wonderful impersonation by Duse at Drury Lane, when she first played the part here last year. Mrs Campbell has not lived long enough to get as much work cram · med into her entire repertory as Duse gets into every ten minutes of her Magda. Nor has she had sufficient stage experience to polish off the part with the businesslike competence of the golden Sarah, coming down with her infallible stroke on every good stage point in the dialogue, and never letting the play drag for an instant. But even if the audience had never seen either Bernhardt or Duse, it could not have mistaken Mrs Campbell for a competent Magda, although it might very possibly have mistaken the play for a dull and prosy one. The fact is, if Mrs Campbell's irresistible physical gifts and her cunning eye for surface effects had only allowed her to look as silly as she really was in the part (and in one or two passages she very nearly achieved this), her failure would have been as obvious to the greenest novice in the house as it was to me. Take such a dramatic moment, for instance, as that in which Magda receives, first the card, and then the visit of Von Keller, the runaway father of her child. Let us leave Duse's incomparable acting of that scene out of the ques-

146

tion, even if it is impossible to forget it. But with Mrs Campbell it was not merely a falling short of Duse that one had to complain of. She literally did nothing. From the point at which Miss Caldwell, as the servant, brought in the card, to the point at which Magda, her emotion mastered, good-humoredly shakes hands with the fellow (how capitally vulgarly Sarah did that!), Mrs Campbell did not display as much feeling as an ordinary woman of fifty does at the arrival of the postman. Whether her nonentity at this point was the paralysis of a novice who does not know how to express what she feels, or whether it was the vacuity of a woman who does not feel at all, I cannot determine. The result was that the audience did not realize that anything particular was supposed to be happening; and those who had seen the play before wondered why it should be so much less intelligible in English than in a foreign language.

Let me give one other instance. Quite the easiest line in the piece is the prima donna's remark, when she hears about Marie's lieutenant lover, "A lieutenant! with us it's always a tenor." Mrs Campbell actually succeeded in delivering that speech without making anyone smile. At the other end of the compass of the piece we have the terrible line which strikes the Colonel dead at the end—"How do you know that he was the only one?" (meaning "How do you know that this man Von Keller, whom you want me to marry to make an honest woman of me, is the only man who has been my lover?"). Mrs Campbell made an obvious attempt to do something with this line at the last moment. But there is nothing to be done with it except prepare its effect by acting beforehand so as to make the situation live, and then let it do its own work. Between these two failures I can recall no success; indeed, I can hardly recall any effort that went far enough to expose Mrs Campbell to the risk of active failure. Although she was apparently doing her best with the part, her best let its best slip by her, and only retained its commonplaces.

The part of Magda is no doubt one in which a young actress may very well be excused for failing. But from the broad point of view of our national interest in art, it is necessary, when work of the class of Sudermann's is in question, to insist on the claim of the public to have the best dramas of the day presented in English by the fittest talent. Mrs Campbell was entitled to her turn; but now that it is clear that the part does not suit her, are we to have it locked up lest any other actress should demonstrate that it can be done better? Are we to have no chance of seeing how it would come out in the hands of the actresses who have shewn a special aptitude for this class of work? Miss Elizabeth Robins would certainly not play Militza half as effectively as Mrs Campbell; but can it be doubted by anyone who has seen her play Hilda Wangel that she would play Magda, especially in the self-assertive scenes, twenty times better than Mrs Campbell? Miss Robins can assert herself more youthfully, and pity herself more pathetically, than any actress on our stage. Doubtless she might fail to convince us in the sympathetic, grandly maternal phases of the character; but what about Miss Janet Achurch for that side of it? Miss Achurch, with no copyright monopoly of A Doll's House, has never been approached as Nora Helmer: Mrs Campbell's attempt at Magda is the merest baby-play in comparison with that performance. These able and energetic women who pioneered the new movement have had, so far, little to repay them except unlimited opportunities of looking on at fashionable dramas, in which placidly pretty and pleasant actresses enjoy a heyday of popular success by exhibiting themselves in expensive frocks, and going amiably through half a dozen tricks which they probably amuse themselves by teaching to their poodles when they are at a loss for something better to do. The managers are quite right to keep actresses of the calibre of Miss Achurch and Miss Robins out of such business: they would be more likely to knock an ordinary fashionable play to pieces than to become popular pets in it—after all, one does not want a Great Western locomotive to carry one's afternoon tea upstairs. But if the managers are going in for Sudermann and Ibsen, and serious work generally, then in the name of common sense let them shew us something more of the people who have proved themselves able to handle such work, and keep their pretty dolls for dolls' work.

However, if Mrs Patrick Campbell has just shewn that she is not yet a great actress, she is at any rate an artist; and nobody can complain of her having tried Magda, if only there is no attempt to prevent others from trying also. The circumstances were not altogether favorable to her. It is true that she was supported by the best Pastor Hefferdingh we have seen—Mr Forbes Robertson was admirable in the character; but the all-important Colonel Schwartze was disastrous: Mr Fernandez exhibited every quality of the old actor except the quality of being able to understand his part. Miss Alice Mansfield, as the agitated aunt, forgot that she was playing first-class drama in the Lyceum Theatre, and treated us to the grimaces and burlesque prolongations of her words with which she is accustomed to raise a laugh in farcical comedies. And Mr Gillmore, as Lieutenant Max, had not a touch of the smart German subaltern about him. Otherwise there was nothing to complain of. Mr Scott Buist, whose success as Tesman in Hedda Gabler has taught him the value of thoroughly modern parts, did not, especially in the earlier scenes, adapt himself sufficiently to the large size of the theatre, nor could he surpass the inimitable Von Keller of Sarah Bernhardt's company; but, for all that, he understood the part and played it excellently. Miss Brooke's Marie was spoiled by Mrs Campbell's Magda. She conveyed the impression of being a respectable young woman, with a rather loose and good-for-nothing kind of sister, instead of being clearly weaker in her conventionality than Magda in her independence.

Mr Herman Merivale's adaptation of Divorçons began by putting me out of temper. First, we had the inevitable two servants gossiping about their employers' affairs, their pretended function being to expound the plot, their real one to bore the audience sufficiently to make the principals doubly welcome when they arrive. Why do not those ridiculous people in the gallery who persist in hissing the author when all the mischief is over make themselves useful by venting their destructive rage on those two Sardovian servants? Then the supernumerary persons —the visitors, and so on—were tiresome, and did not know how to behave themselves as people behave in country houses. I do not recommend the manners of a dull country house to actors and actresses in private life: I am well aware that there is no time for them in London, even if they were admirable in themselves; but I do suggest that it is a wasteful mistake to spend a good deal of money in mounting a country-house scene realistically, and then spoil all the illusion by the gush and rush, the violent interest in everything and the eagerly false goodfellowship so characteristic of theatrical at-homes, and so markedly foreign to county society. Then, again, Cyprienne, instead of being translated into her English equivalent, became a purely fantastic person, nominally an Italian lady married to an English squire, but really a purely imaginary incarnation of the pet qualities of her sex. The Italian pretext involved that most exasperating of all theatrical follies and nuisances, the pet resource of the spurious actor who goes to his make-up box for character and to some mimic's trick for his speech, a stage foreign accent. At the end of the first act I was in the worst possible temper with the whole performance, the more so as the incident of the electric bell all but missed fire, partly because the bell, far from being startling, was hardly audible, and partly because the two performers, instead of stopping paralysed, and letting the very funny effect make itself (as it always does in this way infallibly with Chaumont), tried to work it up with excited action and speeches, which, of course, simply distracted attention from it.

But I was unable to maintain this unfavorable attitude. The shelter of a furze bush will give courage to a soldier under fire; and it may be that the tiny shelter from a too ladylike self-consciousness afforded by the foreign accent made Miss Violet Vanbrugh reckless. At all events she let herself go to such purpose that before the second act was over she had completely changed her professional standing. I asked myself could this be the same lady who was lately ambling and undulating, with the most acutely intentional archness and grace, through The Chili Widow, and being admired and tolerated as a popular hostess rather than nailing the attention and interest of her audience as an actress.

At that time I should have abandoned hope of Miss Vanbrugh as a comedian but for my recollection of a certain burlesque of The Master Builder, in which—again, observe, having an excuse for letting herself go—she impressed me prodigiously. I suspect that Miss Vanbrugh has hitherto lamed herself by trying to arrive at Miss Ellen Terry's secret from without inward, instead of working out her own secret from within outward. However that may be, the position into which she sprang last Tuesday, with the most decisive success, is that of Mrs Kendal, which, owing to the prolonged epidemic of handsome idiocy among our leading ladies, and sentimental inanity among our authors, has been vacant for a ridiculously long period. The Queen's Proctor is now the most amusing play in London: it is worth going to for nothing else than to hear Miss Vanbrugh protest, "It is not jealousy, but c——uriosity." Mr Bourchier, a born actor, and in fact the only first-rate light comedian of his generation (the rest either cannot make us laugh or can do nothing else), plays to Miss Violet Vanbrugh as perhaps only a husband can play to his wife—at least with the unmixed approbation of the British public. Although the first act of the piece has been sacrificed somewhat in the adaptation, the adapting device employed in it enables the succeeding acts to follow the original in all its witty liveliness. And now that Mr Bourchier has got a real play and a real part, he no longer trifles with his work. I was never convinced before Tuesday night that his career as a manager was assured; but now that Mrs Bourchier's genius has got loose with such astonishing and delightful suddenness, and he is attacking his own work seriously, the prospects of the combination appear to be unlimited. There is some capital playing in the piece by Mr W. G. Elliot as Cæsar Borgia (our old friend Adhemar), Mr Hendrie, and Mr Kinghorne, who is pathetically funny (much the finest way of being funny) as a Scots waiter. I congratulate Mr Bourchier heartily on his first genuine success.

MISS NETHERSOLE AND MRS KENDAL

CARMEN. A dramatic version of Prosper Mérimée's novel. By Henry Hamilton. In four acts. Gaiety Theatre, 6 June 1896.

THE WANDERER FROM VENUS; OR, TWENTY-FOUR HOURS WITH AN ANGEL. A new and original fanciful comedy. By Robert Buchanan and Charles Marlowe. New Grand Theatre, Croydon, 8 June 1896.

THE GREATEST OF THESE——. A play in four acts. By Sydney Grundy. Garrick Theatre, 10 June 1896.   [13 *June* 1896]

I AM ordinarily a patient man and a culpably indulgent critic; but I fear I must ask the responsible parties, whoever they are, what they mean by this Carmen business at the Gaiety Theatre? Are we to have no credit in London for knowing, I will not say fine art from fashionable art, because that we unfortunately do not know, but at least fashionable art from unfashionable? We may be vague in our notions of the difference between a thirteenth-century church and a seventeenth-century one, a costume designed by a comic-opera costumier and one painted by Benozzo Gozzoli, a Leadenhall Press book and a Kelmscott Press one, or a Mrs Ebbsmith and a Magda; but at all events we can distinguish between Kensington Palace Gardens or Fitzjohn's Avenue and the Old Kent Road, between a suit turned out by a Savile Row tailor and one purchased at a Jamaica Road slopshop, between the Century Magazine and a broadsheet of ballads, and between Mrs Ebbsmith and Maria Martin, the heroine of The Murder in the Red Barn. Why, then, attempt to put us off, at the height of the season, with such a piece of work as this new version of Carmen? I am too goodnatured to deliberately set to work to convey an adequate notion of what a very poor, cheap, tawdry business it is; but some idea of the class of audience to which it has been written down may perhaps be gathered from the fact that when Carmen is cajoling the dragoon in the first act, she repeatedly turns to the audience—the London audience—and remarks, aside, "He thinks I am in earnest" or the like, lest we, unsophisticated yokels as we are, might possibly be misled by her arts into accepting her as the sympathetic heroine. The dialogue only rises, not without effort, to the point of making the bare story intelligible to those of us who know the opera by heart already. I say the opera; for the description of the work as "a dramatic version of Prosper Mérimée's novel" is quite misleading. If it were not for the first scene of the second act—which ought to be cut out—nobody could possibly suspect the author of having ever read a line of Mérimée. The true original is, of course, the libretto; and all the departures made from its scenario are blunders. The superfluous scene just mentioned could only be rendered endurable by very expressive physical acting on the parts of Carmen and José. But the author has so little stagecraft that he makes it take place in the dark, where, accordingly, it is not endurable. Again, in the tavern scene, Dolores-Michaela enters and makes an appeal to Carmen's better nature! And Carmen, after being stabbed, and dying a screaming, gurgling, rattling, "realistic" death, compounded of all the stage colics and convulsions ever imagined, suddenly comes to life and dies over again in the older operatic manner, like Edgardo in Lucia, warbling "I love you, I love you." What is a critic expected to say to such folly?

The execution of this tedious, inept, absurd, and at its most characteristic moments positively asinine play only emphasized its defects. In the course of my musical experiences I have seen a great many Carmens. The earlier ones aimed at something like the Carmen of Mérimée, the gipsy of a gentleman's imagination, a Carmen with holes in her stockings, ready to beg, steal, fight, or trade with her own person as a matter of course, but still a Carmen with her point of honor, scandalized and angry because José jealously killed her hideous old husband with a knife thrust instead of buying her from him in the correct gipsy manner for a few shillings, and brave to grandeur in confronting her death, brought on her, not by the extravagance of her own misconduct, but by the morbid constitutional jealousy of the melancholy hidalgo-dragoon. When Trebelli played the part, for instance, there was not the slightest hint in her performance of the influence of that naturalistic movement which was presently to turn Carmen into a disorderly, lascivious, good-for-nothing factory girl. There was nothing of it even in Selina Dolaro's Carmen, except that the assumption of one of Trebelli's parts by an opera-bouffe artist was itself a sign of the times. The first prima donna who definitely substituted the Zola Carmen for the Mérimée Carmen was Marie Roze, who never did anything quite competently, and yet could coax the public to come to see her do everything incompetently. One forgave her Carmen as one forgives Manon Lescaut: whatever else she may have been, she was lovable. The next notable Carmen was Giulia Ravogli. Nobody but she has given us the free, roving, open-air Carmen, strong of body, prompt of hand, genuinely and not ignobly contemptuous of civilization. But Ravogli, though she played to every turn of the orchestra with a masterly understanding of the score, and a precision and punctuality of pantomimic action which I have never seen surpassed either by the best French performers in ballet of the Enfant Prodigue type, or by such German Wagnerian artists as Alvary in Siegfried, was too roughly real and powerful for what is at best but a delicately flimsy little opera; and the part was left to the pretty pettishnesses and ladylike superficialities of Miss Zélie de Lussan until Calvé took it up. Calvé, an artist of genius, divested Carmen of the last rag of romance and respectability: it is not possible to describe in decent language what a rapscallion she made of her. But the comedy of her audacities was irresistible. Her lewd grin at the officer after her arrest, the hitch of the dress by which she exhibited her ankle and defined the outline of her voluptuous figure for his inspection; her contemptuous lack of all interest in Michaela's face, followed by a jealous inspection of the exuberance of her hips; her self-satisfied glance at her own figure from the same point of view in the looking-glass in the second act when she heard José approaching: all these strokes were not only so many instantaneous dramas in themselves taking you every time into the heart of the character, but were executed with such genuine artistic force that you could no more help enjoying them than you could help enjoying the sottishnesses of Falstaff if only Falstaff were played by a great comedian. Calvé wasted no romantic flattery on her Carmen—allowed her no courage, nothing but rowdiness, no heart, no worth, no positive vice even beyond what her taste for coarse pleasures might lead her to; and she made her die with such frightful art that when the last flopping, reeling, disorganized movement had died out of her, you felt that there was nothing lying there but a lump of carrion. Here you had no mere monkey mimicry of this or that antic of a street girl, but great acting in all its qualities, interpretation, invention, selection, creation, and fine execution, with the true tragi-comic force behind it. And yet it was hard to forgive Calvé for the performance, since the achievement, though striking enough, was, for an artist of her gifts, too cheap to counterbalance the degradation of her beauty and the throwing away of her skill on a study from vulgar life which was, after all, quite foreign to the work on which she imposed it.

Miss Olga Nethersole, in her attempt to exploit the reputation which all these opera-singers have made for Carmen, is too heavily handicapped by the inevitable comparison with them. If her acting version had been made by a dramatist capable of supplying an equivalent for the charm and distinction of Mérimée's narrative or the delicate romance of Bizet's music; or if she herself, by insight, humor, and finesse of execution, were able to impose on the piece, such as it is, a fascinating, quasi-realistic character-fantasy of the Macaire order, she might possibly have made the play tolerable after the opera. But none of these conditions are fulfilled for her. She has the staginess of an old actress with the inexpertness of a young one; her Carmen ridiculously combines the realistic sordidness and vulgarity of a dissolute ragpicker with the old-fashioned modish airs and graces, the mantilla, comb, fan, castanets, and dancing-shoes of the stage Spanish gipsies whom our grandmothers admired; and she has not a spark of humor. Her vocal accomplishments are so slender that, instead of genuinely speaking, like her colleague Miss Alexes Leighton, she intones in the manner of some of our naturally voiceless melodramatic actors; but being unable to complete their effective simulation of a powerful voice by copying their sharp, athletic articulation, she relies rather on mere inflexions, which are intolerably monotonous, and too feeble to send even her vowels clearly across the footlights. Her facial play, obscured by a heavily black-leaded impressionist make-up, seems limited to a couple of expressions: No. 1, drawn mouth and jaw, with stretched, staring eyes for tragic presentiment of fate? No. 2, for seduction, a smile with the eyes exactly as before and the lips strongly retracted to display the lower teeth, both effects being put on and off suddenly like masks. In short, judged by this performance, Miss Nethersole is not yet even a proficient actress, much less a great one. Why, then, it may be asked, have we heard so much of her Carmen? I can only answer that those who really want to know had better go and see it. Acting is not the only spectacle that people will stop to look at, though it is the only one with which I am concerned here.

I note with satisfaction that the suburban theatre has now advanced another step. On Monday a new play by Mr Robert Buchanan and his collaborator, Charles Marlowe, was produced at the new theatre at Croydon—a theatre which is to some of our Strand theatres as a Pullman drawing room car is to an old second-class carriage—with a company which includes Miss Kate Rorke, Mr Oswald Yorke, Mr Beauchamp, Mr Anson, Miss Eva Moore, and Miss Vera Beringer. The band played the inevitable overture to Raymond and Mr German's dances, for all the world as if we were at the Vaudeville. I paid three shillings for a stall, and twopence for a program. Add to this the price of a first-class return ticket from London, three and sixpence (and you are under no compulsion to travel first class if second or third will satisfy your sense of dignity); and the visit to the Croydon Theatre costs three and tenpence less than the bare price of a stall in the Strand. And as Miss Kate Rorke not only plays the part of an angel in her most touching manner, but flies bodily up to heaven at the end of the play, to the intense astonishment of the most hardened playgoers, there is something sensational to talk about afterwards.

The play is a variation on the Pygmalion and Galatea theme. It is full of commonplace ready-made phrases to which Mr Buchanan could easily have given distinction and felicity if he were not absolutely the laziest and most perfunctory workman in the entire universe, save only when he is writing letters to the papers, rehabilitating Satan, or committing literary assault and battery on somebody whose works he has not read. I cannot help suspecting that even the trouble of finding the familiar subject was saved him by a chance glimpse of some review of Mr Wells' last story but one. Yet the play holds your attention and makes you believe in it: the born story-teller's imagination is in it unmistakeably, and saves it from the just retribution provoked by the author's lack of a good craftsman's conscience.

Mrs Kendal should really be more cautious than she was at the Garrick on Wednesday night. When you feed a starving castaway you do not give him a full meal at once: you accustom him gradually to food by giving him small doses of soup. Mrs Kendal, forgetting that London playgoers have been starved for years in the matter of acting, inconsiderately gave them more in the first ten minutes than they have had in the last five years, with the result that the poor wretches became hysterical, and vented their applause in sobs and shrieks. And yet in the old days at the St James's they would have taken it all as a matter of course, and perhaps grumbled at the play into the bargain. Mrs Kendal is actually better than ever, now that the pretty ladylike drama of her earlier triumphs is as obsolete as croquet. It is true that in spite of being on her guard in London, she occasionally throws a word at the heads of the audience in such a declamatory way as to raise a mild suspicion that she has perhaps not been wasting her finest methods on the less cultivated sections of the American nation. But her finish of execution, her individuality and charm of style, her appetizingly witty conception of her effects, her mastery of her art and of herself—that mastery for which her amateurish successors are trying to substitute mere abandonment—are all there, making her still supreme among English actresses in high comedy, whilst even in cheap sentiment, for which she has too much brains and character, and in which, consequently, her methods are entirely artificial, the artifice is so skilful and so sympathetic that she makes her audience cry with the greatest ease. Some years ago there was a tendency to mistake the wearing out of the Scrap of Paper-cum-Ironmaster repertory for the wearing out of Mrs Kendal's long success and great prestige. For my part, I see no reason to doubt that if she can only be convinced that London is as tired of that repertory as she is herself (which is probably putting the case strongly), the most serious part of her career may be beginning instead of ending.

As to Mr Grundy's piece, it has the advantage of being violently polemical and didactic; and there is nothing the British public loves better in a play, provided, of course, that it is also dramatic. The Greatest of These— is dramatic up to the brief but unbearable fourth act, which drops all semblance of drama and is simply and frankly nothing but the chairman's superfluous summing up of the discussion. Ten years ago this play, with its open preaching of the rights of humanity as against virtues, religions, respectabilities, and other manufactured goods—especially the provincial varieties—would have ranked as an insanity only fit for the Independent Theatre. Today, after Ibsen and Nietzsche, the only objection to it is that it is rather too crude, parochial, and old-fashioned an expression of an inspiriting and universal philosophy; and it went down, accordingly, like one of Dr Watts's hymns. The general presentation of the piece was so far inevitably false as a picture of English provincial society that Mrs Kendal was a great deal too clever for Warminster, the atmosphere being that of South Kensington or Regent's Park rather than of Salisbury Plain; but, subject to this qualification, the management was first-rate. Miss Nellie Campbell's Grace Armitage was a good piece of professional work—even the brilliant successes of nowadays are seldom that—and Mr Nutcombe Gould and Mr Kemble were well within their powers in the other parts. Mr Rodney Edgcumbe, no doubt, shocked the principals by describing himself as "stowny browk"; but they will soon get used to that. They have probably found out already that any sort of diction is considered good enough for the stage nowadays. As to Mr Kendal, one can only give him the old advice—get divorced. He is a capital comedian; and yet in the whole course of this play he can only steal one laugh in the first act. For the rest, he outrages his nature and genius faithfully in support of his wife in a hopeless part; and the audience, if not delighted, is at least moved by the melancholy dignity of the sacrifice.

SOME OTHER CRITICS

DRAMATIC ESSAYS. By John Forster and George Henry Lewes. Reprinted from the Examiner (1835–38) and The Leader (1850–54). With Notes and an Introduction by William Archer and Robert Lowe. London: Walter Scott. 1896.

MAM'ZELLE NITOUCHE. A musical comedy in three acts by MM. Meilhac, Millaud, and Hervé. Royal Court Theatre, 1 June 1896. [20 *June* 1896]

THE rate of production at the theatres has been so rapid lately that I am conscious of putting off my remarks on performances just as I habitually put off answering letters, in the hope that the march of events will presently save me the trouble of dealing with them. My labors, it must be remembered, are the labors of Sisyphus: every week I roll my heavy stone to the top of the hill; and every week I find it at the bottom again. To the public the tumbling down of the stone is the point of the whole business: they like to see it plunging and bounding and racing in a flying cloud of dust, blackening the eyes of a beautiful actress here and catching an eminent actor-manager in the wind there, flattening out dramatists, demolishing theatres, and generally taking a great deal on itself, considering its size. But the worst of it (from my point of view) is that when it is all over I am the only person who is a penny the worse. The actresses are as beautiful and popular as ever; the actor-managers wallow in the profits of the plays I have denounced; the dramatists receive redoubled commissions; the theatres reopen with programs foolisher than before; and nothing remains of my toy avalanche but the stone at my feet to be rolled up again before the fatigue of the last heave is out of my bones. Sometimes I ask myself whether anybody ever reads critical articles—whether the whole thing is not a mere editorial illusion, a superstition from the purely academic origin of critical journalism. That I, under the compulsion of my daily needs, should face the weekly task of writing these columns is intelligible enough; but that you, reader (if you exist), should under no compulsion at all face the weekly task of reading them merely to keep me in bread and butter is an amazing, incredible thing to me. Yet people do it. They not only want to hear me chattering about Mrs Patrick Campbell, but actually to hear the ghosts of Forster and Lewes chattering about the ghosts of Macready and Forrest, Charles Kean and Rachel. Here is Mr Walter Scott, a publisher who knows by experience what the public will stand in this way, issuing a handsome three-and-sixpenny volume of the Examiner and Leader articles of these dead and gone critics, edited by Mr Robert Lowe and my colleague, Mr William Archer, who has his own stone to roll up every week. The book contains no portrait of Forster: perhaps the editors thought that Dickens's word-picture of him as "a harbitrary gent" could not be improved on; but there is a photograph of Lewes which suggests to me the fearful question, "Are *we* at all like that?"

I recommend the series of dramatic essays of which this book is the third volume to all actors who pretend to be indifferent to the opinion of such persons as myself; for it proves beyond contradiction that the actor who desires enduring fame must seek it at the hands of the critic, and not of the casual playgoer. Money and applause he may have in plenty from the contemporary mob; but posterity can only see him through the spectacles of the elect: if he displease *them*, his credit will be interred with his bones. The world believes Edmund Kean to have been a much greater actor than Junius Brutus Booth solely because Hazlitt thought so. Its belief in the inferiority of Forrest to Macready is not its own opinion, but Forster's. The one failure of Charles Kean's life that matters now is his failure to impress Lewes in anything higher than melodrama. Some day they will reprint my articles; and then what will all your puffs and long runs and photographs and papered houses and cheap successes avail you, O lovely leading ladies and well-tailored actor-managers? The twentieth century, if it concerns itself about either of us, will see you as I see you. Therefore study my tastes, flatter me, bribe me, and see that your acting-managers are conscious of my existence and impressed with my importance.

Both Lewes and Forster had the cardinal faculty of the critic: they could really and objectively see the stage; and they could analyse what they saw there. In this respect Forster is as good as Hazlitt or Lewes: he is a first-rate demonstrator, and can take an actor to pieces and put him together again as well as anybody. But his outlook on the general human life in relation to which the theatre must always be judged, is not so lofty, keen, and free-minded as that of Hazlitt, who was something of a genius; and he had not Lewes's variety of culture, flexibility, and fun. I consider that Lewes in some respects anticipated me, especially in his free use of vulgarity and impudence whenever they happened to be the proper tools for his job. He had a rare gift of integrity as a critic. When he was at his business, he seldom remembered that he was a gentleman or a scholar. In this he shewed himself a true craftsman, intent on making the measurements and analyses of his criticism as accurate, and their expression as clear and vivid, as possible, instead of allowing himself to be distracted by the vanity of playing the elegant man of letters, or writing with perfect good taste, or hinting in every line that he was above his work. In exacting all this from himself, and taking his revenge by expressing his most labored conclusions with a levity that gave them the air of being the unpremeditated whimsicalities of a man who had perversely taken to writing about the theatre for the sake of the jest latent in his own outrageous unfitness for it, Lewes rolled his stone up the hill quite in the modern manner of Mr Walkley, dissembling its huge weight, and apparently kicking it at random hither and thither in pure wantonness. In fact, he reminds Mr William Archer of a writer called Corno di Bassetto, who was supposed—among other impostures—to have introduced this style of writing when Mr T. P. O'Connor invented the halfpenny evening paper in 1888. But these articles of Lewes's are miles beyond the crudities of Di Bassetto, though the combination of a laborious criticism with a recklessly flippant manner is the same in both. Lewes, by the way, like Bassetto, was a musical critic. He was an adventurous person as critics go; for he not only wrote philosophical treatises and feuilletons, but went on the stage, and was denounced by Barry Sullivan as "a poor creature," perhaps for the feebleness of his execution, but perhaps also a little because he tried to get away from the superhuman style of Barry into the path since opened up by Irving. He also wrote plays of the kind which, as a critic, he particularly disliked. And he was given to singing—nothing will ever persuade me that a certain passage in The Impressions of Theophrastus Such about an amateur vocalist who would persist in wrecking himself on O Ruddier than the Cherry does not refer to Lewes. Finally he was rash enough to contract a morganatic union with the most famous woman writer of his day, a novelist, thereby allowing his miserable affections to triumph over his critical instincts (which he appears, however, to have sometimes indulged clandestinely in spite of himself); and so, having devoted some years to remonstrating with people who persisted in addressing the famous novelist by her maiden name instead of as "Mrs Lewes," he perished after proving conclusively in his own person that "womanly self-sacrifice" is an essential manly weakness. The history of that interesting union yet remains to be written. Neither cynic nor heroine worshipper will ever do it justice; but George Eliot at least paid it the widow's compliment of marrying again, though she did not select a critic this time. These and other features of Lewes's career are dealt with from the point of view of the general reader in Mr Archer's very interesting forty pages of introduction. From my personal point of view, they are, on the whole, a solemn warning. I shall not marry, morganatically or otherwise. Eminent lady novelists will please accept this notice.

Miss May Yohe might, I think, have given us something fresher at the Court Theatre than a revival of Mam'zelle Nitouche.

I take it that Miss Yohe is not now living by her profession and compelled to accept what engagements may come her way, leaving to her managers the responsibility of choosing the piece. She is, is she not, in an independent position, gained by alliance with the British aristocracy, and subject to all the social responsibilities attaching to that sort of independence? These responsibilities do not, of course, demand that she should share in the patriarchal administration of the family estate if she is driven by irresistible instincts to seek her natural activity on the stage as an artist. Nobody can object to that alternative course, nor to her subsidizing the theatre out of her revenues—not earned, be it remembered, by herself, but derived at some point or other from the nation's industries. Clearly the revenues and the artistic activity cannot honorably be wasted on unworthy or stale entertainments merely, as the professional phrase goes, to give the manageress a show. If a lady wants nothing more than that, she must conform to social discipline and take her show in the prescribed ladylike way, either plastering herself with diamonds and sitting in an opera-box like a wax figure in a jeweller's shop window, or dressing herself prettily and driving up and down the Row in the afternoon to be stared at by all the world and his wife. Whether in sanctioning the necessary expenditure for this purpose the nation makes a wise bargain or not, shall not be discussed here. Suffice it to say that it is an extremely liberal one for the lady, and need not be enlarged so as to include appearances on the stage as well as in the auditorium and in the Row. For just consider what would happen if acting under professional conditions became as fashionable as cycling. We should have every theatre in London taken at extravagant rents by fashionable amateurs; and art would be banished to the suburbs and the provinces. If, however, a lady comes forward to supersede the ordinary commercial manager out of pure love of the theatre and a determination to rescue the lighter forms of musical art from the rowdiness and indecency which popular gagging comedians have been allowed to introduce into it of late years, then she is within the sphere of her most serious social duties as much as if she were interesting herself in orphanages and hospitals. This, I take it, is the honorable construction to which Miss May Yohe's enterprise is entitled *prima facie*.

Unfortunately, it is very hard to feel that the Court performance bears out such a view. Miss May Yohe is too clever—too much the expert professional—to be dismissed as a stage-struck fashionable amateur; but, on the other hand, there is nothing either in Mam'zelle Nitouche nor in the style of its performance to explain why any lady should step out of the aristocratic sphere to produce it. I noticed that Mr Mackinder, an agile and clever comedian who sedulously cultivates the style of Mr Arthur Roberts, permitted himself, in the first act, to interrupt Miss Haydon with a quip which might possibly have made a schoolboy grin, but which was disrespectful to the audience, to his fellow-artists, to Miss Yohe as the responsible manager, to his art, and to himself. In the green-rooms of some music-halls they post a notice warning performers not to interpolate any objectionable pleasantries into their songs and dialogue on pain of instant cancelling of their engagement. It seems time to post this notice in all our comic-opera houses except the Savoy. When a lady who bears a title in private life undertakes the management of a West End theatre, one hopes that there, at least, no such precaution could be necessary; and yet, as I have said, Mr Mackinder had not been ten minutes on the stage before he improvised a jest that made every decent person in the theatre shiver, and did it, too, in perfect good faith, with a hardworking desire to shew his smartness and make his part "go." For the rest, there was nothing to complain of, and nothing to admire particularly. Miss Florence Levey gave us a very lively and confident imitation—but only an imitation—of a skilled dancer and singer. Mr Tapley, whom I can remember when he was a tenor, can still inflict certain falsetto tones sufficiently to be called, by a stretch of compliment, a tenorino. Miss Yohe's own extraordinary artificial contralto had so little tone on the first night that it was largely mistaken for an attack of hoarseness; and her sentimental song, with its aborted cadence which sought to make a merit and a feature of its own weakness, was only encored, not quite intentionally, out of politeness. Her sustaining power seems gone: she breathes after every little phrase, and so cannot handle a melody in her old broad, rich manner; but doubtless the remedy for this is a mere matter of getting into condition. As a comic actress she has improved since the days of Little Christopher Columbus; and the personal charm and gay grace of movement, with the suggestion of suppressed wildness beneath them, are all there still, with more than their original bloom on them. But with every possible abuse of the indulgence of which Miss Yohe can always count on more than her fair share, it is impossible to say that she removes the impression that the day for opéra-bouffe has gone by. Opéra-bouffe is dramatically and musically too trivial for modern taste in opera; and in spectacle, variety, and novelty it cannot compete with the string of music-hall turns disguised as "musical comedy" now in vogue. Besides, even our modern music-hall songs and the orchestral "melodrame" which accompanies our acrobats are symphonic in construction and Wagnerian in breadth and richness compared to the couplets and quadrilles of Offenbach and Lecocq; although it is true, all the same, that Offenbach's score of La Grande Duchesse and its libretto are classics compared to anything we seem able to turn out nowadays. Still, if La Grande Duchesse had been entrusted to a mere comic-song tune compiler and a brace of facetious bar-loafers, it would have been none the more up to date now in dramatic weight and musical richness. Miss Yohe had better order a libretto from a witty dramatist and a score from a clever musician, both in touch with the humor of the day, and try her luck with that. She will only waste her time and money if she tries back to cast-off favorites.

By the way, this is musical criticism: why am I writing it? Why do they not send my colleague J. F. R. to these things? How stale it all seems! how hopeless! how heavily the stone of Sisyphus goes up along this track in the hot weather!

THE SECOND DATING OF SHERIDAN

THE SCHOOL FOR SCANDAL. By Sheridan. Lyceum Theatre, 20 June 1896.

ON THE MARCH. A musical comedy in two acts. Prince of Wales Theatre, 22 June 1896. [27 *June* 1896]

IT is impossible to see The School for Scandal without beginning to moralize. I am going to moralize: let the reader skip if he will.

As the world goes on, manners, customs, and morals change their aspect with revolutionary completeness, whilst man remains almost the same. Honor and decency, coats and shirts, cleanliness and politeness, eating and drinking, may persist as names; but the actual habits which the names denote alter so much that no century would tolerate those of its forerunner or successor. Compare the gentleman of Sheridan's time with the gentleman of today. What a change in all that is distinctively gentlemanly!—the dress, the hair, the watch-chain, the manners, the point of honor, the meals, the ablutions, and so on! Yet strip the twain, and they are as like as two eggs: maroon them on Juan Fernandez, and what difference will there be between their habits and those of Robinson Crusoe? Nevertheless, men do change, not only in what they think and what they do, but in what they are. Sometimes they change, just like their fashions, by the abolition of one sort and color of man and the substitution of another—white for black or yellow for red, white being the height of fashion with us. But they also change by slow development of the same kind of man; so that whilst the difference between the institutions of the eighteenth and twentieth centuries may be as complete as the difference between a horse and a bicycle, the difference between the men of those periods is only a trifling increment of efficiency, not nearly so great as that which differentiated Shakespear from the average Elizabethan. That is why Shakespear's plays, though obsolete as representations of fashion and manners, are still far ahead of the public as dramatic studies of humanity.

But I must cut my argument more finely than this. To say that

166

fashions change more rapidly than men is a very crude statement of extremes. Everything has its own rate of change. Fashions change more quickly than manners, manners more quickly than morals, morals more quickly than passions, and, in general, the conscious, reasonable, intellectual life more quickly than the instinctive, wilful, affectionate one. The dramatist who deals with the irony and humor of the relatively durable sides of life, or with their pity and terror, is the one whose comedies and tragedies will last longest —sometimes so long as to lead a book-struck generation to dub him "Immortal," and proclaim him as "not for an age, but for all time." Fashionable dramatists begin to "date," as the critics call it, in a few years: the accusation is rife at present against the earlier plays of Pinero and Grundy, though it is due to these gentlemen to observe that Shakespear's plays must have "dated" far more when they were from twenty to a hundred years old than they have done since the world gave up expecting them to mirror the passing hour. When Caste and Diplomacy were fresh, London Assurance had begun to date most horribly: nowadays Caste and Diplomacy date like the day-before-yesterday's tinned salmon; whereas if London Assurance were revived (and I beg that nothing of the kind be attempted), there would be no more question of dating about it than about the plays of Garrick or Tobin or Mrs Centlivre.

But now observe the consequences, as to this dating business, of the fact that morals change more slowly than costumes and manners, and instincts and passions than morals. It follows, does it not, that every "immortal" play will run the following course? First, like London Assurance, its manners and fashions will begin to date. If its matter is deep enough to tide it over this danger, it will come into repute again, like the comedies of Sheridan or Goldsmith, as a modern classic. But after some time—some centuries, perhaps—it will begin to date again in point of its ethical conception. Yet if it deals so powerfully with the instincts and passions of humanity as to survive this also, it will again regain its place, this time as an antique classic, especially if it tells a capital story. It is impossible now to read, without a curdling of the blood and a bristling of the hair, the frightful but dramatically most powerful speech which David, on his death-bed, delivers to his son about the old enemy whom he had himself sworn to spare. "Thou art a wise man and knowest what thou oughtest to do unto him; but his hoar head bring thou down to the grave with blood." Odysseus, proud of outwitting all men at cheating and lying, and intensely relishing the blood of Penelope's suitors, is equally outside our morality. So is Punch. But David and Ulysses, like Punch and Judy, will survive for many a long day yet. Not until the change has reached our instincts and passions will their stories begin to "date" again for the last time before their final absolescence.

I have been led into this investigation of "dating" by the fact that The School for Scandal, which has got over its first attack of that complaint so triumphantly that its obsolete costumes and manners positively heighten its attraction, dated very perceptibly last Saturday night at the Lyceum in point of morals. Its thesis of the superiority of the good-natured libertine to the ill-natured formalist and hypocrite may pass, though it is only a dramatization of Tom Jones, and hardly demurs to the old morality further than to demonstrate that a bad man is not so bad as a worse. But there is an ancient and fishlike smell about the "villainy" of Joseph and the ladylikeness of Lady Teazle. If you want to bring The School for Scandal up to date, you must make Charles a woman, and Joseph a perfectly sincere moralist. Then you will be in the atmosphere of Ibsen and of The Greatest of These— at once. And it is because there is no sort of hint of this now familiar atmosphere—because Joseph's virtue is a pretence instead of a reality, and because the women in the play are set apart and regarded as absolutely outside the region of free judgment in which the men act, that the play, as aforesaid, "dates."

Formerly, nothing shocked us in the screen scene except Charles's caddishness in making fun of Sir Peter and his wife under very painful circumstances. But, after all, Charles was not so bad as Hamlet rallying Ophelia at the play or Mercutio chaffing the Nurse. What now jars on us is the caddishness of Lady

Teazle, whose conduct for the first time begins to strike us as it would if it were the conduct of a man in the like circumstances. Society forbids a man to compromise a woman; but it also requires him, if he nevertheless does compromise her, to accept as one of the consequences of his action the obligation not to betray her, even if he has to go into the witness-box and swear to her innocence. Suppose Lady Teazle, on being surprised by Sir Peter in Joseph's rooms, had invented a plausible excuse, and had asked Joseph to confirm her. Suppose Joseph had thereupon said, "No, it is false, every word. My slumbering conscience awakens; and I return to the sacred path of truth and duty. Your wife, Sir Peter, is an abandoned woman who came here to tempt me from the path of honor. But for your arrival I might have fallen; but now I see the blackness of her conduct in all its infamy; and I ask you to pardon me, and to accept the sincerity of my contrition as a pledge for my future good conduct." Would any extremity of blackballing, cutting, even kicking, be considered too severe for the man who should try to extricate himself at the expense of his accomplice in that straightforward manner? And yet that is exactly what Lady Teazle does without the least misgiving on the part of the dramatist as to the entire approval and sympathy of the audience. In this, as far as I am concerned, the dramatist is mistaken, and the play consequently dates. I cannot for the life of me see why it is less dishonorable for a woman to kiss and tell than a man. It is sometimes said that the social consequences of exposure are worse for a woman than for a man; but that is certainly not the case in these days of Parnell overthrows and ruinous damages, whatever it may have been in the time of Sheridan —and the commonplace assumptions with regard to that period are probably as erroneous as those current about our own. At all events, when a married woman comes to a man's rooms with the deliberate intention of enjoying a little gallantry, and, on being caught, pleads for sympathy and forgiveness as an innocent young creature misled and seduced by a villain, she strikes a blow at the very foundations of immorality.

The fact that this is not altogether a wise thing to do—that artificial systems of morality, like other dangerous engines, explode when they are worked at high pressure without safety-valves—was cynically admitted in Sheridan's time with regard to men, and sentimentally repudiated with regard to women. But now see what has happened. A terrible, gifted person, a woman speaking for women, Madame Sarah Grand to wit, has arisen to insist that if the morality of her sex can do without safety-valves, so can the morality of "the stronger sex," and to demand that the man shall come to the woman exactly as moral as he insists that she shall come to him. And, of course, not a soul dares deny that claim. On the other hand, the fact that there is an obvious alternative way out of the difficulty does not escape those to whom Madame Sarah Grand's position is a *reductio ad absurdum* of our whole moral system; and accordingly we have Mrs Kendal asking every night at the Garrick why Man—meaning Woman—should be so much more moral than God. As for me, it is not my business as a dramatic critic to pursue the controversy: it concerns me only as the explanation of how Lady Teazle's position is changed by the arrival of audiences who read edition after edition of The Heavenly Twins, and who nightly applaud the point made by the author of The Greatest of These—. Whether they are for greater rigor with the novelist, or for greater charity with the dramatist, they are equally learning to drop the old fast-and-loose system of a masculine morality for the man and a feminine morality for the woman, and to apply instead a human standard impartially to both sexes. And so The School for Scandal dates on the Woman Question almost as badly as The Taming of the Shrew.

That the play is well acted goes without saying. Sheridan wrote for the actor as Handel wrote for the singer, setting him a combination of strokes which, however difficult some of them may be to execute finely, are familiar to all practised actors as the strokes which experience has shewn to be proper to the nature and capacity of the stage-player as a dramatic instrument. With Sheridan you are never in the plight of the gentleman who stamped on a sheet of Beethoven's music in a rage, declaring that what cannot be played should not be written. That difficulty exists today with Ibsen, who abounds in passages that our actors do not know how to play; but The School for Scandal is like Acis and Galatea: you may have the voice and the skill for it or you may not (probably not); but at all events you are never in doubt as to how it ought to be done. To see Mr William Farren play Sir Peter after a long round of modern "character acting" is like hearing Santley sing Nasce al bosco after a seasonful of goat-bleating Spanish tenors and tremulous French baritones shattering themselves on passionately sentimental dithyrambs by Massenet and Saint-Saëns. Mr Forbes Robertson is an excellent Joseph Surface. He gets at the centre of the part by catching its heartlessness and insincerity, from which his good looks acquire a subtle ghastliness, his grace a taint of artifice, and all the pictorial qualities which make him so admirable as a saint or medieval hero an ironical play which has the most delicate hypocritical effect. Mr Fred Terry not only acts as Charles Surface, but acts well. I do not expect this statement to be believed in view of such prior achievements of his as A Leader of Men, The Home Secretary, and so forth; but I am bound to report what I saw. Mr Terry has grown softer—fatter, if he will excuse the remark; and he has caught some of the ways of Miss Julia Neilson, the total result being to make his playing more effeminate than it used to be; but it cannot be denied that he plays Charles Surface with a vivacity and a pleasant adipose grace that has nothing of the stickishness of his modern Bond Street style about it. Mrs Patrick Campbell struck me as being exactly right, for modern purposes, in her performance. In the fourth act she was Lady Teazle, and not an actress using the screen scene as a platform for a powerful but misplaced display of intense emotional acting. No doubt an actress—if she is able to do it—is greatly tempted to say to Joseph Surface "I think we had better leave honor out of the question" with all the dignity and depth of Imogen rebuking Iachimo, and to reveal herself, when the screen falls, as a woman of the richest nature tragically awakened for the first time to its full significance. In ten years' time we shall have Mrs Campbell doing this as unscrupulously as Miss Rehan or any other past-mistress of her art does it now. But it is not the play: it upsets the balance of the comedy and belittles Sir Peter. Nothing deeper is wanted than commonplace thoughtlessness, good-nature, and a girl's revulsion of feeling at the end; and this Mrs Patrick Campbell gives prettily and without exaggeration, with the result that the comedy is seen in its true proportions for the first time within the memory of this generation. It may be held, of course, that the play has only been kept alive by overacting that particular scene; but this view is not borne out by a general comparison of the effect of the Daly and the Lyceum revivals. On Miss Rose Leclercq, Mr Cyril Maude, and Mr Edward Righton as Mrs Candour, Sir Benjamin Backbite, and Sir Oliver, I need not waste compliments: their success was a foregone conclusion. Maria was hardly in Miss Brooke's line; but then Maria is not in anybody's line. Mr Forbes Robertson's reception was extraordinarily enthusiastic. It is evident that the failure of Magda and the escapade of Michael have not shaken his popularity, whatever else it may have cost him. Towards Mrs Campbell, however, there was a disposition to be comparatively sane and critical as well as very friendly. I attribute this, not to any improvement in the public brain, but to a make-up which, though cleverly in character with Lady Teazle, hid all the magnetic fascination of Paula Tanqueray and Fedora.

On the March, at the Prince of Wales' Theatre (now in the hands of Miss Cissy Grahame), is prodigiously superior to Biarritz, which seems to have perished miserably, as it certainly deserved to. It is a variety entertainment of no particular pretensions to smartness; and it must be admitted that the primitive funniments and outlandish dialect of Mr Thomas Murray, the Irish-American comedian who succeeds Mr Arthur Roberts, smacks of the village rather than of the West End. But he is imperturbably good-humored, sings in tune, and surprises the audience into laughing at his childlike jokes several times, on which scores much is forgiven to him. For the rest, the people who come forward to dance can dance, and the singers can sing—one of them, Miss Maud Boyd, so exceptionally well that she recalled the night on which the public first discovered Miss Marie Tempest. Miss Alice Atherton, who is in some danger of bodily outgrowing her reputation, is supported by Mr Horace Mills, a highly successful disciple of Mr Dan Leno. Mr Brookfield throws himself away pitiably for half the evening in order to recover himself very funnily during the other half as an amateur Valentine in Faust. On the whole, though I do not defend the entertainment as "a musical comedy," or the charging of theatre prices for what is really a music-hall entertainment; still, there is no incompetence, no parading of the unskilled, flashy girls who get engaged in theatres solely because their ineptitudes would not be tolerated for a moment in a music-hall; and the music is not rowdy and tiresome, but pretty, with fairly elegantly scored accompaniments. Let On the March, therefore, pass as good of its simple kind.

DE MORTUIS

[4 *July* 1896]

THOSE lazy spectators of the pageant of life who love to reflect on the instability of human greatness have by this time yawned and gone to bed after reading the last of the subsiding rush of paragraphs about the late Sir Augustus Harris. The day after his death one of the greetings addressed to me was, "And so your old enemy is gone." This shocked me at the moment; for, though I had no illusions whatever about his imaginary greatness as an operatic reformer, I did not dislike him personally; and I was naturally in a softer mood after the news of his premature death than I used to be at the time when, as a musical critic, I was making onslaught after onslaught on the spurious artistic prestige of Covent Garden. In those days the relations between us were certainly somewhat strained. There were seasons when I always sat down in my stall at Covent Garden with the virtuous consciousness of having paid hard money for it, instead of being the invited guest of the manager whose scalp it was my business to take. There were times, too, when I was warned that my criticisms were being collated by legal experts for the purpose of proving "prejudice" against me, and crushing me by mulcting my editor in fabulous damages. And, as sure as fate, if that editor had been a skinflint and a coward; if he had corruptly regarded his paper, in its critical relation to the fine arts, solely as a convenient instrument for unlimited sponging on managers, publishers, and picture-dealers for gratuitous boxes, stalls, books, prints, and private-view invitations; if he had been willing to sell his critic for an advertisement or for an invitation to the dinner or garden parties of the smartest partizans of the fashionable tenor or prima donna of the season; or if he had been a hired editor at the mercy of a proprietor of that stamp, then I should have been silenced, as many other critics were silenced. But the late Edmund Yates was not that sort of editor. He had his faults; but he did not run away from his own sword for fear of cutting his fingers with it; he did not beg the tribute he could compel; and he had a strong and loyal *esprit de corps*. The World proved equal to the occasion in the conflict with Covent Garden; and finally my invitations to the Opera were renewed; the impresario made my personal acquaintance, and maintained the pleasantest personal relations with me from that time onward; and so, as I have said, when his death was announced, I was quite taken aback by the reference to our ancient warfare.

I refer to it myself now because it is well that the public should know the truth as to the perils of the relation between the Press, the theatre, and the law. I have sometimes been asked whether the attempt to suppress my criticism was made with a Napoleonic dispassionateness, as part of the routine of a huge commercial enterprise fighting for its monopoly as a matter of life or death, and bent on bringing the Press to heel at any cost, or whether the impresario regarded me as a sort of critical cobra, unable to contain my venom, and subject to fits of blind, purposeless, altogether brutish fits of malicious rage against his splendid and beloved Opera. I reply that even if he had entertained the latter opinion of me—and no doubt, being only human, he may have done so once or twice for a day or so after reading some particularly exasperating sally of mine—yet the practical steps he took to silence or intimidate me were taken in legitimate self-defence, and were as much a part of his business as his advertisements were. All managers do the same—why should they not?—and that is why so few critics say what they think. Personal motives do not count for much in any theatre, even in the case of actor-managers who angrily profess them, simply because the commercial pressure under which a manager works, with his money flying away at the rate of from five hundred to a thousand a week, and no sort of certainty of the receipts amounting to fifty, will nail the touchiest actor to strict business if he is capable of management at all. But if this is true of the theatre, what must be the state of mind of the Covent Garden impresario, whose expenses for one performance would keep a theatre going for a fortnight? Such conditions bring the most wilful and thin-skinned man back to his business interests every time he lapses into petulance or sentimental generosity. Besides, there was one gigantic business obligation which was peculiar to Sir Augustus Harris. In ordinary theatrical management nobody proposes a policy of monopoly. It is quite understood that Mr Alexander must count on the competition of Mr Tree, Mr Hare, Sir Henry Irving, and, in fact, as many competitors as there are suitable theatres in London. But the Augustan policy at Covent Garden was one of monopoly at all costs. The impresario well knew what the old system of two competing operas, one at Her Majesty's and the other at Covent Garden, was like behind the scenes. To issue flashy lying prospectuses; to slip into your theatre by back ways so as to avoid the ambuscades of the unpaid chorus; to hold your artists spellbound with flattering conversations until after bank hour lest they should present their cheques before money could be scraped together to meet them: all these shifts and dodges of the bankrupt two-opera system were no part of the Harris *régime*, under which the credit of the Covent Garden treasury became as that of the Bank of England. Sir Augustus Harris paid more money every year to prevent artists from working for anybody else than some of his predecessors paid for work actually done on their stages. The grievance at Covent Garden was, not that you could not get your money, but that you were not allowed to earn it. He not only held Drury Lane and Covent Garden against all comers, but took Her Majesty's and locked it up until it was demolished. Even in smaller theatres tenants found clauses in their agreements barring Italian Opera. Just as he forestalled possible rivals as a pantomime manager by engaging all the stars of the music-hall, whether he had work for them or not, so, as an impresario, he engaged every operatic artist who shewed the slightest promise of becoming a source of strength to a competitor. When Signor Lago discovered Cavaleria, the Ravoglis, and Ancona, they were bought over his head immediately. There was no malice in the matter. The alternative to monopoly was bankruptcy. Sir Augustus Harris's triumph as a business impresario was his acceptance of that big condition and his achievement of the feat of finance and organization involved by it.

As an artistic impresario, he applied his Drury Lane experience of the stage management of crowds with great effect to a few simple melodramatic operas, notably to William Tell, and afterwards to La Navarraise and L'Attaque du Moulin. But the current notion that he could handle the masterpieces of dramatic music is a ludicrous delusion. I notice that The World, forgetting its back numbers, says, "Sir Augustus Harris's most excellent work was his resuscitation of Grand Opera in England. Hitherto opera had spelt ruin, for it had been slipshod, inartistic, absurd. Sir Augustus Harris labored to cast aside the fatuous conventions of the Italian school, and to adopt all that was best in the German stage." *Sancta simplicitas!* The truth is that he fought obstinately for the Italian fatuities against the German reforms. He was saturated with the obsolete operatic traditions of the days of Tietjens, whose Semiramide and Lucrezia he admired as great tragic impersonations. He described Das Rheingold as "a damned pantomime"; he persisted for years in putting Tannhäuser on the stage with Venusberg effects that would have disgraced a Whitechapel Road gaff, with the twelve horns on the stage replaced by a military band behind the scenes, and with

Rotten Row trappings on the horses; he introduced *opéra-bouffe* warriors—girls with flaxen wigs and Greek helmets—into the Elysian Fields in Gluck's Orfeo; he could not be persuaded to engage a first-rate or even a second-rate conductor, or to make his stage manager at least ask somebody to tell him enough of the stories of the operas to prevent Meyerbeer's Huguenot soldiers from joining in the prayers of the Catholics, or to provide something more plausible for Gilda to die upon than a comfortable sofa placed in the middle of a street in a thunderstorm; he wasted the talents of dramatic singers like Maurel and Giulia Ravogli, who required intelligent management and casting to make the most of them; he could provide unlimited luxury and limelight, but not artistic incentive, for the wonderful bevy of singers, the de Reszkes, Melba, Eames, Calvé, and Plançon, who were the real winners of his success; in short, he did and undid and left undone such things as I dare not set down here at this moment lest I should jog the memory of the Recording Angel to his peril. It was only in the last few years that he began to learn something from Calvé and the young Italian school, from Wagner, from Massenet and Bruneau, and from Verdi's latest works. Had he been merely an ignorant man, it would have been much better for him; for then he might have had that advantage over his predecessors which Mr Archer lays his finger on in speaking of his start as manager of Drury Lane—"he was too young and practical to be in the least degree hampered by tradition." In opera, unfortunately, he was soaked in tradition, and kept London a quarter of a century behind New York and Berlin—down almost to the level of Paris—in dramatic music.

As to his making opera pay, he did not succeed in doing that until he was in business on an enormous scale, and was making one enterprise pay for another, besides raising the price of the stalls on the best nights to twenty-five shillings. Then he at last declared the usual privately subscribed subvention more trouble than it was worth, and did without it. The Opera had by that time grown to dimensions of which his predecessors never dreamt. It overflowed from Covent Garden into Drury Lane;

the superfluous artists, engaged only to secure them from capture by Signor Lago or Mr Mapleson, were turned to account at a second series of performances; the chorus was engaged for the year instead of the season; spring seasons and winter seasons were added; cheap performances of Faust, Cavalleria, The Bohemian Girl, Lohengrin, I Pagliacci, and Hansel and Gretel were kept going like Madame Tussaud's or the Crystal Palace; companies were sent into the provinces; and finally, when the non-musical side of the huge business was brought in as well—the Drury Lane pantomime, the melodramas, and all their offshoots—the fact that this or that summer night at Covent Garden, taken by itself, might not pay, was of no more account than the fact that the billposting, taken by itself, did not pay. I have always said that to criticize Sir Augustus Harris it was not enough to be a musician: one had to be an economist as well; and the columns of elaborate error emptied on his grave abundantly prove how right I was. Quite the most enthralling memorial of him would be the publication of his accounts, if he kept any. Copies should be appended of the contracts imposed by him on the more dependent classes of artists engaged. The extent to which he succeeded in inducing such people to place themselves at his disposal when wanted without exacting any reciprocal obligation would considerably astonish those innocent persons who think of the operatic stage as a specially free and irresponsible profession. You can drive a second-class prima donna to sign an agreement that a mason, a carpenter, or an engine-fitter, backed by their Trade-Unions, would tear up and throw in your face.

To discuss the operations of a commercial organization of this extent as if they were the outcome of the private character of the entrepreneur is idle. It is like discussing whether the battle of Waterloo was a humane proceeding on Wellington's part, or a personally courageous one on Napoleon's. The Reverend Dr Ker Gray, we are told, gave an impressive address at the funeral on the work of the dead man, "honest, honorable, straightforward." But one feels a want of real life in this description—after all, the reverend gentleman may say as much for the next bookmaker he buries, or for Prince Bismarck. Big games are played with the cards on the table; and in businesses where there is no trust all payments are prompt. What the orator meant was, I suspect, that Sir Augustus Harris was impatient of humbug; that he was proud of promising the public nothing, and giving them gorgeous value for their money as a matter of course; and that he pursued his business simply and with integrity, simplicity and integrity being possible in everything, from burglary to martyrdom. But we have not yet heard the devil's advocate on his case. Was he, for instance, a good employer as well as a punctual paymaster—I do not mean to Messieurs de Reszke and Mesdames Melba and Eames, but to "extra" ladies and gentlemen (formerly called "supers"), to the rank and file of his orchestras, and to the multitude of poor people who are needed in the business of a great showman, and who are helplessly at the mercy of their master? Did he, in feasting the public with the annual melodramatic display of stage sport, stage "high life," and jingo stage war, ever sacrifice a farthing to any consideration for the sincerity or morality of the sentiments he was appealing to? Did he produce or encourage the production of any great work of art, new or old, for its own sake? Did the advance that was visible in his later enterprises spring from anything deeper than a famous man's desire to live up to his reputation, and an ambitious plutocrat's pride in having the dearest of everything? I really do not know; and neither do the writers who have been cheapening public applause by writing of him in terms which would flatter a great prime minister.

For my own part I confess to liking the man better than I had any reason to like him. There was a certain pathos about him, with a touch of humor; and I do not doubt the assurances of his friends that he was very sensitive to stories of distress. But I know that he was not a great manager; and I am not convinced that he was even a very clever one. Attentive observers of great "captains of industry" know that their success often comes to them in spite of themselves—that instead of planning and guiding complicated enterprises with a master-hand, they are simply following the slot of the market with a sort of doglike instinct into the centre of all sorts of enterprises which are too big to be upset by their misunderstandings. I am perfectly certain that if Sir Augustus Harris had managed the Opera according to his own ideas, he would have destroyed it quite as effectually as Mr Mapleson did. It seems hardly credible now that I once exhausted myself, in the columns of The World, in apparently hopeless attempts to shame the de Reszkes out of their perpetual Faust and Mephistopheles, Romeo and Laurent, and in poohpooed declarations that there were such works in existence as Die Walküre and Tristan. It was not Sir Augustus Harris that roused Jean de Reszke from his long lethargy, but his own artistic conscience and the shock of Vandyk's brilliant success in Massenet's Manon. Today I am told that Jean de Reszke is playing Tristan with unspeakable glory to Edouard's King Mark; and my World successor is telling his readers—*my* readers—that the performance is "a passion flower on Sir Augustus Harris's grave," and of "the happy expression on his face two years ago, when he told us of the delight he had in preparation for us." My dear Mr Hichens, you should have seen the happy expression on his face five or six years ago, when I used to urge that Tristan, having been composed in 1859, was perhaps a little overdue. I do not grudge the grave its passion flowers; but I do suggest that the next great impresario who takes thirty-seven years to realize the value of a masterpiece must not be surprised if he finds that not even his premature death on the eve of its production will persuade an "old enemy" that he died of artistic enthusiasm.

In short, on this subject, I am, like the gentleman in The Corsican Brothers, "still implacable." I said it all when he was alive; I say it now that he is dead; and I shall say it again whenever I see the Press bowing a little too low before commercial success, and offering it the wreaths that belong to genius and devotion alone.

"THE SPACIOUS TIMES"

DOCTOR FAUSTUS. By Christopher Marlowe. Acted by members
of the Shakespear Reading Society at St George's Hall, on a
stage after the model of the Fortune Playhouse, 2 July 1896.

THE MUMMY. A new and original farce in three acts. By George
D. Day and Allan Reed. Comedy Theatre, 2 July 1896.

SCENES FROM ROMEO AND JULIET, FEDORA, and THE COUNTRY
GIRL. By Miss Elizabeth Tyree. Comedy Theatre, 3 July 1896.

BEHIND THE SCENES. A farcical comedy, adapted from The First
Night. By Felix Morris and George P. Hawtrey. Comedy
Theatre, 4 July 1896. [11 *July* 1896]

MR WILLIAM POEL, in drawing up an announcement of the last
exploit of the Elizabethan Stage Society, had no difficulty in citing a number of eminent authorities as to the superlative merits
of Christopher Marlowe. The dotage of Charles Lamb on the
subject of the Elizabethan dramatists has found many imitators,
notably Mr Swinburne, who expresses in verse what he finds in
books as passionately as a poet expresses what he finds in life.
Among them, it appears, is a Mr G. B. Shaw, in quoting whom
Mr Poel was supposed by many persons to be quoting me. But
though I share the gentleman's initials, I do not share his views.
He can admire a fool: I cannot, even when his folly not only expresses itself in blank verse, but actually invents that art form for
the purpose. I admit that Marlowe's blank verse has charm of
color and movement; and I know only too well how its romantic
march caught the literary imagination and founded that barren
and horrible worship of blank verse for its own sake which has
since desolated and laid waste the dramatic poetry of England.
But the fellow was a fool for all that. He often reminds me, in his
abysmally inferior way, of Rossini. Rossini had just the same
trick of beginning with a magnificently impressive exordium,
apparently pregnant with the most tragic developments, and
presently lapsing into arrant triviality. But Rossini lapses amusingly; writes "Excusez du peu" at the double bar which separates

the sublime from the ridiculous; and is gay, tuneful and clever in his frivolity. Marlowe, the moment the exhaustion of the imaginative fit deprives him of the power of raving, becomes childish in thought, vulgar and wooden in humor, and stupid in his attempts at invention. He is the true Elizabethan blank-verse beast, itching to frighten other people with the superstitious terrors and cruelties in which he does not himself believe, and wallowing in blood, violence, muscularity of expression and strenuous animal passion as only literary men do when they become thoroughly depraved by solitary work, sedentary cowardice, and starvation of the sympathetic centres. It is not surprising to learn that Marlowe was stabbed in a tavern brawl: what would be utterly unbelievable would be his having succeeded in stabbing anyone else. On paper the whole obscene crew of these blank-verse rhetoricians could outdare Lucifer himself: Nature can produce no murderer cruel enough for Webster, nor any hero bully enough for Chapman, devout disciples, both of them, of Kit Marlowe. But you do not believe in their martial ardor as you believe in the valor of Sidney or Cervantes. One calls the Elizabethan dramatists imaginative, as one might say the same of a man in delirium tremens; but even that flatters them; for whereas the drinker can imagine rats and snakes and beetles which have some sort of resemblance to real ones, your typical Elizabethan heroes of the mighty line, having neither the eyes to see anything real nor the brains to observe it, could no more conceive a natural or convincing stage figure than a blind man can conceive a rainbow or a deaf one the sound of an orchestra. Such success as they have had is the success which any fluent braggart and liar may secure in a pothouse. Their swagger and fustian, and their scraps of Cicero and Aristotle, passed for poetry and learning in their own day because their public was Philistine and ignorant. Today, without having by any means lost this advantage, they enjoy in addition the quaintness of their obsolescence, and, above all, the splendor of the light reflected on them from the reputation of Shakespear. Without that light they would now be as invisible as they are insufferable. In condemning them indiscriminately, I am only doing what Time would have done if Shakespear had not rescued them. I am quite aware that they did not get their reputations for nothing; that there were degrees of badness among them; that Greene was really amusing, Marston spirited and silly-clever, Cyril Tourneur able to string together lines of which any couple picked out and quoted separately might pass as a fragment of a real organic poem, and so on. Even the brutish pedant Jonson was not heartless, and could turn out prettily affectionate verses and foolishly affectionate criticisms; whilst the plausible firm of Beaumont and Fletcher, humbugs as they were, could produce plays which were, all things considered, not worse than The Lady of Lyons. But these distinctions are not worth making now. There is much variety in a dust-heap, even when the rag-picker is done with it; but we throw it indiscriminately into the "destructor" for all that. There is only one use left for the Elizabethan dramatists, and that is the purification of Shakespear's reputation from its spurious elements. Just as you can cure people of talking patronizingly about "Mozartian melody" by shewing them that the tunes they imagine to be his distinctive characteristic were the commonplaces of his time, so it is possible, perhaps, to cure people of admiring, as distinctively characteristic of Shakespear, the false, forced rhetoric, the callous sensation-mongering in murder and lust, the ghosts and combats, and the venal expenditure of all the treasures of his genius on the bedizenment of plays which are, as wholes, stupid toys. When Sir Henry Irving presently revives Cymbeline at the Lyceum, the numerous descendants of the learned Shakespearean enthusiast who went down on his knees and kissed the Ireland forgeries will see no difference between the great dramatist who changed Imogen from a mere name in a story to a living woman, and the manager-showman who exhibited her with the gory trunk of a newly beheaded man in her arms. But why should we, the heirs of so many greater ages, with the dramatic poems of Goethe and Ibsen in our hands, and the music of a great dynasty of musicians, from Bach to Wagner, in our ears—why should we waste our time on the rank and file of the Elizabethans, or encourage foolish modern persons to imitate them, or talk about Shakespear as if his moral platitudes, his jingo claptraps, his tavern pleasantries, his bombast and drivel, and his incapacity for following up the scraps of philosophy he stole so aptly, were as admirable as the mastery of poetic speech, the feeling for nature, and the knack of character-drawing, fun, and heart wisdom which he was ready, like a true son of the theatre, to prostitute to any subject, any occasion, and any theatrical employment? The fact is, we are growing out of Shakespear. Byron declined to put up with his reputation at the beginning of the nineteenth century; and now, at the beginning of the twentieth, he is nothing but a household pet. His characters still live; his word pictures of woodland and wayside still give us a Bank-holiday breath of country air; his verse still charms us; his sublimities still stir us; the commonplaces and trumperies of the wisdom which age and experience bring to all of us are still expressed by him better than by anybody else; but we have nothing to hope from him and nothing to learn from him—not even how to write plays, though he does that so much better than most modern dramatists. And if this is true of Shakespear, what is to be said of Kit Marlowe?

Kit Marlowe, however, did not bore me at St George's Hall as he has always bored me when I have tried to read him without skipping. The more I see of these performances by the Elizabethan Stage Society, the more I am convinced that their method of presenting an Elizabethan play is not only the right method for that particular sort of play but that any play performed on a platform amidst the audience gets closer home to its hearers than when it is presented as a picture framed by a proscenium. Also, that we are less conscious of the artificiality of the stage when a few well-understood conventions, adroitly handled, are substituted for attempts at an impossible scenic verisimilitude. All the old-fashioned tale-of-adventure plays, with their frequent changes of scene, and all the new problem plays, with their intense intimacies, should be done in this way.

The E. S. S. made very free with Doctor Faustus. Their devils, Baliol and Belcher to wit, were not theatrical devils with huge pasteboard heads, but pictorial Temptation-of-St-Anthony devils such as Martin Schongauer drew. The angels were Florentine fifteenth-century angels, with their draperies sewn into Botticellian folds and tucks. The Emperor's bodyguard had Maximilianesque uniforms copied from Holbein. Mephistophilis made his first appearance as Mr Joseph Pennell's favorite devil from the roof of Notre Dame, and, when commanded to appear as a Franciscan friar, still proclaimed his modernity by wearing an electric bulb in his cowl. The Seven Deadly Sins were *tout ce qu'il y a de plus fin de siècle*, the five worst of them being so attractive that they got rounds of applause on the strength of their appearance alone. In short, Mr William Poel gave us an artistic rather than a literal presentation of Elizabethan conditions, the result being, as always happens in such cases, that the picture of the past was really a picture of the future. For which result he is, in my judgment, to be highly praised. The performance was a wonder of artistic discipline in this lawless age. It is true, since the performers were only three or four instead of fifty times as skilful as ordinary professional actors, that Mr Poel has had to give up all impetuosity and spontaneity of execution, and to have the work done very slowly and carefully. But it is to be noted that even Marlowe, treated in this thorough way, is not tedious; whereas Shakespear, rattled and rushed and spouted and clattered through in the ordinary professional manner, all but kills the audience with tedium. For instance, Mephistophilis was as joyless and leaden as a devil need be—it was clear that no stage-manager had ever exhorted him, like a lagging horse, to get the long speeches over as fast as possible, old chap—and yet he never for a moment bored us as Prince Hal and Poins bore us at the Haymarket. The actor who hurries reminds the spectators of the flight of time, which it is his business to make them forget. Twenty years ago the symphonies of Beethoven used to be rushed through in London with the sole object of shortening the agony of the audience. They were then highly unpopular. When Richter arrived he took the opposite point of view, playing them so as to prolong the delight of the audience; and Mottl dwells more lovingly on Wagner than Richter does on Beethoven. The result is that Beethoven and Wagner are now popular. Mr Poel has proved that the same result will be attained as soon as blank-verse plays are produced under the control of managers who like them, instead of openly and shamelessly treating them as inflictions to be curtailed to the utmost. The representation at St George's Hall went without a hitch from beginning to end, a miracle of diligent preparedness. Mr Mannering, as Faustus, had the longest and the hardest task; and he performed it conscientiously, punctually, and well. The others did no less with what they had to do. The relief of seeing actors come on the stage with the simplicity and abnegation of children, instead of bounding on to an enthusiastic reception with the "Here I am again" expression of the popular favorites of the ordinary stage, is hardly to be described. Our professional actors are now looked at by the public from behind the scenes; and they accept that situation and glory in it for the sake of the "personal popularity" it involves. What a gigantic reform Mr Poel will make if his Elizabethan Stage should lead to such a novelty as a theatre to which people go to see the play instead of to see the cast!

There has been a plague of matinées lately; but the matinée is the opportunity of the incompetent casual acting-manager; and the incompetent casual acting-manager's opportunity often proves the holiday of the eminent dramatic critic, whose invitation, being the main thing that the casual one is engaged to look after, is generally forgotten. Nevertheless, I was captured no less than thrice last week. The Mummy is ingenious enough to have a narrow miss of being a successful play; but unfortunately in these matters a miss is as good as a mile. What is wrong with it is the perfunctory flimsiness of the figures who surround the mummy. It is not enough to provide a squad of rag dolls for your mummy to confuse himself in: they must be real people in whom we can feel some interest, and who can make us believe that an ancient Egyptian is actually walking about in a modern household. The play only lives whilst Mr Brough, whose trained physical self-command and professional skill were never more useful, is on the stage. Our younger generation of stage bunglers, who take such prodigious trouble to prevent perfectly simple effects from making themselves, doubtless often ask themselves why the public can be so unjust and foolish as to laugh at an actor who can apparently do nothing but stare helplessly at his own success. The reason is, of course, that Mr Lionel Brough never stands between the public and Mr Lionel Brough's part. This seems simple but just try to do it, and you will appreciate the training that it costs to make a capable actor.

Miss Elizabeth Tyree, late of Mr Daniel Frohman's company at the Lyceum Theatre, New York, invited London to see what she could do as Juliet, Fedora, and the Country Girl. Like most American executive artists, musical and dramatic, Miss Tyree shewed signs of having attempted to qualify herself by some systematic physical training for her profession. But she does not appreciate the degree of beauty of execution and distinction of style that are required by such parts as Juliet and Fedora. She played Juliet, amusingly enough, to Mr Will Dennis's Romeo, exactly as Miss Maude Millet plays the comic relief young lady in a modern comedy to Mr Sidney Brough's comic relief young gentleman. The performance proved, not that Miss Tyree can play Juliet, but that the balcony scene makes a capital one-act comedietta. Her Fedora was out of the question: it was as remote from the effect planned by Sardou as Brixton is from St Petersburg. The Country Girl was adequate; but then we have a dozen young ladies on our own stage who could do it as well if any one wanted them to. Frankly, since Miss Tyree must be understood as asking whether she has the power that crosses frontiers, I must reply, Not yet. The work she can do so far can be done in any country without sending to America for assistance. And the sort of character for which she seems best fitted by her temperament is precisely that in which English actresses excel. If Miss Elizabeth Robins or Miss Olga Brandon were to return to their native shores, it would not be easy to name their successors in their best parts, not only because of their professional skill, but because their temperaments are of a kind that England does not produce very freely. We can and do produce Miss Tyree's temperament by the dozen.

I congratulate Mr Felix Morris on the success with which, returning to this country after a long absence, he has persuaded us to revive two hopelessly obsolete plays for his sake. On 'Change was pardonable; but a new version of The First Night is really too much; Achille Dufard is as dead as Alfred Wigan. There are, however, three scenes in the new version which should be rescued from Dufard's grave. The outfaced dunning grocer, with his "Arf a mo: give a man a chance," is very funny; and the rehearsal, with the leading lady on the rampage, as well as the scene at the end of the first act, should certainly be seen again, if only to let London enjoy a most amusing and spontaneous piece of acting by Miss Alma Stanley. Shade of Lady Dedlock, who would have supposed that she could have done this excellent thing! Mr Ernest Cosham was capital as the grocer. The piece was, indeed, exceptionally well played on all hands; but Mr Felix Morris and Miss Sarah Brooke, though they did all that was possible, could not justify the survival of their part of the business. Mr Morris's French accent, by the way, was a triumph of accurate aural observation.

DALY UNDAUNTED

THE COUNTESS GUCKI. An entirely new comedy in three acts, adapted from the original of Franz von Schonthan by Augustin Daly. Comedy Theatre, 11 July 1896.

THE LIAR. Comedy in two acts, by Samuel Foote. Royalty Theatre, 9 July 1896. (A Revival.)

THE HONORABLE MEMBER. A new three-act comedy drama by A. W. Gattie. Court Theatre, 14 July 1896. [18 *July* 1896]

O MR DALY! Unfortunate Mr Daly! What a play! And we are actually assured that The Countess Gucki was received with delight in America! Well, perhaps it is true. After all, it may very well be that a nation plunged by its political circumstances into the study of tracts on bimetallism may have found this "entirely new comedy" quite a page of romance after so many pages of the ratio between gold and silver. But in London, at the end of a season of undistracted gaiety, it is about as interesting as a second-hand ball dress of the last season but ten. When the curtain goes up, we are in Carlsbad in 1819, talking glibly about Goethe and Beethoven for the sake of local and temporal color. Two young lovers, who provide what one may call the melancholy relief to Miss Rehan, enter upon a maddeningly tedious exposition of the relationship and movements of a number of persons with long German titles. As none of these people have anything to do with the play as subsequently developed, the audience is perhaps expected to discover, when the curtain falls, that the exposition was a practical joke at their expense, and to go home laughing good-humoredly at their own discomfiture. But I was far too broken-spirited for any such merriment. These wretched lovers are supposed to be a dull, timid couple, too shy to come to the point; and as the luckless artists who impersonate them have no comic power, they present the pair with such conscientious seriousness that reality itself could produce nothing more insufferably tiresome. At last Miss Rehan appears, her entry being worked up with music—O Mr Daly, Mr Daly, when will you learn the time of day in London?—in a hideous Madame de Staël costume which emphasizes the fact that Miss Rehan, a woman in the prime of life with a splendid physique, is so careless of her bodily training that she looks as old as I do. She, too, talks about Goethe and Beethoven, and, having the merest chambermaid's part, proceeds heartlessly to exhibit a selection of strokes and touches broken off from the old parts in which she has so often enchanted us. This rifling of the cherished trophies of her art to make a miserable bag of tricks for a part and a play which the meekest leading lady in London would rebel against, was to me downright sacrilege: I leave Miss Rehan to defend it if she can. The play, such as it is, begins with the entry of a gigantic coxcomb who lays siege to the ladies of the household in a manner meant by the dramatist to be engaging and interesting. In real life a barmaid would rebuke his intolerable gallantries: on the stage Miss Rehan is supposed to be fascinated by them. Later on comes the one feeble morsel of stale sentiment which saves the play from the summary damnation it deserves. An old General, the coxcomb's uncle, loved the Countess Gucki when she was sixteen. They meet again: the General still cherishes his old romance: the lady is touched by his devotion. The dramatist thrusts this ready-made piece of pathos in your face as artlessly as a village boy thrusts a turnip-headed bogie; but, like the bogie, it has its effect on simple folk; and Miss Rehan, with callous cleverness, turns on one of her best Twelfth Night effects, and arrests the sentimental moment with a power which, wasted on such trivial stuff, is positively cynical and shocking. But this oasis is soon left behind. The old General, not having a line that is worth speaking, looks solemn and kisses Miss Rehan's hand five or six times every minute; the coxcomb suddenly takes the part of circus clown, and, in pretended transports of jealousy, thrusts a map between the pair, and shifts it up and down whilst they dodge him by trying to see one another over or under it. But, well as we by this time know Mr Daly's idea of high comedy, I doubt if I shall be believed if I describe the play too closely. The whole affair, as a comedy presented at a West End house to a London audience by a manager "starring" a first-rate actress, ought to be incredible—ought to indicate that the manager is in his second childhood. But I suppose it only indicates that audiences are in their first childhood. If it pays, I have no more to say.

Mr Lewis and Mrs Gilbert, like Miss Rehan, are still faithful to Mr Daly, in spite of his wasting their talent on trash utterly unworthy of them. Remonstrance, I suppose, is useless. At best it could only drive Mr Daly into another of his fricassees of Shakespear.

Mr Bourchier's revival of The Liar produced an effect out of all proportion to the merits of the play by the contrast between Foote's clever dialogue and the witlessness of our contemporary drama. The part of Young Wilding gives no trouble to a comedian of Mr Bourchier's address; and Mr Hendrie as Old Wilding was equal to the occasion; but the rest clowned in the most graceless amateur fashion. The very commonplaces of deportment are vanishing from the stage. The women cannot even make a curtsey: they sit down on their heels with a flop and a smirk, and think that that is what Mr Turveydrop taught their grandmothers. Even Miss Irene Vanbrugh is far too off-hand and easily self-satisfied. Actors, it seems to me, will not be persuaded nowadays to begin at the right end of their profession. Instead of acquiring the cultivated speech, gesture, movement, and personality which distinguish acting as a fine art from acting in the ordinary sense in which everybody acts, they dismiss it as a mere word which signifies to be, to do, or to suffer, like Lindley Murray's verb, and proceed to inflame their imaginations with romantic literature and green-room journalism until such time as their great opportunity will come. Off the stage, be it observed, people are now better trained physically than they ever were before, and therefore more impatient of exhibitions of ugliness and clumsiness. Any good dancing-master could take half a dozen ordinary active young ladies and gentlemen, and in four lessons make them go through the whole stage business of The Liar much more handsomely than the Royalty company. It is a great pity that all actors and actresses are not presented at Court: it would force them, for once in their lives at least, to study the pageantry of their profession, instead of idly nursing their ambitions, and dreaming of "conceptions" which they could not execute if they were put to the proof.

The Honorable Member, produced at a matinée at the Court last Tuesday, is a remarkable play; not because the author, Mr Gattie, is either a great dramatic poet or even, so far, a finished playwright; but because he seems conversant with ethical, social, and political ideas which have been fermenting for the last fifteen years in England and America, and which have considerably modified the assumptions upon which writers of penny novelettes and fashionable dramas depend for popular sympathy. The social judgments pronounced in the play are unmistakeably those of reaction against unsocial commercialism and political party ser-

vice, with here and there a touch of the cultured variety of anar-
chism. The hero is openly impatient of the scruples the heroine
makes about going to live with him, she being unfortunately
married to a felon. "You say it is wrong," he says: "what you
mean is that some person in a horsehair wig will shew that it is
against the law." When some one takes a high moral tone against
betting, he uses up the point made in Mr Wordsworth Donisthorpe's essays, that a life insurance is a pure bet made by the
insurance company with the person insured. A dramatist who
has read Mr Donisthorpe comes as a refreshing surprise in a
theatrical generation which pouts at Mr Henry Arthur Jones's
plays because their ideas are as modern as those of Pusey and
Maurice, Ruskin and Dickens. I suggest, however, to Mr Gattie
that people's ideas, however useful they may be for embroidery,
especially in passages of comedy, are not the true stuff of drama,
which is always the naïve feeling underlying the ideas. As one
who has had somewhat exceptional opportunities of observing
the world in which these new ideas are current, I can testify that
they afford no clue to the individual character of the person holding them. A Socialist view of industrial questions, and an Individualist view of certain moral questions, may strongly differentiate the rising public man of today from the rising public man
of twenty-five years ago, but not one rising public man of today
from another rising public man of today. I know a dozen men
who talk and think just as Mr Gattie's editor-hero talks and thinks;
but they differ from one another as widely as Pistol differs from
Hamlet. The same thing is true of the Liberal-Capitalist persons
who talk and think just the other way: they differ as widely as
Mr Gladstone differs from Mr Jabez Balfour. I quite see that since
we shall always have a dozen dramatists who can handle conventions for every one who can handle character, we are coming
fast to a melodramatic formula in which the villain shall be a bad
employer and the hero a Socialist; but that formula is no truer
to life than the old one in which the villain was a lawyer and the
hero a Jack Tar. It is less than four years since the Independent
Theatre, then in desperate straits for a play of native growth,

extracted from my dustheap of forgotten MSS. a play called Widowers' Houses, in which I brought on the stage the slum landlord and domineering employer who is, in private life, a scrupulously respectable gentleman. Also his bullied, sweated rent-collector. Take Widowers' Houses; cut out the passages which convict the audience of being just as responsible for the slums as the landlord is; make the hero a ranting Socialist instead of a perfectly commonplace young gentleman; make the heroine an angel instead of her father's daughter only one genera-tion removed from the wash-tub; and you have the successful melodrama of tomorrow. Mr Gattie, who probably never saw my play, has taken a long step in this direction. His Samuel Ditherby, M.P., bullying the wretched clerk Beamer, is my Sar-torius bullying the rent-collector Lickcheese; and the relationship is emphasized by the fact that just as my play was rescued from the fury of an outraged public by Mr James Welch's creation of Lickcheese, The Honorable Member was helped through an intolerably hot July afternoon by the same actor's impersona-tion of Beamer. Unfortunately for Mr Welch, the third act of Widowers' Houses presented Lickcheese in a comic aspect, and so left an impression that Mr Welch had made his great hit in a comic part. But, though Mr Welch has a considerable power of being funny, he has done no purely comic part that half a dozen other comedians could not do as well or better; whereas his power of pathos in realism—a power which is sufficient to awaken the sympathy and hush the attention of the whole house before he utters a word—distinguishes him from every other actor in his line on our stage; entitles him, indeed, to rank as an actor of genius. His Petkoff in Arms and the Man, and his postboy in Rosemary, are all very well; but what difficulty would there be in replacing him in either part? But his first entry and scene as Lickcheese, his curate in Alan's Wife, and this new part of Beamer—all pathetic work—which of our actors could touch them after him? Beamer is technically even a greater triumph than Lickcheese, because—though I say it who should not—the author has been less considerate to the actor. Mr Welch's exit in

dead silence in the first act of Widowers' Houses brought down
the house; but it was bound to do so if only (a large "if," I
admit) the actor had driven home the preceding scene up to the
hilt. But Beamer has to turn at the door and deliver what I take
to be one of the most dangerous exit speeches ever penned, being
nothing less than "Curse you! Curse you! Damn you to hell!"
That speech is one of the author's mistakes; but Mr Welch pulled
it through so successfully that his exit was again the hit of the
piece. Surely it cannot take our managers more than another
twenty years—or, say, twenty-five—to realize that the parts for
Mr Welch are strong and real pathetic parts instead of silly clown-
ing ones.

Here, then, we have the popular elements in Sartorius and
Lickcheese, with an angel heroine of the unjustly accused variety,
and a hero who, if not aggressively a Socialist, is a high-toned
young man of the American ethical sort, ready to try the same
experiment of living down prejudice that George Henry Lewes
tried with George Eliot. The plot is very old and simple—La
Gazza Ladra over again, except that it is Beamer instead of a
magpie who brings the heroine under suspicion of stealing the
family diamonds. The audience swallowed all the heterodox
sentiments as if they were the platitudes of an archbishop. The
play might be lightened and smartened considerably by the
excision of a number of bits and scraps which, good enough for
conversation, are not good enough for drama. Miss Madge Mc-
Intosh played the heroine so naturally that she was neither more
nor less interesting than if the play had been real. This is more
than I could say for all actresses; but I do not mean it as a compliment for all that. Unless an actress can be at least ten times as
interesting as a real lady, why should she leave the drawing room
and go on the stage? Mr Graham Brown's impersonation of the
plain-clothes policeman was a clever bit of mimicry. The other
parts were in familiar hands—those of Mr Anson, Mrs Edmund
Phelps, Mr Bernage, and Mr Scott Buist.

BLAMING THE BARD

CYMBELINE. By Shakespear. Lyceum Theatre, 22 September 1896.
[26 *September* 1896]

I CONFESS to a difficulty in feeling civilized just at present. Flying from the country, where the gentlemen of England are in an ecstasy of chicken-butchering, I return to town to find the higher wits assembled at a play three hundred years old, in which the sensation scene exhibits a woman waking up to find her husband reposing gorily in her arms with his head cut off.

Pray understand, therefore, that I do not defend Cymbeline. It is for the most part stagey trash of the lowest melodramatic order, in parts abominably written, throughout intellectually vulgar, and, judged in point of thought by modern intellectual standards, vulgar, foolish, offensive, indecent, and exasperating beyond all tolerance. There are moments when one asks despairingly why our stage should ever have been cursed with this "immortal" pilferer of other men's stories and ideas, with his monstrous rhetorical fustian, his unbearable platitudes, his pretentious reduction of the subtlest problems of life to commonplaces against which a Polytechnic debating club would revolt, his incredible unsuggestiveness, his sententious combination of ready reflection with complete intellectual sterility, and his consequent incapacity for getting out of the depth of even the most ignorant audience, except when he solemnly says something so transcendently platitudinous that his more humble-minded hearers cannot bring themselves to believe that so great a man really meant to talk like their grandmothers. With the single exception of Homer, there is no eminent writer, not even Sir Walter Scott, whom I can despise so entirely as I despise Shakespear when I measure my mind against his. The intensity of my impatience with him occasionally reaches such a pitch, that it would positively be a relief to me to dig him up and throw stones at him, knowing as I do how incapable he and his worshippers are of understanding any less obvious form of indignity. To read Cymbeline and to think of Goethe, of Wagner, of Ibsen, is, for me, to imperil the habit of studied moderation of statement which years of public responsibility as a journalist have made almost second nature in me.

But I am bound to add that I pity the man who cannot enjoy Shakespear. He has outlasted thousands of abler thinkers, and will outlast a thousand more. His gift of telling a story (provided some one else told it to him first); his enormous power over language, as conspicuous in his senseless and silly abuse of it as in his miracles of expression; his humor; his sense of idiosyncratic character; and his prodigious fund of that vital energy which is, it seems, the true differentiating property behind the faculties, good, bad, or indifferent, of the man of genius, enable him to entertain us so effectively that the imaginary scenes and people he has created become more real to us than our actual life—at least, until our knowledge and grip of actual life begins to deepen and glow beyond the common. When I was twenty I knew everybody in Shakespear, from Hamlet to Abhorson, much more intimately than I knew my living contemporaries; and to this day, if the name of Pistol or Polonius catches my eye in a newspaper, I turn to the passage with more curiosity than if the name were that of—but perhaps I had better not mention any one in particular.

How many new acquaintances, then, do you make in reading Cymbeline, provided you have the patience to break your way into it through all the fustian, and are old enough to be free from the modern idea that Cymbeline must be the name of a cosmetic and Imogen of the latest scientific discovery in the nature of a hitherto unknown gas? Cymbeline is nothing; his queen nothing, though some attempt is made to justify her description as "a woman that bears all down with her brain"; Posthumus, nothing—most fortunately, as otherwise he would be an unendurably contemptible hound; Belarius, nothing—at least, not after Kent in King Lear (just as the Queen is nothing after Lady Macbeth); Iachimo, not much—only a *diabolus ex machina* made plausible; and Pisanio, less than Iachimo. On the other hand, we have Cloten, the prince of numbsculls, whose part, indecencies and all, is a literary masterpiece from the first line to the last; the two princes—fine presentments of that impressive and generous myth, the noble savage; Caius Lucius, the Roman general, urbane among the barbarians; and, above all, Imogen. But do, please, remember that there are two Imogens. One is a solemn and elaborate example of what, in Shakespear's opinion, a real lady ought to be. With this unspeakable person virtuous indignation is chronic. Her object in life is to vindicate her own propriety and to suspect everybody else's, especially her husband's. Like Lothaw in the jeweller's shop in Bret Harte's burlesque novel, she cannot be left alone with unconsidered trifles of portable silver without officiously assuring the proprietors that she has stolen naught, nor would not, though she had found gold strewed i' the floor. Her fertility and spontaneity in nasty ideas is not to be described: there is hardly a speech in her part that you can read without wincing. But this Imogen has another one tied to her with ropes of blank verse (which can fortunately be cut)—the Imogen of Shakespear's genius, an enchanting person of the most delicate sensitiveness, full of sudden transitions from ecstasies of tenderness to transports of childish rage, and reckless of consequences in both, instantly hurt and instantly appeased, and of the highest breeding and courage. But for this Imogen, Cymbeline would stand about as much chance of being revived now as Titus Andronicus.

The instinctive Imogen, like the real live part of the rest of the play, has to be disentangled from a mass of stuff which, though it might be recited with effect and appropriateness by young amateurs at a performance by the Elizabethan Stage Society, is absolutely unactable and unutterable in the modern theatre, where a direct illusion of reality is aimed at, and where the repugnance of the best actors to play false passages is practically insuperable. For the purposes of the Lyceum, therefore, Cymbeline had to be cut, and cut liberally. Not that there was any reason to apprehend that the manager would flinch from the operation: quite the contrary. In a true republic of art Sir Henry Irving would ere this have expiated his acting versions on the scaffold. He does not merely cut plays: he disembowels them. In Cymbeline he has quite surpassed himself by extirpating the antiphonal third verse of the famous dirge. A man who would do that would do anything—cut the coda out of the first movement of Beethoven's Ninth Symphony, or shorten one of Velasquez's Philips into a kitcat to make it fit over his drawing room mantelpiece. The grotesque character tracery of Cloten's lines, which is surely not beyond the appreciation of an age educated by Stevenson, is defaced with Cromwellian ruthlessness; and the patriotic scene, with the Queen's great speech about the natural bravery of our isle, magnificent in its Walkürenritt swing, is shorn away, though it might easily have been introduced in the Garden scene. And yet, long screeds of rubbish about "slander, whose edge is sharper than the sword," and so on, are preserved with superstitious veneration.

This curious want of connoisseurship in literature would disable Sir Henry Irving seriously if he were an interpretative actor. But it is, happily, the fault of a great quality—the creative quality. A prodigious deal of nonsense has been written about Sir Henry Irving's conception of this, that, and the other Shakespearean character. The truth is that he has never in his life conceived or interpreted the characters of any author except himself. He is really as incapable of acting another man's play as Wagner was of setting another man's libretto; and he should, like Wagner, have written his plays for himself. But as he did not find himself out until it was too late for him to learn that supplementary trade, he was compelled to use other men's plays as the framework for his own creations. His first great success in this sort of adaptation was with the Merchant of Venice. There was no question then of a bad Shylock or a good Shylock: he was simply not Shylock at all; and when his own creation came into conflict with Shakespear's, as it did quite openly in the Trial scene, he simply played in flat contradiction of the lines, and positively acted Shakespear off the stage. This was an original policy, and an intensely interesting one from the critical point of view; but it was obvious that its difficulty must increase with the vividness and force of the dramatist's creation. Shakespear at his highest pitch cannot be set aside by any mortal actor, however gifted; and when Sir Henry Irving tried to interpolate a most singular and fantastic notion of an old man between the lines of a fearfully mutilated acting version of King Lear, he was smashed. On the other hand, in plays by persons of no importance, where the dramatist's part of the business is the merest trash, his creative activity is unhampered and uncontradicted; and the author's futility is the opportunity for the actor's masterpiece. Now I have already described Shakespear's Iachimo as little better than any of the lay figures in Cymbeline—a mere *diabolus ex machina*. But Irving's Iachimo is a very different affair. It is a new and independent creation. I knew Shakespear's play inside and out before last Tuesday; but this Iachimo was quite fresh and novel to me. I witnessed it with unqualified delight: it was no vulgar bagful of "points," but a true impersonation, unbroken in its life-current from end to end, varied on the surface with the finest comedy, and without a single lapse in the sustained beauty of its execution. It is only after such work that an artist can with perfect naturalness and dignity address himself to his audience as "their faithful and loving servant"; and I wish I could add that the audience had an equal right to offer him their applause as a worthy acknowledgment of his merit. But when a house distributes its officious first-night plaudits impartially between the fine artist and the blunderer who roars a few lines violently and rushes off the stage after compressing the entire art of How Not to Act into five intolerable minutes, it had better be told to reserve its impertinent and obstreperous demonstrations until it has learnt to bestow them with some sort of discrimination. Our first-night people mean well, and will, no doubt, accept my assurance that they are donkeys with all possible good humor; but they should remember that to applaud for the sake of applauding, as schoolboys will cheer for the sake of cheering, is to destroy our own power of complimenting those who, as the greatest among us, are the servants of all the rest.

Over the performances of the other gentlemen in the cast let me skate as lightly as possible. Mr Norman Forbes's Cloten, though a fatuous idiot rather than the brawny "beef-witted" fool whom Shakespear took from his own Ajax in Troilus and Cressida, is effective and amusing, so that one feels acutely the mangling of his part, especially the cutting of that immortal musical criticism of his upon the serenade. Mr Gordon Craig and Mr Webster are desperate failures as the two noble savages. They are as spirited and picturesque as possible; but every pose, every flirt of their elfin locks, proclaims the wild freedom of Bedford Park. They recite the poor maimed dirge admirably, Mr Craig being the more musical of the twain; and Mr Webster's sword-and-cudgel fight with Cloten is very lively; but their utter deficiency in the grave, rather sombre, uncivilized primeval strength and Mohican dignity so finely suggested by Shakespear, takes all the ballast out of the fourth act, and combines with the inappropriate prettiness and sunniness of the landscape scenery to handicap Miss Ellen Terry most cruelly in the trying scene of her awakening by the side of the flower-decked corpse: a scene which, without every accessory to heighten its mystery, terror, and pathos, is utterly and heart-breakingly impossible for any actress, even if she were Duse, Ristori, Mrs Siddons, and Miss Terry rolled into one. When I saw this gross and palpable oversight, and heard people talking about the Lyceum stage management as superb, I with difficulty restrained myself from tearing out my hair in handfuls and scattering it with imprecations to the four winds. That cave of the three mountaineers wants nothing but a trellised porch, a bamboo bicycle, and a nice little bed of standard roses, to complete its absurdity.

With Mr Frederic Robinson as Belarius, and Mr Tyars as Pisanio, there is no reasonable fault to find, except that they might, perhaps, be a little brighter with advantage; and of the rest of their male colleagues I think I shall ask to be allowed to say nothing at all, even at the cost of omitting a tribute to Mr Fuller Mellish's discreet impersonation of the harmless necessary Philario. There remains Miss Geneviève Ward, whose part, with the Neptune's park speech lopped off, was not worth her playing, and

Miss Ellen Terry, who invariably fascinates me so much that I have not the smallest confidence in my own judgment respecting her. There was no Bedford Park about the effect she made as she stepped into the King's garden; still less any of the atmosphere of ancient Britain. At the first glance, we were in the Italian fifteenth century; and the house, unversed in the cinquecento, but dazzled all the same, proceeded to roar until it stopped from exhaustion. There is one scene in Cymbeline, the one in which Imogen receives the summons to "that same blessed Milford," which might have been written for Miss Terry, so perfectly does its innocent rapture and frank gladness fit into her hand. Her repulse of Iachimo brought down the house as a matter of course, though I am convinced that the older Shakespeareans present had a vague impression that it could not be properly done except by a stout, turnip-headed matron, with her black hair folded smoothly over her ears and secured in a classic bun. Miss Terry had evidently cut her own part; at all events the odious Mrs Grundyish Imogen had been dissected out of it so skilfully that it went without a single jar. The circumstances under which she was asked to play the fourth act were, as I have explained, impossible. To wake up in the gloom amid the wolf and robber-haunted mountain gorges which formed the Welsh mountains of Shakespear's imagination in the days before the Great Western existed is one thing: to wake up at about three on a nice Bank-holiday afternoon in a charming spot near the valley of the Wye is quite another. With all her force, Miss Terry gave us faithfully the whole process which Shakespear has presented with such dramatic cunning—Imogen's bewilderment, between dreaming and waking, as to where she is; the vague discerning of some strange bedfellow there; the wondering examination of the flowers with which he is so oddly covered; the frightful discovery of blood on the flowers, with the hideous climax that the man is headless and that his clothes are her husband's; and it was all ruined by that blazing, idiotic, prosaic sunlight in which everything leapt to the eye at once, rendering the mystery and the slowly growing clearness of perception incredible and unintelligible, and spoiling a scene which, properly stage-managed, would have been a triumph of histrionic intelligence. Cannot somebody be hanged for this?— men perish every week for lesser crimes. What consolation is it to me that Miss Terry, playing with infinite charm and delicacy of appeal, made up her lost ground in other directions, and had more than as much success as the roaring gallery could feel the want of?

A musical accompaniment to the drama has been specially composed; and its numbers are set forth in the bill of the play, with the words "LOST PROPERTY" in conspicuous red capitals in the margin. Perhaps I can be of some use in restoring at least some of the articles to their rightful owner. The prelude to the fourth act belongs to Beethoven—first movement of the Seventh Symphony. The theme played by "the ingenious instrument" in the cave is Handel's, and is familiar to lovers of Judas Maccabeus as O never bow we down to the rude stock or sculptured stone. J. F. R. will, I feel sure, be happy to carry the work of identification further if necessary.

Sir Henry Irving's next appearance will be on Bosworth Field. He was obviously astonished by the startling shout of approbation with which the announcement was received. We all have an old weakness for Richard. After that, Madame Sans-Gêne, with Sardou's Napoleon.

MAINLY ABOUT MELODRAMAS

THE DUCHESS OF COOLGARDIE. A romance of the Australian goldfields. In five acts. By Euston Leigh and Cyril Clare. Drury Lane, 19 September 1896.

THE CO-RESPONDENT. A new and original farcical comedy. In four acts. By G. W. Appleton. Theatre Métropole, Camberwell, 21 September 1896.

TWO LITTLE VAGABONDS. A new and original melodrama. By G. R. Sims and Arthur Shirley. Princess's Theatre, 23 September 1896.   [3 *October* 1896]

IN the interests of my own craft of literature, I really must protest against the notion that a popular play can be knocked together by any handy person who knows the ways of the stage and the follies of the public. I do not claim any greater mystery for the playwright's craft than for the scene-painter's or costumier's; but then actors and managers have not yet taken to painting their own scenes or stitching their own doublets. When they do, I shall lose no time in pointing out that painting and tailoring are none the less skilled trades because everyone can see how they are done, and can even sew on a button or make a sketch in an amateur way on occasion. So far, the amateur offers himself as a cheap and convenient substitute for the author only. I therefore beg to observe, politely but firmly, that dramatic authorship, even of the routine kind, is a highly skilled trade as trades go, and that a gentleman may be an experienced actor and manager, an enthusiastic student of the stage, qualified to write and speak interestingly about it, and better versed in its illusions and those of the public than many authors, and yet be quite unable to write a play that would not be dear at the traditional tariff of five shillings an act. There is at present running at Drury Lane an entertainment called The Duchess of Coolgardie, which is not a play at all in any serious technical sense of the word. Mr John Coleman offers it as the work of "Euston Leigh and Cyril Clare," a flourish which we may take as a humorous avowal that some person or persons of no consequence have jumbled all the stage incidents they can remember into an entertainment wherewith to fool the public to the top of its bent. There is only one hypothesis on which Mr Coleman can be excused for this: to wit, that "Euston Leigh and Cyril Clare" are no other than Mr Coleman himself. In that case, I am willing to allow that Mr Coleman cannot be blamed for his share of the inveterate delusion of the old actor that an audience can be interested in incidents and situations without believing in or caring for the people to whom these incidents and situations occur. If that were so, a shooting-gallery would be as interesting as a battlefield: the mere flash, smoke, and bang of the thing would be enough. But it is not so; and the proof is that all the shocks, disclosures, fights, rescues, escapes, assassinations, murder trials, and recognitions of long-lost brothers which are crowded into

The Duchess of Coolgardie at the rate of a dozen per act, do not produce as much interest as Box and Cox, simply because the preliminary dramatic illusion which changes painted cloths into places and actors and actresses into heroes and heroines has been left out. Nobody wants to see Mr Glenney and Mr Vanderfeldt, in their own persons, firing blank cartridges at one another, or drearily shamming misunderstandings with Miss Hilda Spong in *her* own person. It is no doubt hard for an actor to believe that he cannot himself create any illusion, and that the very gesture, word, look, and deed with which he has infallibly brought down the house twenty times will fall flat or excite derisive laughter the twenty-first time merely because it occurs in a different play; but the public knows only too well how easily that may happen. I do not believe there is an experienced melodramatic actor in the world who has not in his head, if not actually in manuscript, a drama which must surpass all previous dramas in stage effect, since he has combined in it all the effects of all the successful melodramas of the past thirty years. Sometimes that wonderful play gets produced, with the result that not a single squib in the whole catherine wheel can be induced to catch fire; and the manager is left lamenting that he did not rather speculate in Ibsen or Maeterlinck. The author of such a work can only be compared to a man who, having noticed that many persons furtively treasure up and carry about a withered rose petal or two, should open a shop for the sale of faded flowers.

Nevertheless, some of us have breathed more freely at The Duchess of Coolgardie than we did at the Harrisian melodramas, because we were glad to be rid of their open exploitation of the popular worship of sport, fashion, and jingoism, in scenes which it did nobody any good to gloat over. In The Duchess there is an air of returning to the simple, hearty, honest sentiments of ideal primeval humanity. But an attentive examination of the play from the ethical point of view will suggest that the main difference is one of expense. The Harrisian scenes on the racecourse and parade-ground, and in the Row, were dear. Primitive sentiment is cheap. When I see nuggets, chests of gold, and pocket books containing twenty thousand pounds, sticking all over a melodrama like raisins in an unwholesome cake—when I detect acute appreciation on the dramatist's part of the spell which a profuse handing round of champagne casts on a world which can only afford to drink beer—when I see threats, blows, oaths, fights, and, above all, that hypocritical savagery which revels in the moral pastime of hounding down a criminal, I may admire the economy and simplicity of Mr Coleman's methods as compared with those of the late Sir Augustus Harris; but the moral atmosphere does not strike me as being at all more bracing. His patriotism, in particular, is a miracle of cheapness. As an Irishman, I have, of course, noticed that the ceremony of drinking the health of my native land never palls on a true British audience. In no country is patriotism more popular than in England, especially Irish, Polish, Italian, and Balkan patriotism. In the same way, English patriotism, expressed by a British tar with a Union Jack and an aptitude for the hornpipe, is by no means unacceptable in Ireland. This is natural enough; for the country you have never lived in is the one about which you are most likely to have romantic illusions. It was, therefore, shrewd enough of Mr Coleman to discard all the expensive Jingo machinery of Sir Augustus Harris, with its troopships and battles and magazine-gun fusillades, and to replace it by a single Irish actor, especially when there was so clever a one at hand as Mr J. L. Shine, certainly the best sympathetic stage Irishman we have had since Boucicault, and a past master at the sort of humbug which the Irishman learns in England in the course of his attempts to impose on the inhabitants.

Where Mr Coleman has truly distinguished himself is by the discrimination with which he has chosen his company. For some years past our managers and authors have been for the most part so incapable of distinguishing good acting from bad, or even competent professionalism from cautious helplessness, that, in spite of the share of the stage in the general and inevitable march of progress, there is really some foundation for the complaint that the better an actor knows his business the harder he finds it to get engagements. All the marketable qualities are negative ones; and all the positive ones are stamped as dangerous, as they of course are at a theatre where the manager does not know how to employ them. Mr Coleman, however, has secured a highly efficient cast; and had he but indulged himself and the public with a real dramatic author as well, the combination might have proved a great managerial success. Mr Vanderfeldt for the villain is as happy a choice as Mr Shine for the Paddy: he succeeds in holding together and individualizing a shamelessly absurd part. Mr Hermann Vezin supplies the requisite importance to the Warden without trouble to himself; and Mr Charles Glenney, Mr Laurence Cautley, Mr Lowne, and Mr Oswald Yorke are all judiciously cast. Miss Hilda Spong plays with grace and sympathy: her good looks are not a mere stage effect, nor her refinement an affectation. Miss Laura Johnson appears as an aboriginal black boy in a part which is an obvious silk patch on a shoddy play. She plays it with refreshing audacity and aptitude, her keenness, and the peculiar jarring, bird-of-prey note in her voice, serving her well on this occasion. On the whole, The Duchess of Coolgardie seems to me to prove that, with Mr Coleman to choose the actors and somebody else to choose the play, Drury Lane might hold its own for some time yet.

Albeit not used to the melting mood, the critics sobbed most pathetically over Two Little Vagabonds at the Princess's. This excessive appreciation of a drop of sentiment in a thirsty land is, perhaps, natural; but in my case Nature has not been so prodigal in her gift of tears as to justify me, a prudent man, in wasting many of them on Wally and Dick. I remember once, when a play of my own was accused of being a pamphlet, replying that I heartily wished the accusation were true, as there was nothing so popular on the stage as a dramatized pamphlet, except a dramatized tract. This pregnant observation has not been lost on Mr Sims. He has saturated himself with the sentiment of Dr Watts's My Mother, and made it the agent of salvation in a dramatic version of the familiar tract of the boy thief who suddenly finds conviction of sin, and resolves to steal no more. This crisis is brought about by the well-known situation of the Bishop and the candlesticks in Les Misérables, with the mother as the Bishop, her purse as the candlesticks, and the boy-thief (her own son, needless to observe, though she does not know it) as Jean Valjean. All this is not so bad: indeed, the situation in the third act, where the mother, after taking an unfortunate little waif to her house as her son, and completely gaining his affection, discovers that he is a changeling, and is afraid to break his heart by telling him so, is touching and fresh. Besides, Mr Sims is a humorist, and has some genuine faculty as a storyteller. With such a safe subject as these two modern Babes in the Wood he can easily keep an audience amused if they are not too exacting about his workmanship and the truth of his touches of nature. Unfortunately there is a good deal more than this in Two Little Vagabonds. It begins with that repulsive piece of stale nonsense, the impossible misunderstanding which leads the hero to believe that the heroine is the mother of her sister's illegitimate child, and thereupon to behave towards her with the unspeakable baseness and folly vulgarly supposed proper to men of honor on such occasions. Then there is a silly sensation scene, void of all interest or credibility, which the gallery receive partly with derision and partly with the sort of approbation we give to things we do not value, when, since we are accustomed to have them provided for us, they cannot be omitted without slighting us. The attitude of the sixpenny and shilling playgoer on this point is exactly like that of the pedestrian who, when you are bicycling, curses you if you pass him without ringing your bell, not that he has been unaware of your approach, or is in the slightest danger from you, but because, conceiving that he is entitled by law to have a bell rung in his honor, he feels belittled by any neglect of that ceremony. In dealing with cognate demands in the theatre a dramatist has to choose between offending the foolish playgoers and the sensible ones; and as I happen to be, in my own opinion, one of the sensible ones (as far as a fundamentally foolish business admits of sensibleness), the sensation scene at the Princess's so completely broke my interest in the play that I left immediately after it, though I foresaw that Wally was going to die with intense pathos in the last act.

However, short of senselessly pretending to enjoy what no properly qualified London critic could possibly take seriously, or to be impressed with devices which everyone connected with the theatre speaks of in private as despicably ridiculous, I am anxious to shew my sense of the enterprise of the management at the Princess's, where popular drama at reasonable prices has been kept going with great energy throughout the year. It seems to me, by the way, that the critics of the Sunday papers might help a good deal by a vigorous remonstrance with the frequenters of the gallery for their occasional lapses into blackguardism. The majority of the gods are no doubt perfectly decent people, quite sincere in their applause of the chivalrous sentiments uttered upon the stage. But they should not allow the minority to discredit them by insulting every actress whose part requires her to make some demonstration of affection to her stage lover. Acting is impossible under such conditions; and an audience which cannot keep order in this respect spoils the entertainment it has just paid for, and makes fine artists very reluctant to accept engagements to act to it, not to mention that it disgraces itself.

The cast of Two Little Vagabonds includes Miss Geraldine Oliffe, who must rather envy Miss Tyndall and Miss Fairbrother their easy and popular parts as the two boys. It is quite up to the west end standard, and is, in fact, rather thrown away on the play, which, though quite likely to be successful, does not suggest any standard at all.

At the Métropole Theatre in Camberwell Mr Mulholland last week produced a new farcical comedy called The Co-Respondent, by Mr G. W. Appleton. The house laughed a good deal, and as I joined in the merriment, I suppose I cannot honestly say that the play missed its mark, though I should certainly advise Mr Frank Wyatt and Miss Violet Melnotte to think twice before transferring it to the west end.

WILLIAM MORRIS AS ACTOR AND DRAMATIST

[10 *October* 1896]

AMONG the many articles which have been written about William Morris during the past week, I have seen none which deal with him as dramatist and actor. Yet I have been present at a play by William Morris; and I have seen him act, and act, too, much better than an average professional of the twenty-pound-a-week class. I need therefore make no apology for making him the subject of an article on the theatre.

Morris was a quite unaffected and accessible person. All and sundry were welcome to know him to the full extent of their capacity for such acquaintance (which was usually not saying much) as far as a busy and sensitive man could make himself common property without intolerable boredom and waste of time. Even to the Press, which was generally—bless its innocence!—either ignorantly insolent to him or fatuously patronizing, as if he were some delightful curio, appreciable only by persons of taste and fancy, he was willing to be helpful. Journalist though I am, he put up with me with the friendliest patience, though I am afraid I must sometimes have been a fearful trial to him.

I need hardly say that I have often talked copiously to him on many of his favorite subjects, especially the artistic subjects. What is more to the point, he has occasionally talked to me about them. No art was indifferent to him. He declared that nobody could pass a picture without looking at it—that even a smoky cracked old mezzotint in a pawnbroker's window would stop you for at least a moment. Some idiot, I notice, takes it on himself to assure the world that he had no musical sense. As a matter of fact, he had a perfect ear, a most musical singing voice, and so fine a sense of beauty in sound (as in everything else) that he could not endure the clatter of the pianoforte or the squalling and shouting of the average singer. When I told him that the Amsterdam choir, brought over here by M. de Lange, had discovered the secret of the beauty of medieval music, and sang it with surpass-

ing excellence, he was full of regret for having missed it; and the
viol concerts of M. Dolmetsch pleased him greatly. Indeed once,
during his illness, when M. Dolmetsch played him some really
beautiful music on a really beautiful instrument, he was quite
overcome by it. I once urged him to revive the manufacture of
musical instruments and rescue us from the vulgar handsome-
ness of the trade articles with which our orchestras are equipped;
and he was by no means averse to the idea, having always, he
avowed, thought he should like to make a good fiddle. Only
neither in music nor in anything else could you engage him in any
sort of intellectual dilettantism: he would not waste his time and
energy on the curiosities and fashions of art, but went straight to
its highest point in the direct and simple production of beauty.
He was ultra-modern—not merely up to date, but far ahead of
it: his wall papers, his hangings, his tapestries, and his printed
books have the twentieth century in every touch of them; whilst
as to his prose word-weaving, our worn-out nineteenth-century
Macaulayese is rancid by comparison. He started from the thirteenth century simply because he wished to start from the most
advanced point instead of from the most backward one—say
1850 or thereabout. When people called him "archaic," he explained, with the indulgence of perfect knowledge, that they were
fools, only they did not know it. In short, the man was a complete artist, who became great by a pre-eminent sense of beauty,
and practical ability enough (and to spare) to give effect to it.

And yet—and yet—and yet—! I am sorry to have to say it; but
I never could induce him to take the smallest interest in the contemporary theatrical routine of the Strand. As far as I am aware,
I share with Mr Henry Arthur Jones the distinction of being the
only modern dramatist whose plays were witnessed by him (except Charley's Aunt, which bored him); and I greatly fear that
neither of us dare claim his visits as a spontaneous act of homage
to modern acting and the modern drama. Now, when Morris
would not take an interest in anything, and would not talk about
it—and his capacity for this sort of resistance, both passive and
active, was remarkably obstinate—it generally meant that he had

made up his mind, on good grounds, that it was not worth talking about. A man's mouth may be shut and his mind closed much more effectually by his knowing all about a subject than by his knowing nothing about it; and whenever Morris suddenly developed a downright mulishness about anything, it was a sure sign that he knew it through and through and had quarrelled with it. Thus, when an enthusiast for some fashionable movement or reaction in art would force it into the conversation, he would often behave so as to convey an impression of invincible prejudice and intolerant ignorance, and so get rid of it. But later on he would let slip something that shewed, in a flash, that he had taken in the whole movement at its very first demonstration, and had neither prejudices nor illusions about it. When you knew the subject yourself, and could see beyond it and around it, putting it in its proper place and accepting its limits, he would talk fast enough about it; but it did not amuse him to allow novices to break a lance with him, because he had no special facility for brilliant critical demonstration, and required too much patience for his work to waste any of it on idle discussions. Consequently there was a certain intellectual roguery about him of which his intimate friends were very well aware; so that if a subject was thrust on him, the aggressor was sure to be ridiculously taken in if he did not calculate on Morris's knowing much more about it than he pretended to.

On the subject of the theatre, an enthusiastic young first-nighter would probably have given Morris up, after the first attempt to gather his opinion of The Second Mrs Tanqueray, as an ordinary citizen who had never formed the habit of playgoing, and neither knew nor cared anything about the theatre except as a treat for children once a year during the pantomime season. But Morris would have written for the stage if there had been any stage that a poet and artist could write for. When the Socialist League once proposed to raise the wind by a dramatic entertainment, and suggested that he should provide the play, he set to at once and provided it. And what kind of play was it? Was it a miracle play on the lines of those scenes in the Towneley mysteries between the "shepherds abiding in the field," which he used to quote with great relish as his idea of a good bit of comedy? Not at all: it was a topical extravaganza, entitled Nupkins Awakened, the chief "character parts" being Sir Peter Edlin, Tennyson, and an imaginary Archbishop of Canterbury. Sir Peter owed the compliment to his activity at that time in sending Socialists to prison on charges of "obstruction," which was always proved by getting a policeman to swear that if any passer-by or vehicle had wished to pass over the particular spot in a thoroughfare on which the speaker or his audience happened to be standing, their presence would have obstructed him. This contention, which was regarded as quite sensible and unanswerable by the newspapers of the day, was put into a nutshell in the course of Sir Peter's summing-up in the play. "In fact, gentlemen, it is a matter of grave doubt whether we are not all of us continually committing this offence from our cradles to our graves." This speech, which the real Sir Peter of course never made, though he certainly would have done so had he had wit enough to see the absurdity of solemnly sending a man to prison for two months because another man could not walk through him—especially when it would have been so easy to lock him up for three on some respectable pretext—will probably keep Sir Peter's memory green when all his actual judicial utterances are forgotten. As to Tennyson, Morris took a Socialist who happened to combine the right sort of beard with a melancholy temperament, and drilled him in a certain portentous incivility of speech which, taken with the quality of his remarks, threw a light on Morris's opinion of Tennyson which was all the more instructive because he delighted in Tennyson's verse as keenly as Wagner delighted in the music of Mendelssohn, whose credit for qualities of larger scope he, nevertheless, wrote down and destroyed. Morris played the ideal Archbishop himself. He made no attempt to make up the part in the ordinary stage fashion. He always contended that no more was necessary for stage illusion than some distinct conventional symbol, such as a halo for a saint, a crook for a bishop, or, if you liked, a cloak and dagger for the

villain, and a red wig for the comedian. A pair of clerical bands
and black stockings proclaimed the archbishop: the rest he did
by obliterating his humor and intelligence, and presenting his own
person to the audience like a lantern with the light blown out,
with a dull absorption in his own dignity which several minutes
of the wildest screaming laughter at him when he entered could
not disturb. I laughed immoderately myself; and I can still see
quite clearly the long top floor of that warehouse in the Farring-
don Road as I saw it in glimpses between my paroxysms with
Morris gravely on the stage in his bands at one end; Mrs Still-
man, a tall and beautiful figure, rising like a delicate spire above
a skyline of city chimney-pots at the other; and a motley sea of
rolling, wallowing, guffawing Socialists between. There has been
no other such successful first night within living memory, I believe; but I only remember one dramatic critic who took care to
be present—Mr William Archer. Morris was so interested by his
experiment in this sort of composition that he for some time
talked of trying his hand at a serious drama, and would no doubt
have done it had there been any practical occasion for it, or any
means of consummating it by stage representation under proper
conditions without spending more time on the job than it was
worth. Later, at one of the annual festivities of the Hammersmith
Socialist Society, he played the old gentleman in the bath-chair
in a short piece called The Duchess of Bayswater (*not* by himself), which once served its turn at the Haymarket as a curtain
raiser. It was impossible for such a born teller and devourer of
stories as he was to be indifferent to an art which is nothing more
than the most vivid and real of all ways of story-telling. No man
would more willingly have seen his figures move and heard their
voices than he.

Why, then, did he so seldom go to the theatre? Well, come,
gentle reader, why doesnt anybody go to the theatre? Do you
suppose that even I would go to the theatre twice a year except
on business? You would never dream of asking why Morris did
not read penny novelettes, or hang his rooms with Christmas-
number chromolithographs. We have no theatre for men like

Morris: indeed, we have no theatre for quite ordinary cultivated people. I am a person of fairly catholic interests: it is my privilege to enjoy the acquaintance of a few representative people in various vortices of culture. I know some of the most active-minded and intelligent of the workers in social and political reform. They read stories with an avidity that amazes me; but they dont go to the theatre. I know the people who are struggling for the regeneration of the arts and crafts. They dont go to the theatre. I know people who amuse their leisure with edition after edition of the novels of Mrs Humphry Ward, Madame Sarah Grand, and Mr Harold Frederic, and who could not for their lives struggle through two chapters of Miss Corelli, Mr Rider Haggard, or Mr Hall Caine. They dont go to the theatre. I know the lovers of music who support the Richter and Mottl concerts and go to Bayreuth if they can afford it. They dont go to the theatre. I know the staff of this paper. It doesnt go to the theatre—even the musical critic is an incorrigible shirk when his duties involve a visit thither. Nobody goes to the theatre except the people who also go to Madame Tussaud's. Nobody writes for it, unless he is hopelessly stage struck and cannot help himself. It has no share in the leadership of thought: it does not even reflect its current. It does not create beauty: it apes fashion. It does not produce personal skill: our actors and actresses, with the exception of a few persons with natural gifts and graces, mostly miscultivated or half cultivated, are simply the middle-class section of the residuum. The curt insult with which Matthew Arnold dismissed it from consideration found it and left it utterly defenceless. And yet you ask me why Morris did not go to the theatre. In the name of common sense, why should he have gone?

When I say these things to stupid people, they have a feeble way of retorting, "What about the Lyceum?" That is just the question I have been asking for years; and the reply always is that the Lyceum is occupied exclusively with the works of a sixteenth-seventeenth century author, in whose social views no educated and capable person today has the faintest interest, and whose art is partly so villainously artificial and foolish as to produce no effect on a thirteenth-twentieth century artist like Morris except one of impatience and discomfort, and partly so fine as to defy satisfactory treatment at a theatre where there are only two competent performers, who are neither of them in their proper element in the seventeenth century. Morris was willing to go to a street corner and tell the people something that they very badly needed to be told, even when he could depend on being arrested by a policeman for his trouble; but he drew the line at fashionably modernized Shakespear. If you had told him what a pretty fifteenth-century picture Miss Terry makes in her flower wreath in Cymbeline's garden, you might have induced him to peep for a moment at that; but the first blast of the queen's rhetoric would have sent him flying into the fresh air again. You could not persuade Morris that he was being amused when he was, as a matter of fact, being bored; and you could not persuade him that music was harmonious by playing it on vulgar instruments, or that verse was verse when uttered by people with either no delivery at all or the delivery of an auctioneer or toastmaster. In short, you could not induce him to accept ugliness as art, no matter how brilliant, how fashionable, how sentimental, or how intellectually interesting you might make it. And you certainly could not palm off a mess of Tappertitian sentiment daubed over some sham love affair on him as a good story. This, alas, is as much as to say that you could not induce him to spend his evenings at a modern theatre. And yet he was not in the least an Impossibilist: he revelled in Dickens and the elder Dumas; he was enthusiastic about the acting of Robson, and greatly admired Jefferson; if he had started a Kelmscott Theatre instead of the Kelmscott Press, I am quite confident that in a few months, without going half a mile afield for his company, he would have produced work that would within ten years have affected every theatre on earth, from London to St Petersburg, and from New York to Alexandria. At all events, I should be glad to hear any gentleman point out an instance in which he undertook to find the way, and did not make us come along with him. We kicked and screamed, it is true: some of our poor obituarists kicked and screamed—even brayed—at his funeral the other day: but we have had to come along. No man was more liberal in his attempts to improve Morris's mind than I was; but I always found that, in so far as I was not making a most horrible idiot of myself out of misknowledge (I could forgive myself for pure ignorance), he could afford to listen to me with the patience of a man who had taught my teachers. There were people whom we tried to run him down with—Tennysons, Swinburnes, and so on; but their opinions about things did not make any difference. Morris's did.

I must apologize to Mr Arthur Roberts and Mr Hawtrey for postponing consideration of their new parts and plays until next week. I do so from lack of space, not from any sense that the occasion is too melancholy for a word about their gaieties. I feel nothing but elation when I think of Morris. My intercourse with him was so satisfying that I should be the most ungrateful of men if I asked for more. You can lose a man like that by your own death, but not by his. And so, until then, let us rejoice in him.

TWO PLAYS

Mr Martin. A new play, in three acts, by Charles Hawtrey. Comedy Theatre, 3 October 1896.

The White Silk Dress. A musical farce in two acts, by H. J. W. Dam. Music by A. McLean and R. Somerville. Prince of Wales Theatre, 3 October 1896. [17 *October* 1896]

When an actor-manager allows either literary vanity or confidence in his command of clap-trap to tempt him to write his own play, he can be depended on to write a bad one. But when he has a genuine desire to represent certain aspects of life that tickle his imagination and appeal to his mimetic genius, and finds that all the light-handed fictional talent of his time turns away from the theatre to journalism and novel-writing, and so never learns the technique of the stage, he may plunge into authorship with no worse fortune than any other beginner. There has been of late some tentative pottering in this direction, notably by Mr Brook-field, who, without achieving a complete drama, has made himself the predominant partner in various collaborations, avowed and unavowed, mainly by scraps of caricature and mimicry of real life which have seemed quite vivid by contrast with the deadliness of their setting. Mr Charles Hawtrey is a promising member of the same school; and now at last we have an entire comedy from his pen, with Mr Brookfield in the cast. As comedies go nowadays, Mr Martin may almost be called a masterpiece of observation. It cannot be compared to the comedies of Mr Oscar Wilde, because Mr Wilde has creative imagination, philosophic humor, and original wit, besides being a master of language; whilst Mr Hawtrey observes, mimics, and derides quite thoughtlessly; yields to the fascination of stale jokes about "tarts" and the like; offers the most trivial curiosities of slang, pointed profusely by the word "bally," as felicities of diction; makes the hero threaten the villain with "as good a hiding as ever he got in his life," at which the ten most foolish people in the house applaud frantically, whilst the civilized remainder look on with a frozen stare; and otherwise keeps on the hither side of the boundary which separates the clever *flâneur* from the dramatist. But within these limits the work is very smart, especially in its caricatures of social types. The affable, greedy Irishwoman, whose pleasant, flattering, conciliatory ways are the result of a combination of instinctive tact and sympathy with a total absence of respect for the truth, for herself or for anybody else, is excellent—quite a document in sociology. The jovial Bamfylde, who roars with laughter at everything, and clears the way for his weakness and selfishness by sheer force of hilarity, is a slighter but not less lifelike sketch. Some of the other characters are perhaps not less typical in their set; but their set is an insignificant one, consisting mainly of Bohemian artists and people who do their best to shirk the common lot by living what is called a life of pleasure, mostly to their own confusion and undoing. For instance, the brainless, but cunning and rapacious, young lady from the Gaiety, whose inexperience gets her out of her depth at every turn in society, and who suspects impropriety in every shift and whimsicality of the smart conversation she is unable to follow, is not very interesting, possibly because people in false positions never are interesting: it is only when they have found their level that they become worth considering. And the good-hearted music-hall star who *has* found her level, and who, in her rather rowdy way, and upon a charitable construction of all the circumstances, is a very decent, honest, estimable person, smacks of the ideal too much for a comedy of observation.

The chief character, played by Mr Hawtrey, is that familiar modern development of Horatio, the sentimentally imagined man about town who consorts on easy terms with publicans and sinners, but, when touched by an appeal to some past disappointment in love, or to the memory of his mother, can reconcile parents and children, outwit villains, raise money, in short, do everything that conduces to a happy ending. This child of fancy is so familiar on the stage that it is distressing to find him invested with the personal peculiarities of some real person whom Mr Hawtrey has a fancy for imitating. Mr Walkley, in a learned criticism, has proved out of Aristotle that this is bad art on Mr Hawtrey's part; and I admit that here the Stagyrite has anticipated my own theoretic conclusions, not for the first time. But, practically, I do not mind whom Mr Hawtrey imitates, provided he gives artistic quality to his imitation. As it is, unhappily, he merely copies faults of speech which are neither amusing nor characteristic, and which certainly in no way help the verisimilitude of the complication which leads to his being mistaken for an American. They are simply ugly, and consequently painful to listen to. Why persist in them?

The very staleness of the three principal characters—the American sharper, the hero, and the music-hall singer—shews how much Mr Hawtrey has been able to gain by a little sincerity of treatment. It is true that their evolutions are so maladroitly planned that they have to fall back again and again on the explanatory soliloquy in its most childish form; and the time-honored mistaking of one man for another is far-fetched, and lands the author in more difficulties than it gets him out of. Yet, though we thus get old characters, old sentiments, and old situations handled, as far as stage construction goes, in an old and sometimes even obsolete way, the substitution of modern behavior and modern ideas for the customary stage conventions of conduct comes as a huge relief to the playgoer, and gives the comedy a plausible air of fresh cleverness and originality. The usual artificial happy ending, which has made so many plays, even by our best dramatists, break down miserably in the last act, is avoided as successfully as the still worse tragic ending—a Shakespearean inheritance—in which the playwright gets rid of his embarrassments by slaughtering them. In Mr Martin things settle down sensibly enough: the good-natured young lady has to give up her lover, it is true; but though she does not like it, she lumps it with tolerable grace and good sense. The villain is an ordinary blackguard, not distinguishable in his principles or his appearance and manners from the honest members of his set, and therefore not objected to until, on a question of conduct, it is found that any trifling pecuniary advantage will overcome his theoretical objection to be a liar and a thief. This is just as it should be. As society becomes more honest and intelligent, it becomes apparently more cynical. It perceives that the formulation of a code of honor applicable to all possible circumstances is neither possible nor desirable. Consequently, those strenuous professions of devotion to all the articles of the code which seem to have been permissible and even fashionable when Joseph Surface came upon the stage, go out of fashion, and eventually become the mark of a fool or a rogue, although the code still retains enough of its authority with the masses to give pungency to jests at its expense. The congenital blackguard then finds the tone of society on moral questions quite unembarrassing to him. Nobody professes code-morality; nobody is shocked, and many people are amused and interested, by witty verbal professions of code-immorality. The blackguard, having no moral sense, and therefore no consciousness of the existence of morality apart from code-morality, thinks that the reign of morality is over. He does something wrong. As he expected, he is not preached at. As he did not expect, he is promptly and inexorably dropped, and must either efface himself and make a fresh beginning in disguise, or else consort with loose people to the end of his days. But on the English stage, behind the times as it is, code-morality is still in the ascendent. The stage villain utters anti-social sentiments which arouse outspoken horror; and when he is found out, he is preached at, mobbed, cuffed, and often handcuffed. The Hawtrey school avoids this anachronism. In a recent play collaborated in by Mr Brookfield, and called, I think, A Woman's Reason (or some other formula for a Man's Imagination), the villain's part, played by Mr Coghlan, made a lasting impression because it was treated with perfect modernity. And in Mr Martin, Mr Hawtrey, save only for that unhappy touch about giving the villain a good hiding, produces something of the same effect in the same way. Certainly, the villain moves in such a shady set that he has to dive rather energetically into the abysses of card-sharping and avoidable wife-beating in order to get distinctly below his surroundings; but at all events they do not persecute him for his principles: they simply cut him for his conduct. Which is just what would happen to him in real life.

The acting of Mr Martin is exceptionally good. Miss Lottie Venne, Miss Rose Leclercq, and Miss Nina Boucicault, with Messrs Charles and William Hawtrey, Mr Kemble, Mr Brookfield, and Mr Volpe make a brilliant cast. The nominally leading parts, filled by Mr Lovell and Miss Jessie Bateman, are mere routine.

The White Silk Dress at the Prince of Wales' shews that the management of that theatre is not wholly beyond grace, and that the failure of Biarritz was not lost on its conscience. There is an immense improvement in stage discipline, and an obvious attempt to insist on the fact that the piece has a plot. Unfortunately, repentant sinners are seldom happy in their first unaccustomed attempts at virtue; and on the first night, when it became apparent that Mr Dam's laboriously emphasized and tediously expounded plot was no plot at all, the house yelled with rage, and called for the author in a manner that decided him not to accept the invitation. The piece, however, is not an insult to the public; indeed, after Biarritz, it is quite a compliment.

Far—though not too far—from having the old air of an entertainment contrived by a billiard marker for an audience of barloafers, it may quite conceivably have been written by a gentleman for the amusement of gentlemen—not very strong-minded gentlemen, perhaps, but still, persons to whom even a musical farce is something better than an excuse for indecent jesting. In my gratitude for these reforms I shall not criticize the play too closely. Mr Arthur Roberts works as hard as ever, and almost as successfully as ever, to whip up the public sense of humor and carry his admirers along with him; but as he grows older and riper, the old tomfoolery becomes perceptibly less congenial to himself and less convincing to the audience. In a few years more his misgivings, not only as to the dignity of his tricks, but as to their effectiveness, will so paralyse him that he will begin to cling nervously to the author's text. Perhaps he will even take to pathos, and open a theatre with The Porter's Knot and The Cricket on the Hearth. At all events, he is getting suspiciously fond of his songs of senile pathos; and his comic business, once apparently infinite in the variety of its silliness, is reducing itself to a small bag of about four tricks—hardly enough to improvise safely with. Miss Kitty Loftus as "the beautiful Eleanor Bailey"—a conception not wholly untouched with hostess-poetry and a sense of character—is, as usual, fruitlessly industrious in her dancing, only a little better in her singing, but not at all bad in her passages of comedy. Who knows whether she, too, may not yet be brought down to mere acting? The rest of the company is better than might have been expected. It includes Miss Decima Moore, Mrs Brooke, Miss Singleton, Messrs Kelly, Furneaux Cook, Traill, Cheesman, and others who are not merely lay figures round Mr Roberts. On the whole, if each future production proves as great an improvement on its predecessor as The White Silk Dress is on Biarritz, the Prince of Wales' will take serious rank as a light opera house before it is fifty years older.

THE RED ROBE

UNDER THE RED ROBE. A romantic play in four acts, adapted
by Edward Rose from the novel by Stanley Weyman. Haymarket Theatre, 17 October 1896.   [24 *October* 1896]

IF the people who delight in the romances of Mr Stanley Weyman
and the detective stories of Mr Conan Doyle belonged to the
same social stratum as those who formerly read Les Trois Mous-
quetaires and The Murders in the Rue Morgue, I should conclude
that we were in a period of precipitous degeneration. I was
brought up, romantically speaking, on D'Artagnan and Bussy
d'Amboise; and I cannot say that I find Gil de Berault in any
way up to their standard; whilst the descent from that ingenious
automaton, Detective Dupin, to such a prince of duffers and
dullards as Sherlock Holmes is one which, after a couple of
attempts, I have given up as impossible. I therefore approach
Under the Red Robe full of prejudice against it. The very name
appears to me a fatuity: it suggests a companion piece to The
White Silk Dress.

On the other hand, it is impossible to feel ill-disposed towards
the new Haymarket enterprise. Mr Harrison's management at
the Lyceum was exceptionally brilliant, even among first-class
managements. Mr Cyril Maude and Miss Winifred Emery are
among the most solidly popular of those happy couples who,
by giving the sanction of an irreproachable domesticity to the
wickedest of the arts, hallow the dissipations of the respectable
London playgoer. Besides, I, as critic-dramatist, notoriously have
a corrupt personal motive for doing all I can to enhance the
prestige of the Maude-Harrison combination, and making success
a matter of course at the Haymarket. On the whole, I think my
prejudice is sufficiently balanced by my prepossession to allow
me to proceed to the slaughter with a plausible pretence of open-
mindedness.

I began by reading the book—a better policy on the whole
than the alternative one of making a merit of being in the dark

about it. I thought it puerile to the uttermost publishable extreme of jejuniority. It is not without a painful effort that I can bring myself to confess even now that when I was fourteen, some of the romances I wove for myself may have presented me in the character of a dark-souled villain with a gorgeous female passionately denouncing me as "Spy!" "Traitor!" "Villain!" and then remorsefully worshipping me for some act of transcendent magnanimity on my part. But when I was fourteen boys had to keep these audacious imaginings to themselves on pain of intolerable ridicule. Since then the New Public has been manufactured under the Education Act; and nowadays there is a fortune for the literary boy of fourteen, or even the literary adult who can remember vividly what a fool he was at that age.

I do not know how old Mr Stanley Weyman is, but I can certify most positively that his Gil de Berault and Renée de Cocheforêt are nothing but the dark-souled villain-hero and the gorgeous female aforesaid, and that the old situation between them has accumulated nothing round it but a few commonplace duels and adventures, with a very feeble composite photograph of the Richelieus of Dumas and Lytton, and a bold annexation of the Lyttonian incident of the Cardinal pretending to send the hero to execution whilst really sending him to the arms of his lady love.

Mr Edward Rose, in dramatizing such a novel, had to dramatize situation without character—that is, to make bricks without straw. Worse than that, he had to dramatize a situation the boyishness of which must become so flagrantly obvious to the wise under the searching glare of the footlights, that his only hope of acceptance lay in the as yet unfathomed abysses of the literary infancy of the New Public. Whether that public will support him is exactly what we are all wondering at present. As for me, I am getting on in life; I used to make my bread by my wit, and now have to make it by my reputation for wit; and I simply cannot afford to pretend that Under the Red Robe as a play has any charm for me. As a novel, I can pass my idle hour with it, just as Bismarck used to pass his with the police novels of Du

Boisgobey; for, after all, Mr Stanley Weyman is a bit of a story-teller—is, indeed, a rather concise and forcible narrator; and his books serve when the newspaper becomes unendurable. But as a play, involving the effort of making up one's mind to go to the theatre, booking one's seat, going out at night, and so on—no, thank you. At least, not unless the adapter and the performers create some attraction not to be found in the book.

I must sorrowfully add that, for me at least, that attraction is not forthcoming; and I can only hope that the villain-hero and the gorgeous female may pull the play through and cover my disparagements with shame. Even if I accept the romance on its own ground, I have still to complain that the conventions of the theatre prevent Mr Rose from faithfully carrying out the conception of the villain-hero. In the first chapter of the novel there is no mistake about the darkness of Gil de Berault's soul. He rooks an English lad by watching his cards in a mirror. A duel follows, in which, just as the lad perceives that he is hopelessly overmatched, an accident places his antagonist at his mercy. Being too young to understand that if you fight at all, you must fight to win, he refuses to avail himself of what he conceives as an unfair advantage. Gil teaches him not to confuse poetry with business by promptly running him through, and only escapes being lynched by the crowd through the most liberal exercise of his accomplishments as a bully. At the Haymarket all this is nonsensed by an endeavor to steer between Mr Stanley Weyman's rights as author of the story and the prescriptive right of the leading actor to fight popularly and heroically against heavy odds. The Englishman is a giant and a swashbuckler. Instead of sparing Gil when he slips and falls, he rushes to make an end of him, and has his thrust parried by a miracle of address on the part of the prostrate hero, quite in the manner of the combat between the two Master Crummleses. Then the adapter suddenly returns to the book; so that a gallant Frenchman, who, in the presence of a French crowd, has just fought and beaten a gigantic English bully of extra-special insular arrogance, is frantically mobbed by that French crowd for his behavior. In the interval between the first and second acts I asked several persons who had not read the book whether they could understand the behavior of the crowd. They were all, of course, completely bewildered by it.

Yet this first act is lucidity itself compared to the second, in which the necessity for collecting under one roof and into half an hour's time the incidents scattered by Mr Weyman over many leagues and many days has driven Mr Rose into desperate courses. In the novel Renée convicts Gil of spying by luring him to dog her for miles round the country, and then lying low for him round a corner. The Haymarket stage not being large enough for a paperchase, Mr Rose has been driven to make Renée have Gil locked into his bedroom on the top-floor, and then catch him emerging deceitfully from the chimney (Mr Waring calls it a secret passage; but the original conception is too obvious) on the ground-floor. Furthermore, Gil, instead of accidentally finding the diamonds in the street, breaks open the knife-drawer in the sideboard with his dagger, and steals them from that eligible hiding-place, declaring that "he never betrays the hand that pays him," a piece of morality—borrowed from the bravo in Le Roi s'amuse—which plunges the audience into deeper bewilderment every time Mr Waring reiterates it. When at last the gorgeous female gets her chance to heap her disdain on his head, the audience, though prepared for a good deal, is not more prepared for that than for anything else, and is too broken in spirit to rise to the situation. Not until the second scene of the third act does Gil at last make up his mind to be a hero; and the house, with a gasp of relief, exclaims, "Now we know where we are," and settles down to enjoy itself without further misgivings as to the relevance of the Tennysonian couplet on the playbill:

> His honor rooted in dishonor stood;
> And faith unfaithful kept him falsely true.

I suggest that a happier selection would have been the epitaph which Jo Gargery could not afford to have cut on his father's tomb:

> But whatsome'er the failings on his part,
> Remember, reader, he were that good in his heart.

As to the acting, it must be remembered that there is not the ghost of a character in the whole story. When this is allowed for, it will be admitted that the performance is a joyful sight. On the whole, I think I preferred—on the score of conciseness—Mr Holman Clark's impersonation of Clon, the servant whose tongue had been cut out, and who made me regret occasionally that the same operation had not been performed on the others. Next to him my favorite was Mr Cyril Maude, who wisely resolved that, since he could not make sense of his part, he would at any rate make fun of it. He frankly made Captain Larolle a pantaloon, and a very amusing pantaloon too. Judge, then, of the dismay of the audience when, before the play was half over, Clon suddenly seized Captain Larolle round the waist, and rolled with him over a fearful precipice. For a moment we all had a desperate hope that Mr Maude would bounce up through a star trap at the other side of the stage; take a harlequin's leap through the first-floor window of the château; and roll out again through the letter-box, closely pursued by Clon; but it was not to be: Captain Larolle was gone for ever; and I, for one, spent the rest of the evening lamenting his premature decease.

Mr Waring's task was, on the whole, the easiest. When an actor has been condemned for years to move about the stage in ugly Bond Street tailorings, producing an effect of suppressed emotion by his anxiety to avoid creasing them, the effect of suddenly letting him loose as a swordsman in a picturesque costume is dazzling, astonishing, breath-bereaving. Here is Mr Waring, who has created Torvald Helmer and Master Builder Solness in England, and who has played a dozen other parts at least better than this Gil de Berault; and yet, solely because he has exchanged the costume of a funeral mute for that of a cavalier, and fights a duel instead of handing his overcoat to a valet (always a most important incident in a coat-and-waistcoat play), he is suddenly hailed as a man who, after a meritorious but uneventful apprenticeship, has suddenly burst on the world as a great actor. Oh, the New Public! the New Public! indifferent or uncomfortable over fine work: enthusiastic over cheap jobs! Of course, Mr

Waring does the thing on his head, so to speak; but how can I compliment an actor who has done what he has done on stuff like that?

Miss Winifred Emery has no such advantage as Mr Waring. For a man, a Louis Treize costume is a miracle of elegance and romantic fascination compared to the costume of today; but the woman's costume of that time is too matronly for modern ideas of active womanhood. And then not only is the part an unblushingly bad one, limited to the merest mechanical feeding of the play with its one situation, but its verbal style is of that artificial kind which Miss Emery positively refuses (quite rightly) to take seriously. Unfortunately, nothing will cure Mr Rose of this style. He writes it exactly as he might collect miniatures and snuffboxes; and I am convinced that in his heart he longs to make Miss Emery play in feathers and a train held up by two black boys. He sticks in gratuitous asides as pure curiosities, and occasionally goes the length of a bit of Shakespear—for instance, "Youre mad to say so," when the burglary is discovered. My personal regard for Mr Rose changes into malevolent exasperation under this treatment, especially when Miss Winifred Emery acts as the executioner. For when it comes to tall talk and sham antique, Miss Emery takes an attitude which is intolerably humiliating to any sensitive playgoer. The actress who consummated her reputation in The Benefit of the Doubt disappears; and in her place we have a cold, disgusted lady indulging an audience of foolish grown-up men with an exhibition for which she does not disguise her contempt. If one could detect the smallest gleam of humorous enjoyment in her delivery of the obsolete staginesses of Bazilide and Renée, one could accept them as burlesque; but no such relenting is anywhere apparent. Even before she speaks, when she acknowledges her enthusiastic reception with that little catch of the lip and suffusion of the eye which is one of her most irresistible effects, there is scorn in her nostril. As she goes on she makes me feel indescribably abject: if her glance accidentally lights anywhere near me, I instinctively dive under the stall in front, and make a miserable pretence of having dropped some-

227

thing. If only I could get up and assure her that I at least am not taken in by such trash, and am wholly innocent of the folly of the rest of my crawling sex, it would be a relief to me; but she unnerves me so that I dare not. She threw the business of Renée de Cocheforêt to that silly audience as she might have flung a bone to a troublesome dog; and they wagged their tails, and licked her hands, and yelped, and gobbled it as if it were the choicest morsel thay had ever tasted, even from her. After all, why should she waste good acting on such baby-gabies?

In the scenic department some special effects of lighting were tried; but on the first night they were not quite up to the Bayreuth standard, though no doubt they are by this time working smoothly. The plan of representing firelight in an interior by making the footlights jump needs a more complete concealment of the gas flames—especially for people who are nervous about fire. In the decorations of the second act, instead of actual suits of armor, painted canvas profiles are used, perhaps in compliance with the demands of Mr Rose for something old-fashioned. This seems to me to be mere atavism; but it does not matter much. The orchestra, which was put out of sight in Mr Tree's time, is now put out of hearing. There has been a valuable addition to the depth of the stage; and very effective use is made of it in the last act. That reminds me, by the way, of Richelieu, which gave Mr Sydney Valentine an opening for a bit of acting which was duly received as an astonishing rarity. Mr Bernard Gould, made up as a Constable of France of the rugged warrior type, persuaded the audience that he had a fine part, mainly by dint of concealing the fact that he privately knew better.

Altogether, a silly piece of business. Probably it will run for two seasons at least.

ON DEADHEADS AND OTHER MATTERS

LOVE IN IDLENESS. An original comedy in three acts. By Louis
N. Parker and Edward J. Goodman. Terry's Theatre, 21
October 1896.

HIS LITTLE DODGE. A comedy in three acts. By Justin Huntly
McCarthy. From Le Système Ribadier, by MM. Georges
Feydeau and Maurice Hennequin. Royalty Theatre, 24 Oc-
tober 1896.

THE STORM. A play in one act and two tableaux. By Ian Robertson. Royalty Theatre, 24 October 1896.   [31 *October* 1896]

WHY must a farcical comedy always break down in the third act?
One way of answering is to question the fact, citing Pink Dominos as an example of a three-act farcical comedy in which the
third act was the best of the three. But what Pink Dominos really
proved was that three acts of farce is too much for human endurance, no matter how brilliantly it may be kept going to the
end. The public is apt to believe that it cannot have too much of
a good thing. I remember stealing about four dozen apples from
the orchard of a relative when I was a small boy, and retiring to
a loft with a confederate to eat them. But when I had eaten eigh-
teen I found, though I was still in robust health, that it was better
fun to pelt the hens with the remaining apples than to continue
the banquet. Many grown persons have made cognate miscal-
culations. I have known a man, during the craze for Nancy Lee,
engage a street piano to play it continuously for two hours. I
have known another bribe a hairdresser to brush his hair by
machinery for an unlimited period. Both these voluptuaries, of
course, discovered that the art of torture is the art of prolonging
not agony, but ecstasy. If we were to represent theatrical sensation by graphic curves in the manner of Jevons, we should find
that the more acute the sensation, the more rapidly does its curve
of enjoyment descend and dive into the negative. This is specially true of the enjoyment to be derived from farcical comedy.
It is an unsympathetic enjoyment, and therefore an abuse of

nature. The very dullest drama in five acts that ever attained for half a moment to some stir of feeling, leaves the spectator, however it may have bored him, happier and fresher than three acts of farcical comedy at which he has been worried into laughing incessantly with an empty heart. Mind, I am not moralizing about farcical comedy: I am simply giving the observed physical facts concerning it. In this clinical spirit I have over and over again warned the dramatist and the manager not to dwell too long on galvanic substitutes for genuine vivacity. When the vogue of farcical comedy was at its utmost, Mr Gilbert applied its galvanic methods to public life and fashion instead of merely to clandestine sprees and adulterous intrigues. But he tried it cautiously in one act at first, and never ventured on more than two, with lavish allurements of song, dance, and spectacle to give it life and color, in spite of which the two acts always proved quite enough. The fact is, the end of the second act is the point at which the spectators usually realize that the friendly interest in the persons of the drama which sustained them, and gave generosity and humanity to their merriment during the earlier scenes, is entirely undeserved, and that the pretty husband and handsome wife are the merest marionettes with witty dialogue stuck into their mouths. The worst thing that can happen in a play is that the people with whom the audience makes friends at first should disappoint it afterwards. Mr Gilbert carried this disappointment further: he would put forward a paradox which at first promised to be one of those humane truths which so many modern men of fine spiritual insight, from William Blake onward, have worded so as to flash out their contradiction of some weighty rule of our systematized morality, and would then let it slip through his fingers, leaving nothing but a mechanical topsy-turvitude. Farcical comedy combines the two disappointments. Its philosophy is as much a sham as its humanity.

His Little Dodge is no exception to the two-act rule. At the outset Miss Ellis Jeffreys, suddenly developing a delightful talent for comedy, succeeds in winning all possible charm of expectation and indulgent interest for Lady Miranda. Mr Weedon Gros-

smith, by a piece of acting so masterly in its combination of irresistibly comic effect with complete matter-of-courseness (there
is not the faintest touch of grotesque in his dress, face, voice, or
gesture from one end of the piece to the other) that I have seen
nothing so artistic of its kind since Jefferson was here, filled us
with the liveliest curiosity about the Honorable Mandeville Hobb.
Mr Fred Terry, as Sir Hercules, was genial enough to engage our
good will; and Mr Maltby, with his comic conviction, and his
unfailing appreciation of the right dramatic point of his part,
made himself more than welcome. For a moment we were cheated
into believing that we had met some real and likeable people; and
nobody could deny that the play was outrageously funny. But
our disenchantment was all the more irritating. The moment it
became apparent that all these interesting and promising people
were only puppets in a piece of farcical clockwork, the old disappointment, the old worry, the old rather peevish impatience
with the remaining turns of the mechanism set in. A genuine
dramatic development, founded on our interest in Lady Miranda
as suggested to us by Miss Jeffreys in the first act, would have
been followed with the most expectant attention; but hope
changed to weary disgust when her husband picked up a waistcoat strap, and accused her of an intrigue with the gardener,
whose waistcoat was deficient in that particular.

In Love in Idleness there is no such mistake as this. Mr Parker
knows only too well the value of an affectionate relation between
the audience and the persons of the drama. Mortimer Pendlebury,
the hero, is a lovable nincompoop, who muddles the affairs of all
his friends, but so endears himself to Providence by his good-
heartedness that they muddle themselves right again in the most
cheerful way imaginable, and unite him to his long lost love, a
nice old lady in lavender, impersonated by Miss Bella Pateman.
Mr Edward Terry, in a popular and not particularly trying part,
hits the character exactly, and plays not only with comic force,
but with tact and delicacy. But the acting success of the play is
Mr De Lange's fire-eating French Colonel, a perfectly original,
absolutely convincing, and extremely funny version of a part

which, in any other hands, would have come out the most hackneyed stuff in the world. It is not often that two such impersonations as Pendlebury and Gondinot are to be seen at the same theatre; and if there is such a thing still surviving in London as an unprofessional connoisseur of acting, he will do well to see Love in Idleness for their sakes.

By the way, I forgot that His Little Dodge is preceded at the Royalty by a new piece called The Storm, by Mr Ian Robertson. It is like an adaptation of a sentimental Academy picture.

Mr Alexander has been driven to take the Royalty as a chapel of ease to the St James's by The Prisoner of Zenda, which is now a permanent institution, like Madame Tussaud's. I saw it again the other night; and after The Red Robe I do not hesitate to pronounce it a perfectly delectable play. It has gained greatly in smoothness and charm since its first representation, except in the prologue, which is stagey and overplayed. Mr Alexander as Rassendyl is as fresh as paint: so is Mr Vernon as Sapt. Mr H. B. Irving now plays Hentzau, and enjoys himself immensely over it, after his manner. He is, perhaps, our ablest exponent of acting as an amusement for young gentlemen, as his father is our ablest exponent of acting as a fine art and serious profession. Miss Julia Neilson now plays Flavia, and is a little less the princess and more the actress than Miss Millard. Mr Aubrey Smith, as the black Elphberg, suffices in place of Mr Waring, who was wasted on it; but the new Mayor's wife is hardly as fascinating as Miss Olga Brandon. Miss Ellis Jeffreys has made so brilliant a success in comedy at the Royalty, thereby very happily confirming the opinion of her real strength which I ventured upon when Mr Pinero miscast her in Mrs Ebbsmith, that she can afford to forgive me if I confess that her Antoinette de Mauban struck me as being the very worst piece of acting an artist of her ability could conceivably perpetrate.

I am afraid Mrs Kendal's opinion of the Press will not be improved by the printing of a letter of hers which was obviously not intended for publication. However, the blunder has incidentally done a public service by making known Mrs Kendal's very sensible opinion that critics should pay for their seats. Of course they should: the complimentary invitation system is pure, unmitigated, indefensible corruption and blackmail, and nothing else. But are we alone to blame in the matter? When the managers abolish fees they put in their programs a request that the public will not persist in offering them. Why then do they not only bribe me, but force me to accept the bribe? I must attend on the first night. If I try to book a stall as a member of the general public, I am told that there are none to be disposed of, all being reserved for invited guests, including the Press. If I declare my identity, I am immediately accommodated, but not allowed to pay. From time to time we have virtuous announcements from beginners that they are going to do away with the system and pay for all their seats. That only proves that they *are* beginners, and are either making a virtue of necessity, or else are too inexperienced to know how the invitation system works. The public may take it that for the present it is practically compulsory. All that can be said for it is that it is at least an improvement on the abominable old system of "orders," under which newspapers claimed and exercised the right to give orders of admission to the theatres to anyone they pleased, the recipients being mostly tradesmen advertising in their papers. Nowadays, if an editor wants a free seat, he has to ask the manager for it; and some editors, I regret to say, still place themselves under heavy obligations to managers in this way. There are many papers just worth a ticket from the point of view of the experienced acting-manager if they deluge the house with constant and fulsome praise; and this is largely supplied by young men for no other consideration than the first-night stall, the result being, of course, a mass of corrupt puffery for which the complimentary Press ticket is solely responsible. Need I add that the personal position of a critic under the system is by no means a satisfactory one? Under some managements he can always feel secure of his footing as at least the guest of a gentleman—though even that is a false position for him; but he cannot confine himself to theatres so managed. I remember on one occasion, at no less a place than the Royal Italian Opera, a certain State official, well known and respected as a scholarly musician and writer on music, pitched into the Opera in the columns of this journal. Some time afterwards he appeared at Covent Garden in the box of a critic of the first standing, representing a very eminent daily paper. Sir Augustus Harris promptly objected to his complimentary box being used to harbor audacious persons who found fault with him. Of course the eminent daily paper immediately bought its box and went over the eminent *impresario* like a steam-roller; but the incident shews how little a manager who is also a man of the world is disposed to admit the independence of the critic as long as he has to oblige him. It is easy to say that it is a "mutual convenience"; but, in fact, it is a mutual inconvenience. If the incident just narrated had occurred at an ordinary theatre, where the necessary sort of seat for a critic is not always to be obtained on a first night for money, instead of at the Opera, where seats can practically always be bought, the manager might have seriously inconvenienced the critic, especially as the paper was a daily one, by boycotting him.

Let me mention another more recent and equally significant incident. At a first night last week a popular young actor of juvenile parts, in a theatre which he has himself managed, went out between the acts into the hall, which was crowded with critics, and announced in a loud voice, with indignant earnestness, that he had just seen no less revolting a spectacle than the critic of a leading newspaper walking into "the stalls of a London theatre" *not* in evening dress. He added many passionate expressions of his disgust for the benefit of the company, at least half a dozen of whom, including myself, wore simply the dress in which statesmen address public meetings and gentlemen go to church. And yet I rather sympathized with his irritation. The theatrical deadhead gets his ticket on the implied condition that he "dresses the house." If he comes in morning dress, or allows the ladies who accompany him to look dowdy, he is struck off the free-list. To this actor-manager we critics were not his fellow-guests, but simply deadheads whose business it was to "dress the house" and write puffs. What else do we get our free tickets for? Frankly, I dont know. If a critic is an honest critic, he will write the same notice from a purchased seat as from a presented one. He is not free to stay away if he is not invited: a newspaper *must* notice a new play, just as much as it must notice an election. He keeps money out of the house by occupying a seat that would otherwise be sold to the public: therefore he costs the management half a guinea. As I have said, he cannot help himself; but that does not alter the fact, or make it less mischievous. Mrs Kendal, who thinks we should pay for our tickets, is quite right; the impetuous ex-manager who thinks we should dress resplendently in return for our free tickets is quite right; and we are absolutely and defencelessly in the wrong.

As to the remedy, I shall deal with that another time.

IBSEN AHEAD!

DONNA DIANA. A poetical comedy in four acts. Adapted, and to a great extent rewritten, from the German version of Moreto's El Desden con el Desden, by Westland Marston. Special revival. Prince of Wales Theatre, 4 November 1896.

[7 *November* 1896]

FEW performances have struck such terror into me as that of Westland Marston's Donna Diana on Wednesday afternoon. Hitherto I have looked tranquilly on at such reversions to the classically romantic phase which held the English stage from the time of Otway to that of Sheridan Knowles and Westland Marston, because the trick of its execution had been so completely lost that the performances were usually as senselessly ridiculous as an attempt to give one of Hasse's operas at Bayreuth with Sucher and Vogl in the principal parts would be. But such occasions have always provoked the disquieting reflection that since it is quite certain Mrs Siddons produced extraordinary effects in such plays in times when they were, except in point of ceremonious manners, just as remote from real life as they are at present, there must clearly be some way of attacking them so as to get hold of an audience and escape all suggestion of derision. And on that came the threatening thought—suppose this way should be rediscovered, could any mortal power prevent the plays coming back to their kingdom and resuming their rightful supremacy? I say rightful; for they have irresistible credentials in their staginess. The theatrical imagination, the love of the boards, produced this art and nursed it. When it was at its height the touches of nature in Shakespear were not endured: the passages were altered and the events reshaped until they were of a piece with the pure-bred drama engendered solely by the passion of the stage-struck, uncrossed by nature, character, poetry, philosophy, social criticism, or any other alien stock. Stage kings and queens, stage lovers, stage tyrants, stage parents, stage villains, and stage heroes were alone to be found in it; and, naturally, they alone were fit for the stage or in their proper place there. Generations of shallow critics, mostly amateurs, have laughed at Partridge for admiring the King in Hamlet more than Hamlet himself (with Garrick in the part), because "anyone could see that the King was an actor." But surely Partridge was right. He went to the theatre to see, not a real limited monarch, but a stage king, speaking as Partridges like to hear a king speaking, and able to have people's heads cut off, or to browbeat treason from behind an invisible hedge of majestically asserted divinity. Fielding misunderstood the matter because in a world of Fieldings there would be neither kings nor Partridges. It is all very well for Hamlet to declare that the business of the theatre is to hold the mirror up to nature. He is allowed to do it out of respect for the bard, just as he is allowed to say to a minor actor, "Do not saw the air thus," though he has himself been sawing the air all the evening, and the unfortunate minor actor has hardly had the chance of cutting a chip off with a penknife. But everybody knows perfectly well that the function of the theatre is to realize for the spectators certain pictures which their imagination craves for, the said pictures being fantastic as the dreams of Alnaschar. Nature is only brought in as an accomplice in the illusion: for example, the actress puts rouge on her cheek instead of burnt cork because it looks more natural;

but the moment the illusion is sacrificed to nature, the house is up in arms and the play is chivied from the stage. I began my own dramatic career by writing plays in which I faithfully held the mirror up to nature. They are much admired in private reading by social reformers, industrial investigators, and revolted daughters; but on one of them being rashly exhibited behind the footlights, it was received with a paroxysm of execration, whilst the mere perusal of the others induces loathing in every person, including myself, in whom the theatrical instinct flourishes in its integrity. Shakespear made exactly one attempt, in Troilus and Cressida, to hold the mirror up to nature; and he probably nearly ruined himself by it. At all events, he never did it again; and practical experience of what was really popular in the rest of his plays led to Venice Preserved and Donna Diana. It was the stagey element that held the stage, not the natural element. In this way, too, the style of execution proper to these plays, an excessively stagey style, was evolved and perfected, the "palmy days" being the days when nature, except as a means of illusion, had totally vanished from both plays and acting. I need not tell over again the story of the late eclipse of the stagey drama during the quarter-century beginning with the success of Robertson, who, by changing the costume and the form of dialogue, and taking the Du Maurieresque, or garden party, plane, introduced a style of execution which effectually broke the tradition of stagey acting, and has left us at the present moment with a rising generation of actors who do not know their business. But ever since the garden-party play suddenly weakened and gave way to The Sign of the Cross and The Red Robe—ever since Mr Lewis Waller as Hotspur, Mr Alexander as King Rassendyl, and Mr Waring as Gil de Berault have suddenly soared from a position of general esteem as well-tailored sticks into enthusiastic repute as vigorous and imaginative actors—it has become only too probable that the genuine old stagey drama only needs for its revival artists who, either by instinct or under the guidance of the Nestors of the profession, shall hit on the right method of execution.

Judge, then, of my consternation when Miss Violet Vanbrugh,

with Nestor Hermann Vezin looking on from a box, and offici-
ally announced as the artistic counsellor of the management, at-
tacked the part of Donna Diana in Westland Marston's obsolete
play with the superbly charged bearing, the picturesque plas-
tique, and the impassioned declamation which one associates with
the Siddons school! More terrifying still, the play began to live
and move under this treatment. Cold drops stood on my brow
as, turning to Mr Archer, whose gloomy and bodeful eye seemed
to look through and through Donna Diana to immeasurable
disaster beyond, I said, "If this succeeds, we shall have the whole
Siddons repertory back again." And, in a way, it did succeed.
If Westland Marston had been a trifle less tamely sensible and
sedately literary, and if the rest of the company had been able to
play up to Miss Vanbrugh's pitch, it might have succeeded with
frightful completeness. Fortunately none of the others quite attained the palmy plane. Mr Vibart's defiant convexity of attitude
had not the true classic balance—in fact, there were moments
when his keeping any balance at all seemed to disprove gravita-
tion. Mr Bourchier, if one must be quite frank, is spreading himself at the waist so rapidly that he is losing his smartness and vocal
resonance, and will, at his present rate of expansion, be fit for no
part except Falstaff in a few years more. The actor who drinks is
in a bad way; but the actor who eats is lost. Why, with such
excellent domestic influences around him, is Mr Bourchier not
restrained from the pleasures of the table? He has also a trick of
dashing at the end of a speech so impetuously that he is carried
fully three words into the next before he can stop himself. If he
has to say "How do you do? Glad to see you. Is your mother
quite well?" it comes out thus: "How do you do glad to. See you
is your mother. Quite well." All of which, though alleviated by
tunics, tights, and blank verse, is the harder to bear because Mr
Bourchier would be one of our best comedians if only he would
exact that much, and nothing less, from himself. Mr Elliot,
cheered to find the old style looking up again, played Perin with
excellent discretion—was, indeed, the only male member of the
cast who materially helped the play; and Mr Kinghorne, though

seemingly more bewildered than encouraged by the setting back of the clock, took his turn as "the sovereign duke of Barcelona" like a man to whom such crazy adventures had once been quite familiar. Miss Irene Vanbrugh, as the malapert waiting wench who, ever since the spacious times of great Elizabeth, has been the genteel blankversemonger's notion of comic relief, fulfilled her doom with a not too ghastly sprightliness; but the other ladies were out of the question: they had not a touch of the requisite carriage and style, and presented themselves as two shapeless anachronisms, like a couple of English housemaids at the Court of Spain. Let us by all means congratulate ourselves to the full on the fact that our young actresses are at least not stagey; but let us also be careful not to confuse the actress who knows too much to be stagey with the actress who does not know enough.

For the rest, all I can say is that I was glad to look again on the front scenes of my youth, and to see Miss Vanbrugh, after announcing her skill as a lute player, appear with an imitation lyre, wrenched from the pedals of an old-fashioned grand piano, and gracefully pluck with her jewelled fingers at four brass bars about an eighth of an inch thick. If Miss Vanbrugh will apply to Mr Arnold Dolmetsch, he will, I have no doubt, be glad to shew her a real lute. She can return the service by shewing him how very effective a pretty woman looks when she is playing it the right way. Though, indeed, that can be learnt from so many fifteenth-century painters that the wonder is that Miss Vanbrugh should not know all about it.

What, then, is to be the end of all this revival of staginess? Is the mirror never again to be held up to nature in the theatre? Do not be alarmed, pious playgoer: people get tired of everything, and of nothing sooner than of what they most like. They will soon begin to loathe these romantic dreams of theirs, and crave to be tormented, vivisected, lectured, sermonized, appalled by the truths which they passionately denounce as monstrosities. Already, on the very top of the wave of stage illusion, rises Ibsen, with his mercilessly set mouth and seer's forehead, menacing us with a new play. Whereupon we realize how we have shirked the last one—how we have put off the torture of Little Eyolf as one puts off a visit to the dentist. But the torture tempts us in spite of ourselves; we feel that it must be gone through with; and now, accordingly, comes Miss Hedda Hilda Gabler Wangel Robins, christened Elizabeth, and bids us not only prepare to be tortured, but subscribe to enable her to buy the rack. A monstrous proposition, but one that has been instantly embraced. No sooner was it made than Mrs Patrick Campbell volunteered for the Ratwife, the smallest part in Little Eyolf, consisting of a couple of dozen speeches in the first act only. (Clever Mrs Pat! it is, between ourselves, the most fascinating page of the play.) Miss Janet Achurch, the original and only Nora Helmer, jumped at the appalling part of Rita, whom nobody else on the stage dare tackle, for all her "gold and green forests." The subscriptions poured in so fast that the rack is now ready, and the executioners are practising so that no pang may miss a moan of its utmost excruciation. Miss Robins herself will play Asta, the sympathetic sister without whom, I verily believe, human nature could not bear this most horrible play. The performances are announced to take place on successive afternoons from the 23rd to the 27th inclusive, at the Avenue Theatre; and there is a sort of hideous humor in the addition that if three people wish to get racked together, they can secure that privilege in the stalls at eight shillings apiece, provided they apply before the subscription closes on the 16th.

It will be remarked as a significant fact that though the women's parts in Little Eyolf have attracted a volunteer cast which no expenditure could better—enormously the strongest that has ever been brought to bear in England on an Ibsen play—we do not hear of eminent actors volunteering for the part of Allmers (to be played, I understand, by Mr Courtenay Thorpe, whose Oswald, in Ghosts, made an impression in America). The reason is that the actor who plays the man's part in Ibsen has to go under the harrow equally with the audience, suffering the shameful extremity of a weak soul stripped naked before an audience looking to him for heroism. Women do not mind ill usage so much, because the strongest position for a woman is that of a victim: besides, Ibsen is evidently highly susceptible to women, on which account they will forgive him anything, even such remorseless brutalities as Rita's reproach to her husband for his indifference to his conjugal privileges: "There stood your champagne; but you tasted it not," which would be an outrage if it were not a masterstroke. Apart from the sensational scene of the drowning of Little Eyolf at the end of the first act, the theatre and its characteristic imaginings are ruthlessly set aside for the relentless holding up of the mirror to nature as seen under Ibsen rays that pierce our most secret cupboards and reveal the grin of the skeleton there. The remorseless exposure and analysis of the marriage founded on passion and beauty and gold and green forests, the identity of its love with the cruellest hate, and of this same hate with the affection excited by the child (the Kreutzer Sonata theme), goes on, without the smallest concession to the claims of staginess, until the pair are finally dismissed, somewhat tritely, to cure themselves as best they can by sea air and work in an orphanage. Yes, we shall have rare afternoons at the Avenue Theatre. If we do not get our eight shillings' worth of anguish it will not be Ibsen's fault.

Oddly enough, Miss Robins announces that the profits of the torture chamber will go towards a fund, under distinguished auditorship, for the performance of other plays, the first being the ultra-romantic, ultra-stagey Mariana of Echegaray. When, on the publication of that play by Mr Fisher Unwin, I urged its suitability for production, nobody would believe me, because events had not then proved the sagacity of my repeated assertions that the public were tired of tailormade plays, and were ripe for a revival of color and costume; and now, alas! my prophecies are forgotten in the excitement created by their fulfilment. That is the tragedy of my career. I shall die as I have lived, poor and unlucky, because I am like a clock that goes fast: I always strike twelve an hour before noon.

BEETHOVEN'S SYMPHONIES

BEETHOVEN AND HIS NINE SYMPHONIES. By George Grove, C.B.
London and New York: Novello, Ewer & Co. 1896.

[14 *November* 1896]

ON cold Saturday afternoons in winter, as I sit in the theatrical desert, making my bread with great bitterness by chronicling insignificant plays and criticizing incompetent players, it sometimes comes upon me that I have forgotten something—omitted something—missed some all-important appointment. This is a legacy from my old occupation of musical critic. All my old occupations leave me such legacies. When I was in my teens I had certain official duties to perform, which involved every day the very strict and punctual discharge of certain annual payments, which were set down in a perpetual diary. I sometimes dream now that I am back at those duties again, but with an amazed consciousness of having allowed them to fall into ruinous arrear for a long time past. My Saturday afternoon misgivings are just like that. They mean that for several years I passed those afternoons in that section of the gallery of the Crystal Palace concert-room which is sacred to Sir George Grove and to the Press. There were two people there who never grew older—Beethoven and Sir George. August Manns's hair changed from raven black to swan white as the years passed; young critics grew middle-aged and middle-aged critics grew old; Rossini lost caste and was shouldered into the promenade; the fire-new overture to Tannhäuser began to wear as threadbare as William Tell; Arabella Goddard went and Sophie Menter came; Joachim, Hallé, Norman Neruda, and Santley no longer struck the rising generations with the old sense of belonging to tomorrow, like Isaye, Paderewski, and Bispham; the men whom I had shocked as an iconoclastic upstart Wagnerian, braying derisively when they observed that "the second subject, appearing in the key of the dominant, contrasts effectively with its predecessor, not only in tonality, but by its suave, melodious character," lived to see me

242

shocked and wounded in my turn by the audacities of J. F. R.; new evening papers launched into musical criticism, and were read publicly by Mr Smith, the eminent drummer, whenever he had fifty bars rest; a hundred trifles marked the flight of time; but Sir George Grove fed on Beethoven's symphonies as the gods in Das Rheingold fed on the apples of Freia, and grew no older. Sometimes, when Mendelssohn's Scotch symphony, or Schubert's Ninth in C, were in the program, he got positively younger, clearing ten years backward in as many minutes when Manns and the band were at their best. I remonstrated with him more than once on this unnatural conduct; and he was always extremely apologetic, assuring me that he was getting on as fast as he could. He even succeeded in producing a wrinkle or two under stress of Berlioz and Raff, Liszt and Wagner; but presently some pianist would come along with the concerto in E flat; and then, if I sat next him, strangers would say to me "Your son, sir, appears to be a very enthusiastic musician." And I could not very well explain that the real bond between us was the fact that Beethoven never ceased to grow on us. In my personality, my views, and my style of criticism there was so much to forgive that many highly amiable persons never quite succeeded in doing it. To Sir George I must have been a positively obnoxious person, not in the least because I was on the extreme left in politics and other matters, but because I openly declared that the finale of Schubert's symphony in C could have been done at half the length and with twice the effect by Rossini. But I knew Beethoven's symphonies from the opening bar of the first to the final chord of the ninth, and yet made new discoveries about them at every fresh performance. And I am convinced that "G" regarded this as evidence of a fundamental rectitude in me which would bear any quantity of superficial aberrations. Which is quite my own opinion too.

It may be asked why I have just permitted myself to write of so eminent a man as Sir George Grove by his initial. That question would not have been asked thirty years ago, when "G," the rhapsodist who wrote the Crystal Palace programs, was one of the best ridiculed men in London. At that time the average pro-grammist would unblushingly write, "Here the composer, by one of those licenses which are, perhaps, permissible under ex-ceptional circumstances to men of genius, but which cannot be too carefully avoided by students desirous of forming a legiti-mate style, has abruptly introduced the dominant seventh of the key of C major into the key of A flat, in order to recover, by a forced modulation, the key relationship proper to the second sub-ject of a movement in F—an awkward device which he might have spared himself by simply introducing his second subject in its true key of C." "G," who was "no musician," cultivated this style in vain. His most conscientious attempts at it never brought him any nearer than "The lovely melody then passes, by a tran-sition of remarkable beauty, into the key of C major, in which it seems to go straight up to heaven." Naturally the average English-man was profoundly impressed by the inscrutable learning of the first style (which I could teach to a poodle in two hours), and thought "G's" obvious sentimentality idiotic. It did not occur to the average Englishman that perhaps Beethoven's symphonies were an affair of sentiment and nothing else. This, of course, was the whole secret of them. Beethoven was the first man who used music with absolute integrity as the expression of his own emo-tional life. Others had shewn how it could be done—had done it themselves as a curiosity of their art in rare, self-indulgent, *unprofessional* moments—but Beethoven made this, and nothing else, his business. Stupendous as the resultant difference was be-tween his music and any other ever heard in the world before his time, the distinction is not clearly apprehended to this day, be-cause there was nothing new in the musical expression of emo-tion: every progression in Bach is sanctified by emotion; and Mozart's subtlety, delicacy, and exquisite tender touch and noble feeling were the despair of all the musical world. But Bach's theme was not himself, but his religion; and Mozart was always the dramatist and story-teller, making the men and women of his imagination speak, and dramatizing even the instruments in his orchestra, so that you know their very sex the moment their voices reach you. Haydn really came nearer to Beethoven, for he is neither the praiser of God nor the dramatist, but, always within the limits of good manners and of his primary function as a purveyor of formal decorative music, a man of moods. This is how he created the symphony and put it ready-made into Beethoven's hand. The revolutionary giant at once seized it, and, throwing supernatural religion, conventional good manners, dramatic fiction, and all external standards and objects into the lumber room, took his own humanity as the material of his music, and expressed it all without compromise, from his roughest jocularity to his holiest aspiration after that purely human reign of intense life—of Freude—when

> Alle Menschen werden Brüder,
> Wo dein sanfter Flügel weilt.

In thus fearlessly expressing himself, he has, by his common humanity, expressed us as well, and shewn us how beautifully, how strongly, how trustworthily we can build with our own real selves. This is what is proved by the immense superiority of the Beethoven symphony to any oratorio or opera.

In this light all Beethoven's work becomes clear and simple; and the old nonsense about his obscurity and eccentricity and stage sublimity and so on explains itself as pure misunderstanding. His criticisms, too, become quite consistent and inevitable: for instance, one is no longer tempted to resent his declaration that Mozart wrote nothing worth considering but parts of Die Zauberflöte (those parts, perhaps, in which the beat of "dein sanfter Flügel" is heard), and to retort upon him by silly comparisons of his tunes with Non più andrai and Deh vieni alla finestra. The man who wrote the eighth symphony has a right to rebuke the man who put his raptures of elation, tenderness, and nobility into the mouths of a drunken libertine, a silly peasant girl, and a conventional fine lady, instead of confessing them to himself, glorying in them, and uttering them without motley as the universal inheritance.

I must not make "G" responsible for my own opinions; but

I leave it to his old readers whether his huge success as a program writer was not due to the perfect simplicity with which he seized and followed up this clue to the intention of Beethoven's symphonies. He seeks always for the mood, and is not only delighted at every step by the result of his search, but escapes quite easily and unconsciously from the boggling and blundering of the men who are always wondering why Beethoven did not do what any professor would have done. He is always joyous, always successful, always busy and interesting, never tedious even when he is superfluous (not that the adepts ever found him so), and always as pleased as Punch when he is not too deeply touched. Sometimes, of course, I do not agree with him. Where he detects anger in the Eighth symphony, I find nothing but boundless, thundering elation. In his right insistence on the jocular element in the symphonies, I think he is occasionally led by his personal sense that octave skips on the bassoon and drum are funny to conclude too hastily that Beethoven was always joking when he used them. And I will fight with him to the death on the trio of the Eighth symphony, maintaining passionately against him and against all creation that those cello arpeggios which steal on tiptoe round the theme so as not to disturb its beauty are only fidgety when they are played "à la Mendelssohn," and that they are perfectly tender and inevitable when they are played "à la Wagner." The passage on this point in Wagner's essay on Conducting is really not half strong enough; and when "G" puts it down to "personal bias" and Wagner's "poor opinion of Mendelssohn," it is almost as if someone had accounted in the same way for Beethoven's opinion of Mozart. Wagner was almost as fond of Mendelssohn's music as "G" is; but he had suffered unbearably, as we all have, from the tradition established by Mendelssohn's conducting of Beethoven's symphonies. Mendelssohn's music is all *nervous* music: his allegros, expressing only excitement and impetuosity without any ground, have fire and motion without substance. Therefore the conductor must, above all things, *keep them going*; if he breaks their lambent flight to dwell on any moment of them, he is lost. With Beethoven the longer you dwell on any moment the more you will find in it. Provided only you do not sacrifice his splendid energetic rhythm and masterly self-possessed emphasis to a maudlin preoccupation with his feeling, you cannot possibly play him too sentimentally; for Beethoven is no reserved gentleman, but a man proclaiming the realities of life. Consequently, when for generations they played Beethoven's allegros exactly as it is necessary to play the overture to Ruy Blas, or Stone him to death—a practice which went on until Wagner's righteous ragings stopped it—our performances of the symphonies simply spoiled the tempers of those who really understood them. For the sake of redeeming that lovely trio from "fidgetiness," "G" must let us face this fact even at the cost of admitting that Wagner was right where Mendelssohn was wrong.

But though it is possible thus to differ here and there from "G," he is never on the wrong lines. He is always the true musician: that is, the man the professors call "no musician"— just what they called Beethoven himself. It is delightful to have all the old programs bound into a volume, with the quotations from the score all complete, and the information brought up to date, and largely supplemented. It is altogether the right sort of book about the symphonies, made for practical use in the concert room under the stimulus of a heartfelt need for bringing the public to Beethoven. I hope it will be followed by another volume or two dealing with the pianoforte concertos—or say with the G, the E flat, the choral fantasia, and the three classical violin concertos: Beethoven, Mendelssohn, and Brahms. And then a Schubert-Mendelssohn-Schumann volume. Why, dear G, should these things be hidden away in old concert programs which never circulate beyond Sydenham?

PEER GYNT IN PARIS

PEER GYNT. A dramatic poem in five acts, by Henrik Ibsen. Théâtre de l'Œuvre (Théâtre de la Nouveauté, Rue Blanche, Paris), 12 November 1896.

PEER GYNT. Translated into French prose, with a few passages in rhymed metre, by M. le Comte Prozor, in La Nouvelle Revue, 15 May and 1 and 15 June 1896.

PEER GYNT. Metrical translation into English by Charles and William Archer. London: Walter Scott. 1892.

[21 *November* 1896]

THE humiliation of the English stage is now complete. Paris, that belated capital which makes the intelligent Englishman imagine himself back in the Dublin or Edinburgh of the eighteenth century, has been beforehand with us in producing Peer Gynt. Within five months of its revelation in France through the Comte Prozor's translation, it has been produced by a French actor-manager who did *not* play the principal part himself, but undertook two minor ones which were not even mentioned in the program. We have had the much more complete translation of Messrs William and Charles Archer in our hands for four years; and we may confidently expect the first performance in 1920 or thereabouts, with much trumpeting of the novelty of the piece and the daring of the manager.

Peer Gynt will finally smash anti-Ibsenism in Europe, because Peer is everybody's hero. He has the same effect on the imagination that Hamlet, Faust, and Mozart's Don Juan have had. Thousands of people who will never read another line of Ibsen will read Peer Gynt again and again; and millions will be conscious of him as part of the poetic currency of the world without reading him at all. The witches in Macbeth, the ghost in Hamlet, the statue in Don Juan, and Mephistopheles, will not be more familiar to the twentieth century than the Boyg, the Button Moulder, the Strange Passenger, and the Lean Person. It is of no use to argue about it: nobody who is susceptible to legendary poetry can

248

escape the spell if he once opens the book, or—as I can now affirm from experience—if he once sees even the shabbiest representation of a few scenes from it. Take the most conscientious anti-Ibsenite you can find, and let him enlarge to his heart's content on the defects of Ibsen. Then ask him what about Peer Gynt. He will instantly protest that you have hit him unfairly—that Peer Gynt must be left out of the controversy. I hereby challenge any man in England with a reputation to lose to deny that Peer Gynt is not one of his own and the world's very choicest treasures in its kind. Mind, gentlemen, I do not want to know whether Peer Gynt is right or wrong, good art or bad art: the question is whether you can get away from it—whether you ever had the same sensation before in reading a dramatic poem—whether you ever had even a kindred sensation except from the work of men whose greatness is now beyond question. The only people who have escaped the spell which, for good or evil, pleasurably or painfully, Ibsen's dramas cast on the imagination, are either those light-hearted paragraphists who gather their ideas by listening to one another braying, or else those who are taken out of their depth by Ibsen exactly as the music-hall amateur is taken out of his depth by Beethoven.

The Parisian production has been undertaken by M. Lugné Poë, of the Théâtre de l'Œuvre, whose performances of Ibsen and Maeterlinck here are well remembered. He used the translation by the Comte Prozor, which appeared in La Nouvelle Revue, chiefly in prose, but with a few irresistibly metrical passages done into rhymed verse. Unfortunately it was incomplete, especially in the fourth and fifth acts. The Saeter girls were omitted. The Anitra episode was represented by only one scene. The first part of the soliloquy before Memnon's statue was dovetailed into the last half of the soliloquy before the Sphinx, as if the two monuments were one and the same. In the fifth act the Strange Passenger and the Lean Person (the devil) were altogether sacrificed; and the Button Moulder's explanation to Peer of what "being oneself" really means was cut out of his part—an indefensibly stupid mutilation. The episode of the man who cuts off his finger, with his funeral in the last act, as well as the auction scene which follows, also vanished. M. Lugné Poë, in his acting version, restored the Strange Passenger's first entrance on board the ship; but in other respects he took the Prozor version with all its omissions, and cut it down still more. For instance, all the Egyptian scenes, Memnon, Sphinx, pyramids, Begriffenfeldt, Cairo madhouse and all, went at one slash. The scene in the water after the shipwreck, where Peer pushes the unfortunate cook off the capsized boat, but holds him up by the hair for a moment to allow him to pray without eliciting anything more to the purpose than "Give us this day our daily bread," was cut, with, of course, the vital episode of the second appearance of the Strange Passenger. As the performance nevertheless lasted nearly four hours —including, however, a good deal of silly encoring of Grieg's music, and some avoidable intervals between the scenes—extensive curtailment was inevitable, a complete representation being only possible under Bayreuth conditions.

There was only one instance of deliberate melodramatic vulgarization of the poem. In the fourth act, after Peer has made a hopeless donkey of himself with his Hottentot Venus, and been tricked and robbed by her, he argues his way in his usual fashion back into his own self-respect, arriving in about three minutes at the point of saying,

> It's excusable, sure, if I hold up my head
> And feel my worth as the man, Peer Gynt,
> Also called Human-life's Emperor.

At this point Ibsen introduces the short scene in which we see the woman whom Peer has deserted, and who is faithfully waiting for him in the north, sitting outside the old hut in the sunshine, spinning and tending her goats, and singing her song of blessing on the absent man. Now it is of the essence of the contrast that Peer, excellently qualified at this moment, not to be the hero of Solveig's affectionate faith, but to make an intoxicating success in London at a Metropole banquet as a Nitrate King or big showman, should never think of her (though he is constantly recalling, more or less inaccurately, all sorts of scraps of his old experiences, including his amours with the Green Clad One), but should go on to the climax of his coronation by the lunatic Begriffenfeldt as "Emperor of Himself" with a straw crown in the Cairo bedlam. I regret to say that M. Lugné Poë so completely missed Ibsen's intention here, that he made Peer go to sleep *à propos de bottes*; darkened the stage; and exhibited Solveig to him as a dream vision in the conventional Drury Lane fourth-act style. For which, in my opinion (which is softened by the most friendly personal disposition towards M. Poë), he ought to have been gently led away and guillotined. It is quite clear that Peer Gynt remains absolutely unredeemed all through this elderly period of his career; and even when we meet him in the last act returning to Norway an old man, he is still the same clever, vain, greedy, sentimental, rather fascinating braggart and egoist. When the ship runs down a boat he frantically denounces the inhumanity of the cook and sailors because they will not accept his money to risk their lives in an attempt to save the drowning men. Immediately after, when the ship is wrecked, he drowns the cook to save his own life without a moment's remorse. Then up comes the Strange Passenger out of the depths to ask him whether he has never even once—say once in six months—felt that strange sense (that occasionally desperately dangerous sense, as Ibsen well knows) for which we have dozens of old creed names—"divine grace," "the fear of God," "conviction of sin," and so on—but no quite satisfactory modern one. Peer no more understands what he means than if he were an average London journalist. His glimpse of the fact that the Strange Passenger is not, as he at first feared, the devil, but rather a divine messenger, simply relieves his terror. In the country graveyard where, chancing on the funeral of the hero of the chopped finger, a man completely the reverse of himself, he hears the priest's tribute to the character of the deceased, he says:

> I could almost believe it was I that slept
> And heard in a vision my panegyric.

In these scenes, in the one at the auction, in the wood where, comparing himself to the wild onion he is eating, he strips off the successive layers to find the core of it, and, finding that it is all layers and no core, exclaims, "Nature is witty," there is no sign of the final catastrophe except a certain growing desperation, an ironical finding of himself out, which makes a wonderful emotional undercurrent through the play in this act. It is not until he stumbles on the hut, and hears the woman singing in it, that the blow falls, and for the first time the mysterious sense mentioned by the Strange Passenger seizes him. With this point rightly brought out, the symbolism of the following scenes becomes more vivid and real than all the real horses and real water ever lavished on a popular melodrama. Peer's wild run through the night over the charred heath, stumbling over the threadballs and broken straws, dripped upon by the dewdrops, pelted by the withered leaves that are all that is left of the songs he should have sung, the tears he should have wept, the beliefs he should have proclaimed, the deeds he should have achieved, is fantastic only in so far as it deals with realities that cannot be presented prosaically. As the divine case against Peer is followed up, the interest accumulates in a way that no Adelphi court-martial can even suggest. The reappearance of the Strange Passenger as the Button Moulder commissioned to melt up Peer in his casting ladle as so much unindividualized raw material; Peer's frantic attempts to prove that he has always been pre-eminently himself, and his calling as a witness the old beggared Troll king, who testifies, on the contrary, that Peer is a mere troll, shrunk into nothing by the troll principle of being sufficient to himself; Peer's change of ground, and his attempt to escape even into hell by proving that he had at least risen to some sort of individuality as a great sinner, only to have his poor little list of sins (among which he never dreams of mentioning his desertion of Solveig—the only sin big enough to save him) contemptuously rejected by the devil as not worth wasting brimstone on; and his final conviction and despair, from which he is only rescued by the discovery of "Peer Gynt as himself" in the faith, hope, and love of the blind old woman who takes him to her arms: all this deadly earnest is handled with such ironic vivacity, such grimly intimate humor, and finally with such tragic pathos, that it excites, impresses, and touches even those whom it utterly bewilders. Indeed, the ending is highly popular, since it can so easily be taken as implying the pretty middle-class doctrine that all moral difficulties find their solution in love as the highest of all things—a doctrine which, after several years' attentive observation, and a few careful personal experiments, I take to be the utmost attainable extreme of nonsensical wickedness and folly. The real Ibsenist solution is, of course, that there is no "solution" at all, any more than there is a philosophers' stone.

At the performance by L'Œuvre, this trial of a sinner was very concisely summarized; but the point of it was by no means entirely missed. The Strange Passenger received a round of applause; the Button Moulder was appreciated; and the demonstration elicited by the climax of Peer Gynt's burst of despair, "Qu'on trace ces mots sur ma tombe: Ci-gît personne," shewed how effectually Ibsen, at his most abstract point, can draw blood even from a congenitally unmetaphysical nation, to which the play seems as much a mixture of sentiment and stage *diablerie* as Faust seemed to Gounod. Two other scenes moved the audience deeply. One was where Solveig joins Peer in the mountains, and is left by him with the words, "Be my way long or short, you must wait for me"; and the other, which produced a tremendous effect—we should have Peer Gynt in London this season if any of our actor-managers had been there to witness it—the death of Peer's mother. The rest was listened to with alert interest and occasional amazement, which was not always Ibsen's fault. Only one scene—that with the Boyg—failed, because it was totally unintelligible. It was presented as a continuation of the Dovre scene—in itself puzzling enough; and the audience stared in wonder at a pitchy dark stage, with Peer howling, a strange voice squealing behind the scenes, a woman calling at intervals, and not a word that any one could catch. It was let pass with politely smothered laughter as a characteristic Ibsen insanity;

though whether this verdict would have been materially changed if the dialogue had been clearly followed is an open question; for the Boyg (called Le Tordu by the Comte Prozor, and Le Tortueux in the playbill), having elusiveness as his natural speciality, is particularly hard to lay hold of in the disguise of an allegory.

As to the performance, I am not sure that I know how good the actors were; for Ibsen's grip of humanity is so powerful that almost any presentable performer can count on a degree of illusion in his parts which Duse herself failed to produce when she tried Shakespear. To say that Deval did not exhaust his opportunity as Peer is only to say that he is not quite the greatest tragic, comic, and character actor in the world. He misunderstood the chronology of the play, and made Peer no older on the ship than in Morocco, whilst in the last scene he made him a doddering centenarian. He spoiled the famous comment on the blowing up of the yacht, "God takes fatherly thought for my personal weal; but economical!—no, that he isnt," by an untimely stage fall; but otherwise he managed the part intelligently and played with spirit and feeling. Albert-Mayer played no less than four parts: the Boyg, Aslak the Smith, the Strange Passenger, and the Button Moulder, and was good in all, bar the Boyg. Lugné Poë himself played two parts, Solveig's father and the travelling Englishman, Mr Cotton. Mr Cotton was immense. He was a fair, healthy, good-looking young man, rather heavy in hand, stiff with a quiet determination to hold his own among that gang of damned foreigners, and speaking French with an accent which made it a joy to hear him say "C'est trop dire" ("Say trow deah," with the tongue kept carefully back from the teeth). He certainly did infinite credit to the activity and accuracy of Lugné Poë's observation during his visit to this country. Suzanne Auclare, who will be vividly remembered by all those who saw her here as Hilda Wangel in The Master Builder, was cast for Solveig, not altogether wisely, I think, as the part is too grave and maternal for her. In the last scene, which she chanted in a golden voice very much à la Bernhardt, she did not represent Solveig as blind, nor

did her make-up suggest anything more than a dark Southern
woman of about forty-two, although Peer was clearly at least
ninety-nine, and by no means young for his age: in fact, he might
have been the original pilgrim with the white locks flowing. Her
naïve charm carried her well through the youthful scenes; but
on the whole she was a little afraid of the part, and certainly did
not make the most of it. Madame Barbieri, as Aase, was too much
the stage crone; but she probably had no alternative to that or
betraying her real age, which was much too young. She must
have been abundantly satisfied with the overwhelming effect of
her death scene. The only altogether inefficient member of the
cast was the Green Clad One, who did not understand her part,
and did not attend to Ibsen's directions. And the Brat, unfortunately, was a rather pretty child, very inadequately disfigured
by a dab of burnt cork on the cheek.

Many thousand pounds might be lavished on the scenery and
mounting of Peer Gynt. M. Lugné Poë can hardly have lavished
twenty pounds on it. Peer Gynt's costume as the Prophet was
of the Dumb Crambo order: his caftan was an old dressing-gown,
and his turban, though authentic, hardly new. There was no
horse and—to my bitter disappointment—no pig. A few pantomime masks, with allfours and tails, furnished forth the trolls
in the Dovre scene; and the explosion of the yacht was represented
by somebody upsetting a chair in the wing. Anitra, with black
curtains of hair transfixed by peonies over each ear, a whited
face, and a general air of being made up with the most desperate
inadequacy of person and wardrobe after Mrs Patrick Campbell's
Juliet, insisted upon an encore for a dance which M. Fouquier,
of the Figaro, described, without exaggeration, as "les contorsions
d'un lièvre qui a reçu un coup de feu dans les reins." And yet
this performance took place in a theatre nearly as large as Drury
Lane, completely filled with an audience of much the same class
as one sees here at a Richter concert. Miss Robins would not
dream of presenting Little Eyolf at the Avenue Theatre next
week so cheaply. But it mattered very little. M. Lugné Poë
shewed in London that he could catch more of the atmosphere

of a poetic play with the most primitive arrangements than some of our managers succeed in doing at a ruinous outlay. Of course the characteristic Northern hardheaded, hardfisted humor, the Northern power of presenting the deepest truths in the most homely grotesques, was missed: M. Poë, with all his realism, could no more help presenting the play sentimentally and sublimely than M. Lamoureux can help conducting the overture to Tannhäuser as if it were the Marseillaise; but the universality of Ibsen makes his plays come home to all nations; and Peer Gynt is as good a Frenchman as a Norwegian, just as Dr Stockman is as intelligible in Bermondsey or Bournemouth as he is in his native town.

I have to express my obligation to the editor of La Nouvelle Revue for very kindly lending me his private copy of the numbers containing the Prozor translation. Otherwise I must have gone without, as the rest of the edition was sold out immediately after the performance.

LITTLE EYOLF

LITTLE EYOLF. A play in three acts, by Henrik Ibsen. Avenue Theatre, 23 November 1896.   [28 *November* 1896]

THE happiest and truest epithet that has yet been applied to the Ibsen drama in this country came from Mr Clement Scott when he said that Ibsen was "suburban." That is the whole secret of it. If Mr Scott had only embraced his discovery instead of quarrelling with it, what a splendid Ibsen critic he would have made! Suburbanity at present means modern civilization. The active, germinating life in the households of today cannot be typified by an aristocratic hero, an ingenuous heroine, a gentleman-forger abetted by an Artful Dodger, and a parlormaid who takes half-sovereigns and kisses from the male visitors. Such interiors exist on the stage, and nowhere else: therefore the only people who are accustomed to them and at home in them are the dramatic critics. But if you ask me where you can find the Helmer household, the Allmers household, the Solness household, the Rosmer household, and all the other Ibsen households, I reply, "Jump out of a train anywhere between Wimbledon and Haslemere; walk into the first villa you come to; and there you are." Indeed you need not go so far: Hampstead, Maida Vale, or West Kensington will serve your turn; but it is as well to remind people that the true suburbs are now the forty-mile radius, and that Camberwell and Brixton are no longer the suburbs, but the overflow of Gower Street—the genteel slums, in short. And this suburban life, except in so far as it is totally vegetable and undramatic, is the life depicted by Ibsen. Doubtless some of our critics are quite sincere in thinking it a vulgar life, in considering the conversations which men hold with their wives in it improper, in finding its psychology puzzling and unfamiliar, and in forgetting that its bookshelves and its music cabinets are laden with works which did not exist for them, and which are the daily bread of young women educated very differently from the sisters and wives of their day. No wonder they are not at ease in an atmosphere of ideas and assumptions and attitudes which seem to them bewildering, morbid, affected, extravagant, and altogether incredible as the common currency of suburban life. But Ibsen knows better. His suburban drama is the inevitable outcome of a suburban civilization (meaning a civilization that appreciates fresh air); and the true explanation of Hedda Gabler's vogue is that given by Mr Grant Allen—"I take her in to dinner twice a week."

Another change that the critics have failed to reckon with is the change in fiction. Byron remarked that

> Romances paint at full length people's wooings,
> But only give a bust of marriages.

That was true enough in the days of Sir Walter Scott, when a betrothed heroine with the slightest knowledge of what marriage meant would have shocked the public as much as the same ignorance today would strike it as tragic if real, and indecent if simulated. The result was that the romancer, when he came to a love scene, had frankly to ask his "gentle reader" to allow him to omit the conversation as being necessarily too idiotic to interest anyone. We have fortunately long passed out of that stage in novels. By the time we had reached Vanity Fair and Middlemarch —both pretty old and prim stories now—marriage had become the starting point of our romances. Love is as much the romancer's theme as ever; but married love and the courtships of young people who are appalled by the problems of life and motherhood have left the governesses and curates, the Amandas and Tom Joneses of other days, far out of sight. Ten years ago the stage was as far behind Sir Walter Scott as he is behind Madame Sarah Grand. But when Ibsen took it by the scruff of the neck just as Wagner took the Opera, then, willy nilly, it had to come along. And now what are the critics going to do? The Ibsen drama is pre-eminently the drama of marriage. If dramatic criticism receives it in the spirit of the nurse's husband in Romeo and Juliet, if it grins and makes remarks about "the secrets of the alcove," if it pours forth columns which are half pornographic pleasantry and the other half sham propriety, then the end will be, not in the least that Ibsen will be banned, but that dramatic criticism will cease to be read. And what a frightful blow that would be to English culture!

Little Eyolf is an extraordinarily powerful play, although none of the characters are as fascinatingly individualized as Solness or Rosmer, Hedda or Nora. The theme is a marriage—an ideal marriage from the suburban point of view. A young gentleman, a student and an idealist, is compelled to drudge at teaching to support himself. He meets a beautiful young woman. They fall in love with one another; and by the greatest piece of luck in the world (suburbanly considered) she has plenty of money. Thus he is set free by his marriage to live his own life in his own way. That is just where an ordinary play leaves off, and just where an Ibsen play begins. The husband begins to make those discoveries which everybody makes, except, apparently, the dramatic critics. First, that love, instead of being a perfectly homogeneous, un-changing, unending passion, is of all things the most mutable. It will pass through several well-marked stages in a single evening, and, whilst seeming to slip back to the old starting point the next evening, will yet not slip quite back; so that in the course of years it will appear that the moods of an evening were the anticipation of the evolution of a lifetime. But the evolution does not occur in different people at the same time or in the same order. Consequently the hero of Little Eyolf, being an imaginative, nervous, thoughtful person, finds that he has had enough of caresses, and wants to dream alone among the mountain peaks and solitudes, whilst his wife, a warm-blooded creature, has only found her love intensified to a fiercely jealous covetousness of him. His main refuge from this devouring passion is in his peacefully affectionate relations with his sister, and in certain suburban dreams very common among literary amateurs living on their wives' incomes: to wit, forming the mind and character of his child, and writing a great book (on Human Responsibility if you please). Of course the wife, in her jealousy, hates the sister, hates the child, hates the book, hates her husband for making her jealous of them, and hates herself for her hatreds with the frightful logic of greedy, insatiable love. Enter then our old friend, Ibsen's divine messenger. The Ratwife, alias the Strange Passenger, alias the Button Moulder, alias Ulrik Brendel, comes in to ask whether there are any little gnawing things there of which she can rid the house. They do not understand—the divine messenger in Ibsen is never understood, especially by the critics. So the little gnawing thing in the house—the child—follows the Ratwife and is drowned, leaving the pair awakened by the blow to a frightful consciousness of themselves, the woman as a mere animal, the man as a moonstruck nincompoop, keeping up appearances as a suburban lady and gentleman with nothing to do but enjoy themselves. Even the sister has discovered now that she is not really a sister—also a not unprecedented suburban possibility—and sees that the passionate stage is ahead of her too; so, though she loves the husband, she has to get out of his way by the pre-eminently suburban expedient of marrying a man whom she does not love, and who, like Rita, is warm-blooded and bent on the undivided, unshared possession of the object of his passion. At last the love of the woman passes out of the passionate stage; and immediately, with the practical sense of her sex, she proposes, not to go up into the mountains or to write amateur treatises, but to occupy herself with her duties as landed proprietress, instead of merely spending the revenues of her property in keeping a monogamic harem. The gentleman asks to be allowed to lend a hand; and immediately the storm subsides, easily enough, leaving the couple on solid ground. This is the play, as actual and near to us as the Brighton and South Coast Railway—this is the mercilessly heart-searching sermon, touching all of us somewhere, and some of us everywhere, which we, the critics, have summed up as "secrets of the alcove." Our cheeks, whose whiteness Mr Arthur Roberts has assailed in vain, have mantled at "the coarseness and vulgarity which are noted characteristics of the author" (I am quoting, with awe, my fastidiously high-toned colleague of the Standard). And yet the divine messenger only meant to make us ashamed of ourselves. That is the way divine messengers always do muddle their business.

The performance was of course a very remarkable one. When, in a cast of five, you have the three best yet discovered actresses of their generation, you naturally look for something extraordinary. Miss Achurch was the only one who ran any risk of failure. The Ratwife and Asta are excellent parts; but they are not arduous ones. Rita, on the other hand, is one of the heaviest ever written: any single act of it would exhaust an actress of no more than ordinary resources. But Miss Achurch was more than equal to the occasion. Her power seemed to grow with its own expenditure. The terrible outburst at the end of the first act did not leave a scrape on her voice (which appears to have the compass of a military band) and threw her into victorious action in that tearing second act instead of wrecking her. She played with all her old originality and success, and with more than her old authority over her audience. She had to speak some dangerous lines —lines of a kind that usually find out the vulgar spots in an audience and give an excuse for a laugh—but nobody laughed or wanted to laugh at Miss Achurch. "There stood your champagne;

but you tasted it not," neither shirked nor slurred, but driven home to the last syllable, did not elicit an audible breath from a completely dominated audience. Later on I confess I lost sight of Rita a little in studying the surprising capacity Miss Achurch shewed as a dramatic instrument. For the first time one clearly saw the superfluity of power and the vehemence of intelligence which make her often so reckless as to the beauty of her methods of expression. As Rita she produced almost every sound that a big human voice can, from a creak like the opening of a rusty canal lock to a melodious tenor note that the most robust Siegfried might have envied. She looked at one moment like a young, well-dressed, very pretty woman: at another she was like a desperate creature just fished dripping out of the river by the Thames Police. Yet another moment, and she was the incarnation of impetuous, ungovernable strength. Her face was sometimes winsome, sometimes listlessly wretched, sometimes like the head of a statue of Victory, sometimes suffused, horrible, threatening, like Bellona or Medusa. She would cross from left to right like a queen, and from right to left with, so to speak, her toes turned in, her hair coming down, and her slippers coming off. A more utter recklessness, not only of fashion, but of beauty, could hardly be imagined: beauty to Miss Achurch is only one effect among others to be produced, not a condition of all effects. But then she can do what our beautiful actresses cannot do: attain the force and terror of Sarah Bernhardt's most vehement explosions without Sarah's violence and abandonment, and with every appearance of having reserves of power still held in restraint. With all her cleverness as a realistic actress she must be classed technically as a heroic actress; and I very much doubt whether we shall see her often until she comes into the field with a repertory as highly specialized as that of Sir Henry Irving or Duse. For it is so clear that she would act an average London success to pieces and play an average actor-manager off the stage, that we need not expect to see much of her as that useful and pretty auxiliary, a leading lady.

Being myself a devotee of the beautiful school, I like being enchanted by Mrs Patrick Campbell better than being frightened, harrowed, astonished, conscience-stricken, devastated, and dreadfully delighted in general by Miss Achurch's untamed genius. I have seen Mrs Campbell play the Ratwife twice, once quite enchantingly, and once most disappointingly. On the first occasion Mrs Campbell divined that she was no village harridan, but the messenger of heaven. She played supernaturally, beautifully: the first notes of her voice came as from the spheres into all that suburban prose: she played to the child with a witchery that might have drawn him not only into the sea, but into her very bosom. Nothing jarred except her obedience to Ibsen's stage direction in saying "Down where all the rats are" harshly, instead of getting the effect, in harmony with her own inspired reading, by the most magical tenderness. The next time, to my unspeakable fury, she amused herself by playing like any melodramatic old woman, a profanation for which, whilst my critical life lasts, never will I forgive her. Of Miss Robins's Asta it is difficult to say much, since the part, played as she plays it, does not exhibit anything like the full extent of her powers. Asta is a study of a temperament—the quiet, affectionate, enduring, reassuring, faithful, domestic temperament. That is not in the least Miss Robins's temperament: she is nervous, restless, intensely self-conscious, eagerly energetic. In parts which do not enable her to let herself loose in this, her natural way, she falls back on pathos, on mute misery, on a certain delicate plaintive note in her voice and grace in her bearing which appeal to our sympathy and pity without realizing any individuality for us. She gave us, with instinctive tact and refinement, the "niceness," the considerateness, the ladylikeness, which differentiate Asta from the wilful, passionate, somewhat brutal Rita. Perhaps only an American playing against an Englishwoman could have done it so discriminately; but beyond this and the pathos there was nothing: Asta was only a picture, and, like a picture, did not develop. The picture, being sympathetic and pretty, has been much admired; but those who have not seen Miss Robins play Hilda Wangel have no idea of what she is like when she really acts her part instead of merely giving an urbanely pictorial recommendation of it. As to Allmers, how could he recommend himself to spectators who saw in him everything that they are ashamed of in themselves? Mr Courtenay Thorpe played very intelligently, which, for such a part, and in such a play, is saying a good deal; but he was hampered a little by the change from the small and intimate auditorium in which he has been accustomed to play Ibsen, to the Avenue, which ingeniously combines the acoustic difficulties of a large theatre with the pecuniary capacity of a small one. Master Stewart Dawson, as Eyolf, was one of the best actors in the company. Mr Lowne, as Borgheim, was as much out of tone as a Leader sunset in a Rembrandt picture—no fault of his, of course (the audience evidently liked him), but still a blemish on the play.

And this brings me to a final criticism. The moment I put myself into my old attitude as musical critic, I at once perceive that the performance, as a whole, was an unsatisfactory one. You may remonstrate, and ask me how I can say so after admitting that the performers shewed such extraordinary talent—even genius. It is very simple, nevertheless. Suppose you take Isaye, Sarasate, Joachim, and Hollmann, and tumble them all together to give a scratch performance of one of Beethoven's posthumous quartets at some benefit concert. Suppose you also take the two De Reszkes, Calvé, and Miss Eames, and set them to sing a glee under the same circumstances. They will all shew prodigious individual talent; but the resultant performances of the quartet and glee will be inferior, as wholes, to that of an ordinary glee club or group of musicians who have practised for years together. The Avenue performance was a parallel case. There was nothing like the atmosphere which Lugné Poë got in Rosmersholm. Miss Achurch managed to play the second act as if she had played it every week for twenty years; but otherwise the performance, interesting as it was, was none the less a scratch one. If only the company could keep together for a while! But perhaps that is too much to hope for at present, though it is encouraging to see that the performances are to be continued next week, the five matinees—all crowded, by the way—having by no means exhausted the demand for places.

Several performances during the past fortnight remain to be chronicled; but Ibsen will have his due; and he has not left me room enough to do justice to any one else this week.

TOUJOURS SHAKESPEAR

THE MANXMAN. Dramatized by Wilson Barrett from a novel by Hall Caine. Lyric Theatre, 16 November 1896.

A WHITE ELEPHANT. An original farce in three acts, by R. C. Carton. Comedy Theatre, 19 November 1896.

THE KISS OF DELILAH. By George Grant and James Lisle. Drury Lane, 28 November 1896.

AS YOU LIKE IT. St James's Theatre, 2 December 1896.

[5 *December* 1896]

ON visiting the Lyric Theatre at Mr Wilson Barrett's invitation I was much taken aback to find the Manxman still extant. For did I not slay him at the Shaftesbury, and remonstrate vehemently with Mr Hall Caine for letting him loose? Happily, he is not his old self at the Lyric. He only lends his Manxsome name to an elaborate pretext for a display of acting by Mr Wilson Barrett in a Ham Peggotty part. And a very excellent piece of acting it is too —skilful and well judged in execution to the last degree, with just the right feeling and the right humor, and built, not on a virtuous hero formula, but on a definite idiosyncratic character conception. Add to this central attraction such effects of Mr Wilson Barrett's unrivalled managership as the quiet certainty of the business and effects, the excellent lighting of the stage, the simple touches of verisimilitude just in the right places, the filling of the small parts apparently by picked character actors (though really only by young people who have had a competent adviser instead of being left to themselves or deliberately set wrong, as they are at most theatres), and you have the materials for a success out of all proportion to the merits of The Manxman as a serious modern play. Having an unconquerable respect for a man who knows his business, I find in a production like this a satisfaction proof against the fact that to my mind the virtues of Pete Quilliam would not only justify any woman in leaving him, but must, if she were human, absolutely drive her to do so in spite of all ties. The great merit of Mr Wilson Barrett's version is that it almost dispenses with that profound study of a human soul, the Deemster. Having dismissed him myself, at first sight, with the thumb to the nose, I did not regret his absence. I do not see why Mr Hall Caine should not write excellent dramas if he would give up wallowing in second-hand literary pathos, and realize the value of actual life. But, after all, the people who prefer cheap plays would be the losers; and why should they be sacrificed to please superior persons like me?

A White Elephant at the Comedy is as pleasant as Mr Carton's plays usually are, but has their easy-going defect of not making the most either of itself or of the cast. Nobody is more fertile than Mr Carton in happy notions, both of story and character; and nobody, apparently, is more flippantly incapable of keeping hold of them or working them out to any telling purpose. He has had a capital idea of a part for Mr Hawtrey, which, after all, does not come to much; a capital idea of a part for Miss Boucicault, which comes to less; and a capital idea of a part for Miss Lottie Venne, which so nearly comes to nothing at all that it is with the greatest difficulty that she is brought on the stage for a few minutes in the last act to utter a handful of the poorest lines that ever fell to the lot of an all-but-extra lady in a musical farce. There are only two good parts in the piece: one, Mrs Nickleby at the age of thirty. most amusingly played and perfectly interpreted by Miss Compton, who really does know how to study a character and act it; and the other a fretful middle-class lord of creation, realized with most effective vividness through the energy and concentration of Mr Brookfield, who gains ground instead of losing it by changing from short parts to long ones. Two unimportant parts are raised to prominence by the performers, Mr Kemble being funny as the gouty old guest, whilst Mrs Charles Calvert is quite stupendous as the housekeeper. Her part, as written by Mr Carton, is nothing but a few scraps of Gampish, Mrs Brownish fun, such as any of the staff of Punch could reel off by the yard. As conceived by Mrs Calvert, and developed in eloquent silence between the scraps, it is a creation, not to be contemplated without shrieks of laughter tempered by an awe-struck conviction of its reality. A more perfect example of comic acting based, not on a bag of tricks and a few caricatured poses and grimaces, but on the golden rule, "Take care of the charac-ter, and the lines will take care of themselves," could not be de-sired. Miss Mansfield, on the other hand, is again forced into cari-cature by one of those silly parts which will end by costing her the reputation she gained in The Prude's Progress, by her clever playing of a part which was not silly. Mr Eric Lewis, with Messrs Cecil Ramsay and W. T. Lovell, make up a cast of prodigal bril-liancy.

At Drury Lane we have had another drama, ostensibly by George Grant and James Lisle, but really, I suppose, by Mr John Coleman. My regard for Mr Coleman forbids me to dwell on the results of his amiable but deplorable addiction to dramatic com-position. Mr Hermann Vezin stood between the audience and Mr Coleman's Robespierre with sufficient resolution to get him safely past a not altogether spontaneously assembled audience; and Miss Hilda Spong wrecked herself devotedly on the part of Herminie Vanhove, which I humbly advise her not to play again. Miss Edith Jordan and Mr Sam Johnson added to the devastation by copious doses of "comic relief." Altogether a horribly bad play.

The irony of Fate prevails at the St James's Theatre. For years we have been urging the managers to give us Shakespear's plays as he wrote them, playing them intelligently and enjoyingly as pleasant stories, instead of mutilating them, altering them, and celebrating them as superstitious rites. After three hundred years Mr George Alexander has taken us at our words, as far as the clock permits, and gives us As You Like It at full four hours' length. And, alas! it is just too late: the Bard gets his chance at the moment when his obsolescence has become unendurable.

Nevertheless, we were right; for this production of Mr Alexander's, though the longest, is infinitely the least tedious, and, in those parts which depend on the management, the most delightful I have seen. But yet, what a play! It was in As You Like It that the sententious William first began to openly exploit the fondness of the British Public for sham moralizing and stage "philosophy." It contains one passage that specially exasperates me. Jaques, who spends his time, like Hamlet, in vainly emulating the wisdom of Sancho Panza, comes in laughing in a superior manner because he has met a fool in the forest, who

> Says very wisely, It is ten o'clock.
> Thus we may see [quoth he] how the world wags.
> Tis but an hour ago since it was nine;
> And after one hour more twill be eleven.
> And so, from hour to hour, we ripe and ripe;
> And then, from hour to hour, we rot and rot;
> And thereby hangs a tale.

Now, considering that this fool's platitude is precisely the "philosophy" of Hamlet, Macbeth ("Tomorrow and tomorrow and tomorrow," etc.), Prospero, and the rest of them, there is something unendurably aggravating in Shakespear giving himself airs with Touchstone, as if he, the immortal, ever, even at his sublimest, had anything different or better to say himself. Later on he misses a great chance. Nothing is more significant than the statement that "all the world's a stage." The whole world *is* ruled by theatrical illusion. Between the Cæsars, the emperors, the Christian heroes, the Grand Old Men, the kings, prophets, saints, judges, and heroes of the newspapers and the popular imagination, and the actual Juliuses, Napoleons, Gordons, Gladstones, and so on, there is the same difference as between Hamlet and Sir Henry Irving. The case is not one of fanciful similitude but of identity. The great critics are those who penetrate and understand the illusion: the great men are those who, as dramatists planning the development of nations, or as actors carrying out the drama, are behind the scenes of the world instead of gaping and

gushing in the auditorium after paying their taxes at the doors.
And yet Shakespear, with the rarest opportunities of observing
this, lets his pregnant metaphor slip, and, with his usual incapacity for pursuing any idea, wanders off into a grandmotherly
Elizabethan edition of the advertisement of Cassell's Popular
Educator. How anybody over the age of seven can take any interest in a literary toy so silly in its conceit and common in its
ideas as the Seven Ages of Man passes my understanding.
Even the great metaphor itself is inaccurately expressed; for
the world is a playhouse, not merely a stage; and Shakespear
might have said so without making his blank verse scan
any worse than Richard's exclamation, "All the world to
nothing!"

And then Touchstone, with his rare jests about the knight that
swore by his honor they were good pancakes! Who would endure such humor from anyone but Shakespear?—an Eskimo
would demand his money back if a modern author offered him
such fare. And the comfortable old Duke, symbolical of the
British villa dweller, who likes to find "sermons in stones and
good in everything," and then to have a good dinner! This un-
venerable impostor, expanding on his mixed diet of pious twaddle
and venison, rouses my worst passions. Even when Shakespear,
in his efforts to be a social philosopher, does rise for an instant to
the level of a sixth-rate Kingsley, his solemn self-complacency
infuriates me. And yet, so wonderful is his art, that it is not easy
to disentangle what is unbearable from what is irresistible. Orlando one moment says:

> Whate'er you are
> That in this desert inaccessible
> Under the shade of melancholy boughs
> Lose and neglect the creeping hours of time,

which, though it indicates a thoroughly unhealthy imagination,
and would have been impossible to, for instance, Chaucer, is yet
magically fine of its kind. The next moment he tacks on lines
which would have revolted Mr Pecksniff:

If ever you have looked on better days,
If ever been where bells have knolled to church,

> [*How perfectly the atmosphere of the rented*
> *pew is caught in this incredible line!*]

If ever sat at any good man's feast,
If ever from your eyelids wiped—

I really shall get sick if I quote any more of it. Was ever such canting, snivelling, hypocritical unctuousness exuded by an actor anxious to shew that he was above his profession, and was a thoroughly respectable man in private life? Why cannot all this putrescence be cut out of the play, and only the vital parts—the genuine story-telling, the fun, the poetry, the drama, be retained? Simply because, if nothing were left of Shakespear but his genius, our Shakespearolaters would miss all that they admire in him.

Notwithstanding these drawbacks, the fascination of As You Like It is still very great. It has the overwhelming advantage of being written for the most part in prose instead of in blank verse, which any fool can write. And such prose! The first scene alone, with its energy of exposition, each phrase driving its meaning and feeling in up to the head at one brief, sure stroke, is worth ten acts of the ordinary Elizabethan sing-song. It cannot be said that the blank verse is reserved for those passages which demand a loftier expression, since Le Beau and Corin drop into it, like Mr Silas Wegg, on the most inadequate provocation; but at least there is not much of it. The popularity of Rosalind is due to three main causes. First, she only speaks blank verse for a few minutes. Second, she only wears a skirt for a few minutes (and the dismal effect of the change at the end to the wedding dress ought to convert the stupidest champion of petticoats to rational dress). Third, she makes love to the man instead of waiting for the man to make love to her—a piece of natural history which has kept Shakespear's heroines alive, whilst generations of properly governessed young ladies, taught to say "No" three times at least, have miserably perished.

The performance at the St James's is in some respects very

good and in no respect very bad or even indifferent. Miss Neilson's Rosalind will not bear criticism for a moment; and yet the total effect is pardonable, and even pleasant. She bungles speech after speech; and her attacks of Miss Ellen Terry and Mrs Patrick Campbell are acute, sudden, and numerous; but her personal charm carries her through; and her song is a great success: besides, who ever failed, or could fail, as Rosalind? Miss Fay Davis is the best Celia I ever saw, and Miss Dorothea Baird the prettiest Phœbe, though her part is too much cut to give her any chance of acting. Miss Kate Phillips is an appallingly artificial Audrey; for, her style being either smart or nothing, her conscientious efforts to be lumpish land her in the impossible. And then, what is that artistically metropolitan complexion doing in the Forest of Arden?

Ass as Jaques is, Mr W. H. Vernon made him more tolerable than I can remember. Every successive production at the St James's leaves one with a greater admiration than before for Mr Vernon's talent. That servile apostle of working-class Thrift and Teetotalism (O William Shakespear, Esquire, you who died drunk, WHAT a moral chap you were!) hight Adam, was made about twenty years too old by Mr Loraine, who, on the other hand, made a charming point by bidding farewell to the old home with a smile instead of the conventional tear. Mr Fernandez impersonated the banished Duke as well as it is in the nature of Jaques's Boswell to be impersonated; Mr H. B. Irving plays Oliver very much as anybody else would play Iago, yet with his faults on the right side; Mr Vincent retains his lawful speeches (usually purloined by Jaques) as the First Lord; and Mr Esmond tries the picturesque, attitudinizing, galvanic, Bedford Park style on Touchstone, worrying all effect out of the good lines, but worrying some into the bad ones. Mr Wheeler, as Charles, catches the professional manner very happily; and the wrestling bout is far and away the best I have seen on the stage. To me, the wrestling is always the main attraction of an As You Like It performance, since it is so much easier to find a man who knows how to wrestle than one who knows how to act. Mr Alexander's Orlando

I should like to see again later on. The qualities he shewed in it were those which go without saying in his case; and now that he has disposed of the really big achievement of producing the play with an artistic intelligence and practical ability never, as far as my experience goes, applied to it before, he will have time to elaborate a part lying easily within his powers, and already very attractively played by him. There are ten other gentlemen in the cast; but I can only mention Mr Aubrey Smith, whose appearance as "the humorous Duke" (which Mr Vincent Sternroyd, as Le Beau, seemed to understand as a duke with a sense of humor, like Mr Gilbert's Mikado) was so magnificent that it taxed all his powers to live up to his own aspect.

The scene where the two boys come in and sing It was a lover and his lass to Touchstone has been restored by Mr Alexander with such success that I am inclined to declare it the most delightful moment in the whole representation. Mr Edward German has rearranged his Henry VIII music for the masque of Hymen at the end. Hymen, beauteous to gorgeousness, is impersonated by Miss Opp.

The production at this Christmas season could not be more timely. The children will find the virtue of Adam and the philosophy of Jaques just the thing for them; whilst their elders will be delighted by the pageantry and the wrestling.

IBSEN WITHOUT TEARS

[12 *December* 1896]

LITTLE EYOLF, which began at the Avenue Theatre only the other day as an artistic forlorn hope led by Miss Elizabeth Robins, has been promoted into a full-blown fashionable theatrical speculation, with a Morocco Bound syndicate in the background, unlimited starring and bill-posting, and everything complete. The syndicate promptly set to work to shew us how Ibsen should really be done. They found the whole thing wrong from the root up. The silly Ibsen people had put Miss Achurch, an Ibsenite actress, into the leading part, and Mrs Patrick Campbell, a fashionable actress, into a minor one. This was soon set right. Miss Achurch was got rid of altogether, and her part transferred to Mrs Campbell. Miss Robins, though tainted with Ibsenism, was retained, but only, I presume, because, having command of the stage-right in the play, she could not be replaced—say by Miss Maude Millet—without her own consent. The rest of the arrangements are economical rather than fashionable, the syndicate, to all appearance, being, like most syndicates, an association for the purpose of getting money rather than supplying it.

Mrs Patrick Campbell has entered thoroughly into the spirit of the alterations. She has seen how unladylike, how disturbing, how full of horror even, the part of Rita Allmers is, acted as Miss Achurch acted it. And she has remedied this with a completeness that leaves nothing to be desired—or perhaps only one thing. Was there not a Mr Arcedeckne who, when Thackeray took to lecturing, said, "Have a piano, Thack"? Well, Rita Allmers wants a piano. Mrs Tanqueray had one, and played it so beautifully that I have been her infatuated slave ever since. There need be no difficulty about the matter: the breezy Borgheim has only to say, "Now that Alfred is back, Mrs Allmers, wont you give us that study for the left hand we are all so fond of?" and there you are. However, even without the piano, Mrs Campbell succeeded wonderfully in eliminating all unpleasantness from the play. She looked charming; and her dresses were beyond reproach: she carried a mortgage on the "gold and green forests" on her back. Her performance was infinitely reassuring and pretty: its note was, "You silly people! what are you making all this fuss about? The secret of life is charm and self-possession, and not tantrums about drowned children." The famous line "There stood your champagne; but you tasted it not," was no longer a "secret of the alcove," but a good-humored, mock petulant remonstrance with a man whom there was no pleasing in the matter of wine. There was not a taste of nasty jealousy: this Rita tolerated her dear old stupid's preoccupation with Asta and Eyolf and his books as any sensible (or insensible) woman would. Goodness gracious, I thought, what things that evil-minded Miss Achurch did read into this harmless play! And how nicely Mrs Campbell took the drowning of the child! Just a pretty waving of the fingers, a moderate scream as if she had very nearly walked on a tin tack, and it was all over, without tears, without pain, without more fuss than if she had broken the glass of her watch.

At this rate, it was not long before Rita thoroughly gained the sympathy of the audience. We felt that if she could only get rid of that ridiculous, sentimental Asta (Miss Robins, blind to the object lesson before her, persisted in acting Ibsenitically), and induce her fussing, self-conscious, probably underbred husband not to cry for spilt milk, she would be as happy as any lady in the land. Unfortunately, the behaviour of Mr Allmers became more and more intolerable as the second act progressed, though he could not exhaust Rita's patient, slily humorous tolerance. As usual, he wanted to know whether she would like to go and drown herself; and the sweet, cool way in which she answered, "Oh, I dont know, Alfred. No: I think I should have to stay here with *you*—a *litt*-le while" was a lesson to all wives. What a contrast to Miss Achurch, who so unnecessarily filled the stage with the terror of death in this passage! This is what comes of exaggeration, of over-acting, of forgetting that people go to the theatre to be amused, and not to be upset! When Allmers shook his fist at his beautiful wife—O unworthy the name of Briton!—and shouted "*You* are the guilty one in this," her silent dignity overwhelmed him. Nothing could have been in better taste than her description of the pretty way in which her child had lain in the water when he was drowned—his mother's son all over. All the pain was taken out of it by the way it was approached. "I got Borgheim to go down to the pier with me [so nice of Borgheim, dear fellow!]." "And what," interrupts the stupid Allmers, "did you want there?" Rita gave a little laugh at his obtuseness, a laugh which meant "Why, you dear silly," before she replied, "To question the boys as to how it happened." After all, it is these Ibsenite people that create the objections to Ibsen. If Mrs Campbell had played Rita from the first, not a word would have been said against the play; and the whole business would have been quietly over and the theatre closed by this time. But noth-ing would serve them but their Miss Achurch; and so, instead of a pretty arrangement of the "Eyolf" theme for boudoir pianette, we had it flung to the "Götterdämmerung" orchestra, and blared right into our shrinking souls.

In the third act, the smoothness of the proceedings was some-what marred by the fact that Mrs Campbell, not knowing her words, had to stop acting and frankly bring the book on the stage and read from it. Now Mrs Campbell reads very clearly and nicely; and the result of course was that the Ibsenite atmosphere began to assert itself, just as it would if the play were read aloud in a private room. However, that has been remedied, no doubt, by this time; and the public may rely on an uninterruptedly quiet evening.

The main drawback is that it is impossible not to feel that Mrs Campbell's Rita, with all her charm, is terribly hampered by the unsuitability of the words Ibsen and Mr Archer have put into her mouth. They were all very well for Miss Achurch, who perhaps, if the truth were known, arranged her acting to suit them; but they are forced, strained, out of tune in all sorts of ways in the mouth of Mrs Campbell's latest creation. Why cannot the dia-logue be adapted to her requirements and harmonized with her playing, say by Mr William Black? Ibsen is of no use when any-thing really ladylike is wanted: you might as well put Beethoven to compose Chaminades. It is true that no man can look at the new Rita without wishing that Heaven had sent him just such a wife, whereas the boldest man would hardly have envied Allmers the other Rita if Miss Achurch had allowed him a moment's leisure for such impertinent speculations; but all the same, the evenings at the Avenue Theatre are likely to be a little languid. I had rather look at a beautiful picture than be flogged, as a general thing; but if I were offered my choice between looking at the most beautiful picture in the world continuously for a fortnight and submitting to, say, a dozen, I think I should choose the flog-ging. For just the same reason, if I had to choose between seeing Miss Achurch's Rita again, with all its turns of beauty and flashes of grandeur obliterated, and nothing left but its insane jealousy, its agonizing horror, its lacerating remorse, and its maddening unrest, the alternative being another two hours' contemplation of uneventful feminine fascination as personified by Mrs Patrick Campbell, I should go like a lamb to the slaughter. I prefer Mrs Campbell's Rita to her photograph, because it moves and talks; but otherwise there is not so much difference as I expected. Mrs Campbell, as Magda, could do nothing with a public spoiled by Duse. I greatly fear she will do even less, as Rita, with a public spoiled by Miss Achurch.

The representation generally is considerably affected in its scale and effect by the change of Ritas. Mr Courtenay Thorpe, who, though playing *con tutta la forza*, could hardly avoid seeming to underact with Miss Achurch, has now considerable difficulty in avoiding overacting, since he cannot be even in earnest and anxious without producing an effect of being good-humoredly laughed at by Mrs Campbell. Miss Robins, as Asta, has improved greatly on the genteel misery of the first night. She has got complete hold of the part; and although her old fault of resorting to the lachrymose for all sorts of pathetic expression produces something of its old monotony, and the voice clings to one delicate register until the effect verges on affectation, yet Asta comes out as a distinct person about whose history the audience has learnt something, and not as an actress delivering a string of lines and making a number of points more or less effectively. The difficulty is that in this cheap edition of Little Eyolf Asta, instead of being the tranquillizing element, becomes the centre of disturbance; so that the conduct of Allmers in turning for the sake of peace and quietness from his pretty, coaxing, soothing wife to his agitated high-strung sister becomes nonsensical. I pointed out after the first performance that Miss Robins had not really succeeded in making Asta a peacemaker; but beside Miss Achurch she easily seemed gentle, whereas beside Mrs Campbell she seems a volcano. It is only necessary to recall her playing of the frightful ending to the first act of Alan's Wife, and compare it with Mrs Campbell's finish to the first act of Little Eyolf, to realize the preposterousness of their relative positions in the cast. Mrs Campbell's old part of the Ratwife is now played by Miss Florence Farr. Miss Farr deserves more public sympathy than any of the other Ibsenite actresses; for they have only damaged themselves professionally by appearing in Ibsen's plays, whereas Miss Farr has complicated her difficulties by appearing in mine as well. Further, instead of either devoting herself to the most personally exacting of all the arts or else letting it alone, Miss Farr has written clever novels and erudite works on Babylonish lore; has managed a theatre capably for a season; and has only occasionally acted. For an occasional actress she has been rather successful once or twice in producing singular effects in singular parts—her Rebecca in Rosmersholm was remarkable and promising—but she has not pursued her art with sufficient constancy to attain any authoritative power of carrying out her conceptions, which are, besides, only skin deep. Her Ratwife is a favorable example of her power of producing a certain strangeness of effect; but it is somewhat discounted by want of sustained grip in the execution. Miss Farr will perhaps remedy this if she can find time enough to spare from her other interests to attend to it. The rest of the cast is as before. One has no longer any real belief in the drowning of Master Stewart Dawson, thanks to the gentle method of Mrs Campbell. Mr Lowne's sensible, healthy superiority to all this morbid Ibsen stuff is greatly reinforced now that Rita takes things nicely and easily.

I cannot help thinking it a great pity that the Avenue enterprise, just as it seemed to be capturing that afternoon classical concert public to which I have always looked for the regeneration of the classical drama, should have paid the penalty of its success by the usual evolution into what is evidently half a timid speculation in a "catch-on," and half an attempt to slacken the rate at which the Avenue Theatre is eating its head off in rent. That evolution of course at once found out the utter incoherence of the enterprise. The original production, undertaken largely at Miss Robins's individual risk, was for the benefit of a vaguely announced Fund, as to the constitution and purpose of which

no information was forthcoming, except that it proposed to produce Echegaray's Mariana, with Miss Robins in the title-part. But
neither Miss Robins's nor anyone else's interests in this fund seem
to have been secured in any way. The considerable profit of the
first week of Little Eyolf may, for all that is guaranteed to the
contrary, be devoted to the production of an opera, a shadow
play from Paris, or a drama in which neither Miss Robins nor
any of those who have worked with her may be offered any part
or share whatever. There is already just such a fund in existence
in the treasury of the Independent Theatre, which strove hard
to obtain Little Eyolf for production, and which actually guaranteed part of the booking at the Avenue. But here the same difficulty arose. Miss Achurch would no doubt have trusted the
Independent, for the excellent reason that her husband is one of
the directors; but no other artist playing for it would have had
the smallest security that, had its fortunes been established through
their efforts, they would ever have been cast for a part in its
future productions. On the other hand, Miss Achurch had no
hold on the new fund, which had specially declared its intention
of supporting Miss Robins. This has not prevented the production of Little Eyolf, though it has greatly delayed it; for everybody finally threw security to the winds, and played by friendly
arrangement on such terms as were possible. As it happened,
there was a substantial profit, and it all went to the Fund. Naturally,
however, when the enterprise entered upon a purely commercial
phase, the artists at once refused to work for the profit of a syndicate on the enthusiastic terms (or no terms) on which they had
worked for Ibsen and for one another. The syndicate, on the
other hand, had no idea of wasting so expensive a star as Mrs
Patrick Campbell on a small part that could be filled for a few
pounds, when they could transfer her to the leading part and
save Miss Achurch's salary. If they could have substituted an
inferior artist for Miss Robins, they could have effected a still
further saving, relying on Mrs Pat to draw full houses; but that
was made impossible by Miss Robins's power over the stage-
right. Consequently, the only sufferer was Miss Achurch; but it

is impossible for Miss Robins and Mrs Campbell not to feel that the same thing might have happened to them if there had been no stage-right, and if the syndicate had realized that, when it comes to Ibsen, Miss Achurch is a surer card to play than Mrs Campbell.

Under these circumstances, what likelihood is there of the experiment being resumed or repeated on its old basis? Miss Robins will probably think twice before she creates Mariana without some security that, if she succeeds, the part will not immediately be handed over to Miss Winifred Emery or Miss Julia Neilson. Miss Achurch, triumphantly as she has come out of the comparison with her successor, is not likely to forget her lesson. Mrs Campbell's willingness to enlist in forlorn hopes in the humblest capacity may not improbably be received in future as Laocoon received the offer of the wooden horse. I do not presume to meddle in the affairs of all these actors and authors, patrons and enthusiasts, subscribers and guarantors, though this is quite as much my business as theirs; but after some years' intimate experience of the results of unorganized Ibsenism, I venture to suggest that it would be well to have some equitable form of theatrical organization ready to deal with Ibsen's new play, on the translation of which Mr Archer is already at work.

MR BANCROFT'S PILGRIMAGE

[19 *December* 1896]

MR BANCROFT has emerged from his retirement to start on an errand of mercy through this England of ours. To cool the fevered brow, to moisten the parched lip, to wile away the long sleepless nights of sick children with fairy gifts, to stimulate the demand for chromolithographs of the devoted nurse in her snowy bands, with spoon and bowl and angel eyes: this is the high mission on which Seth Bancroft has gone forth from his comfortable fireside, his method being to read Dickens's Christmas Carol in public and give the proceeds to the hospitals.

I have not seen a single notice of Mr Bancroft's enterprise that has not breathed sympathy, admiration, approval, from beginning to end. Now I dont sympathize; I dont admire; I dont approve. Mr Bancroft is an actor. An opportunity for exercising his art, a sympathetic character to appear in, a wide advertisement, and an outpouring of gratitude and popularity must needs be so highly agreeable to him, that it is quite useless to try to persuade me that they represent any sacrifice on his part. He will not be called on to provide any money for the hospitals: the public will provide that and pay his expenses into the bargain. In refraining from any attempt to make money for himself out of his recreation, Mr Bancroft is only following the ordinary custom of English sportsmen of independent means. As long as Mr Bancroft needed to make money by his public appearances, he did make it. Therefore, I have no hesitation in regarding the pilgrimage, apart from its object, as an act of pure self-indulgence on Mr Bancroft's part. Please understand that Mr Bancroft has not, as far as I am aware, put forward any pretension to the contrary, and that he may rightly regard it as one of the special privileges of his art that it enables him to combine beneficence to others with great enjoyment to himself. But the public does not take the matter in this way; and the critics all speak as if Mr Bancroft had unquestionably placed his country under an obligation. My point is that unless Mr Bancroft can justify, as publicly serviceable, his administration and expenditure of the funds, the obligation is all the other way.

Let me then proceed to look the gift horse carefully in the mouth. Is the reading of Dickens's Christmas Carol likely to have any educational effect on public taste? Clearly none whatever. Half a century ago the Carol had a huge success as an exploitation of pre-existent popular sentiment of the vulgar Christmas kind; and its revival today has no more classical pretension than the forthcoming revival of Black-eyed Susan at the Adelphi. Dickens was a man of genius; but that fact is perfectly well known, except perhaps in literary circles, where it is difficult to make a merit of not being able to write like Dickens without disparaging him somewhat. Besides, it is not exactly on the

Christmas Carol that Dickens's reputation rests. Let us then put the possibility of the pilgrimage being educational and edificational out of the question, and come to the real point—the application of the proceeds.

Now I am loth to shatter Mr Bancroft's kindly illusions; and yet I must tell him bluntly that he would do less harm with the money by spending it at Monte Carlo than in arbitrarily (and most ungratefully) enriching the ratepayers of the towns he visits at the expense of the people who pay for tickets to hear him read. For that, and nothing else, is just precisely what he is doing. Hospitals are not public luxuries, but public necessities: when the private contributor buttons up his pocket—as he invariably now does if he understands what he is about—the result is not that the sick poor are left to perish in their slums, but that a hospital rate is struck, and the hospitals happily rescued from the abuses of practically irresponsible private management (which the rich writers of conscience-money cheques never dream of attempting to control), with income uncertain; authority scrambled for by committee, doctors, chiefs of the nursing staff, and permanent officials; and the angel-eyed nurses, coarsely and carelessly fed, sweated and overworked beyond all endurance except by women to whom the opportunity of pursuing a universally respected occupation with a considerable chance of finally marrying a doctor is worth seizing at any cost. For this the overthrow of the begging, cadging, advertising, voluntary-contribution system means the substitution of the certain income, the vigilant audit, the expert official management, the standard wages and hours of work, the sensitiveness to public opinion, including that of the class to which the patients belong, the subjection to the fierce criticism of party newspapers keen for scandals to be used as local electioneering capital, all of which have been called into action by the immense development in local government under the Acts of the last ten years. Of course, as long as ignorant philanthropists, and people anxious to buy positions as public benefactors, maintain private hospitals by private subscription, the ratepayers and the local authorities will be only too glad to shirk their burdens and duties, just as they would if they could induce Mr Bancroft to light and pave the streets for them; but when the philanthropists learn that the only practical effect of their misplaced bounty on the poor is that the patient gets less accommodation and consideration, and the nurse less pay and no security in return for longer hours of labor, they will begin to understand how all the old objections to pauperizing individuals apply with tenfold force to pauperizing the public. In short, Mr Bancroft is meddling, with the best intentions, in a matter which he has not studied, with the result that every one of his readings may be regarded as so much mischief done to everybody but himself and those who have the pleasure of hearing him read.

This is the more aggravating because, had Mr Bancroft directed his attention to matters that he understands, he would have seen in his own art unlimited openings for his benevolence. As a musical critic I protested with all my might against the handing over, at the provincial festivals, of the money earned by Music from lovers of music to relieve the rates in the name of "charity." The one consoling feature about that scandal was that the cheque with which the operatic prima donna headed the subscription list was always handed to her for the purpose along with her salary. I protest now against the same spoliation of Art in the case of the Drama. Why should Mr Bancroft hand over the proceeds of his reading to the town hospital, which will be the worse for it, when he might just as well hand it over to the town theatre, which might be made the better for it? Mr Bancroft will say "How? On what conditions?" I reply that the conditions are not my business. I am not on the philanthropic platform just at present, and therefore cannot be called on to sit down and gratuitously put in the hard work of thinking out a scheme. But Mr Bancroft has mounted that platform. Very well: let him do something to prove his good faith. I have shown that reading the Carol to enthusiastic audiences, and dropping the money, addressed to some hospital treasurer or other, into the nearest pillar-box, is no more philanthropic work than cricket, yachting, or bicycling. But if Mr Bancroft would sit down and think out the problem of what a man could do for the drama in any given place if he had a fifty-pound note to spend on it, then I should admit that he was doing a public service. Even if he were merely to invite proposals and take the trouble of reading them through, he might get and spread some light on the subject. Suppose, for instance, a clergyman wrote up from some village and said, "If you will guarantee my expenses to such and such an amount, I will take the school children and the Christmas mummers in hand, and produce a Bible play with the local artizans and laborers in the principal parts, as they do in the Bavarian Alps." Or suppose some country Pioneer Club wanted to promote a first-rate performance of A Doll's House, but could not induce the local manager to venture upon it without a subsidy. Suppose the Independent Theatre offered to get up a verbatim performance of Peer Gynt, lasting two nights, on condition of being so far assisted that the exploit could ruin nobody but itself; or that Miss Robins were to undertake an Echegaray cycle on the same conditions. What about that Wagner Theatre on Richmond Hill? What about an Academy or "Royal College" of the Drama, with scholarships, and a library scantily furnished with memoirs and reminiscences, and liberally furnished with technical works, including theatrical construction and stage mechanism? Why not offer Macmillans a subsidy towards a Dictionary of the Drama, uniform with Grove's Dictionary of Music and Musicians, or set on foot an inquiry, like that which supplied the material for Mr Charles Booth's Life and Labor of the People into the life and labor of the actor, dealing also with salaries, agreements, sharing arrangements, backing, syndicating, papering, and bribing critics? The appendix, contributed by retired managers, might consist of balance-sheets and detailed accounts of their most famous productions, especially the "successes" by which they lost most money. A missionary fund for affirming the social importance of the drama, and claiming for municipal theatres as high a place in the collectivist program as municipal gas, water, and tramways, would be quite worth considering. Even a fund for persuading actors not to make foolish second-hand remarks about Ibsen in public would be better than nothing. Surely if all these resources occur to me on the spur of the moment, an actor and manager of Mr Bancroft's ability and experience, with unlimited leisure, could find something to do for his profession with the money which he is now using to keep down the character of our hospitals and—if he will take my word for the political economy of the business—to save our landlords from the final incidence of the hospitals rate.

There is also an artistic objection to this pseudo-charitable business. The curse of our stage at present is the shameless prostitution of the art of acting into the art of pleasing. The actor wants "sympathy": the actress wants affection. They make the theatre a place where the public comes to look at its pets and distribute lumps of sugar to them. Even the critics are debauched: there is no mistaking our disconcerted, pettish note whenever a really great artist—Duse, for example—whilst interpreting a drama for us with exquisite intelligence, and playing it with a skill almost inconceivable when measured by our English stan- dards, absolutely declines to flatter us with any sort of solicitation for a more personal regard. Our reluctant, humiliated, rebuffed admissions of the success of actresses who pursue their profession with complete integrity contrast so shockingly with the officious, smirkingly enthusiastic congratulations we shower on those charming women who throw themselves, as such, on the personal admiration, indulgence, and good fellowship of the public, that the more an actress respects herself and loves her profession, the more she hates the existing relations between the stage and the public. Occasionally an actress's heart is so happily constituted that she can spoil the public as she would spoil a nursery of children, and yet work hard at her art; but the average actress, when the author demands anything "unsympathetic" from her, refuses to act on exactly the same grounds as she might refuse to let her lover see her in curl papers. And the actors are worse than the actresses. Why is it that, with the exception of An Enemy of the People, and (partly) The Master Builder, no play of Ibsen's has been performed on the initiative of an actor since Mr Vernon's experiment years ago with Pillars of Society? Simply because Dr Stockman and Solness are the only Ibsen heroes who can depend on a little vulgar "sympathy." Allmers, Helmar, Hjalmar Ekdal, and even Rosmer may be very interesting, very lifelike; but they are not "sympathetic": they are even ridiculous occasionally: at best they are not readily comprehensible by the average actor fancier—for that is what the word playgoer has come to mean nowadays. A player who is still dependent on his profession for his daily bread may plead that "those who live to please must please to live," though I shall take leave to consider any actor who takes that position as being not only the rogue he confesses himself to be, but a fool into the bargain. But an actor in Mr Bancroft's circumstances, retired and independent, what on earth need has he any longer for a sympathetic part? Of what use is a halo of ready-made Hospital Sunday sentiment to him? Why not attempt to create some new sentiment—if it were only to knock into the heads of his benighted profession the elementary truth that it is the business of the dramatic artist, as of other public men and women, to strive incessantly with the public; to insist on earnest relations with it, and not merely voluptuous ones; to lead it, nerve it, withstand its constant tendency to relapse into carelessness and vulgar familiarity; in short, to attain to public esteem, authority, and needfulness to the national welfare (things undreamt of in the relations between the theatrical profession and the public today), instead of to the camp-follower's refuge of mere popularity?

I have hardly left myself room to commemorate the latest exploit of the Elizabethan Stage Society—its performance of The Two Gentlemen of Verona in a City Company's hall in Threadneedle Street. It seems to me that Mr Poel has now abandoned himself wholly to his fancy in dresses and equipments and stage business. I am no expert in these matters; but if Valentine's Turkish costume was not as purely an eighteenth-century convention as the big drum and cymbals in Mozart's Serai!, I am prepared to eat it. The fantastic outlaws, with their plumes and drum, belonged to the same period. The other costumes were mostly Elizabethan; but, except in the case of the Duke, they were surely bourgeois rather than noble. I am bound to say that the number of lines neither intelligently nor intelligibly delivered was greater than at any previous performance of the Society. This was only partly the fault of the hall, which made a magnificent setting for the performance, but also presented acoustic difficulties which only very practised speakers could have overcome. Valentine and Proteus were the most successful of the company, Proteus playing with plenty of address, and Valentine shewing some promise of talent as an actor. The ladies were not emphatic or distinct enough to make any effect. The gentleman who played Launce did not know the difference between a Shakespearean clown and a Zany: he acted worse than his dog—quite the wrong sort of dog, by the way, but very amusing.

RICHARD HIMSELF AGAIN

RICHARD III. Lyceum Theatre, 19 December 1896.

[26 *December* 1896]

THE world being yet little better than a mischievous schoolboy, I am afraid it cannot be denied that Punch and Judy holds the field still as the most popular of dramatic entertainments. And of all its versions, except those which are quite above the head of the man in the street, Shakespear's Richard III is the best. It has abundant devilry, humor, and character, presented with luxuriant energy of diction in the simplest form of blank verse. Shakespear revels in it with just the sort of artistic unconscionableness that fits the theme. Richard is the prince of Punches: he delights Man by provoking God, and dies unrepentant and game to the last. His incongruous conventional appendages, such as the Punch hump, the conscience, the fear of ghosts, all impart a spice of outrageousness which leaves nothing lacking to the fun of the entertainment, except the solemnity of those spectators who feel bound to take the affair as a profound and subtle historic study.

Punch, whether as Jingle, Macaire, Mephistopheles, or Richard, has always been a favorite part with Sir Henry Irving. The craftily mischievous, the sardonically impudent, tickle him immensely, besides providing him with a welcome relief from the gravity of his serious impersonations. As Richard he drops Punch after the coronation scene, which, in deference to stage tradition, he makes a turning-point at which the virtuoso in mischief, having achieved his ambition, becomes a savage at bay. I do not see why this should be. In the tent scene, Richard says:

> There is no creature loves me;
> And if I die no soul will pity me.

Macbeth repeats this patch of pathos, and immediately proceeds to pity himself unstintedly over it; but Richard no sooner catches the sentimental cadence of his own voice than the mocker in him is awakened at once, and he adds, quite in Punch's vein,

> Nay, wherefore should they? since that I myself
> Find in myself no pity for myself.

Sir Henry Irving omits these lines, because he plays, as he always does, for a pathetically sublime ending. But we have seen the sublime ending before pretty often; and this time it robs us of such strokes as Richard's aristocratically cynical private encouragement to his entourage of peers:

> Our strong arms be our conscience, swords our law.
> March on; join bravely; let us to't pell-mell,
> If not to Heaven, then hand in hand to hell;

followed by his amusingly blackguardly public address to the rank and file, quite in the vein of the famous and more successful appeal to the British troops in the Peninsula. "Will you that are Englishmen fed on beef let yourselves be licked by a lot of —— Spaniards fed on oranges?" Despair, one feels, could bring to Punch-Richard nothing but the exultation of one who loved destruction better than even victory; and the exclamation

> A thousand hearts are great within my bosom

is not the expression of a hero's courage, but the evil ecstasy of the destroyer as he finds himself, after a weak, piping time of peace, back at last in his native element.

Sir Henry Irving's acting edition of the play is so enormously superior to Cibber's, that a playgoer brought up, as I was, on the old version must needs find an overwhelming satisfaction in it. Not that I object to the particular lines which are now always flung in poor Cibber's face. "Off with his head: so much for Buckingham!" is just as worthy of Shakespear as "I'll hear no more. Die, prophet, in thy speech," and distinctly better than "Off with his son George's head."

> Hark! the shrill trumpet sounds. To horse! Away!
> My soul's in arms, and eager for the fray,

is ridiculed because Cibber wrote it; but I cannot for the life of me see that it is inferior to

> Go muster men. My counsel is my shield.
> We must be brief when traitors brave the field.

"Richard's himself again" is capital of its kind. If you object to the kind, the objection is stronger against Shakespear, who set Cibber the example, and was proclaimed immortal for it, than against an unfortunate actor who would never have dreamt of inventing the art of rhetorical balderdash for himself. The plain reason why the public for so many generations could see no difference in merit between the famous Cibber points and

> A horse! A horse! My kingdom for a horse!

was that there was no difference to see. When it came to fustian, Jack was as good as his master.

The real objection to Cibber's version is that it is what we call a "one man show." Shakespear, having no room in a play so full of action for more than one real part, surrounded it with figures whose historical titles and splendid dresses, helped by a line or two at the right moment, impose on our imagination sufficiently to make us see the whole Court of Edward IV. If Hastings, Stanley, the "jockey of Norfolk," the "deep revolving witty Buckingham," and the rest, only bear themselves with sufficient address not to contradict absolutely the dramatist's suggestion of them, the audience will receive enough impression of their reality, and even of their importance, to give Richard an air of moving in a Court as the King's brother. But Cibber could not bear that anyone on the stage should have an air of importance except himself: if the subordinate members of the company could not act so well as he, it seemed to him, not that it was his business as the presenter of a play to conceal their deficiencies, but that the first principles of justice and fair dealing demanded before all things that his superiority should be made evident to the public. (And there are not half a dozen leading actors on the stage today who would not take precisely that view of the situation.) Consequently he handled Richard III so as to make every other actor in it obviously ridiculous and insignificant, except only that Henry VI, in the first act, was allowed to win the pity of the audience in order that the effect might be the greater when Richard stabbed him. No actor could have produced more completely, exactly, and forcibly the effect aimed at by Cibber than Barry Sullivan, the one actor who kept Cibber's Richard on the stage during the present half-century. But it was an exhibition, not a play. Barry Sullivan was full of force, and very clever: if his power had been less exclusively of the infernal order, or if he had devoted himself to the drama instead of devoting the drama to himself as a mere means of self-assertion, one might have said more for him. He managed to make the audience believe in Richard; but as he could not make it believe in the others, and probably did not want to, they destroyed the illusion almost as fast as he created it. This is why Cibber's Richard, though it is so simple that the character plays itself as unmistakeably as the blank verse speaks itself, can only be made endurable by an actor of exceptional personal force. The second and third acts at the Lyceum, with their atmosphere of Court faction and their presentation before the audience of Edward and Clarence, make all the difference between the two versions.

But the Lyceum has by no means emancipated itself from

288

superstition—even gross superstition. Italian opera itself could go no further in folly than the exhibition of a pretty and popular young actress in tights as Prince Edward. No doubt we were glad to see Miss Lena Ashwell—for the matter of that we should have been glad to see Mrs John Wood as the other prince—but from the moment she came on the stage all serious historical illusion necessarily vanished, and was replaced by the most extreme form of theatrical convention. Probably Sir Henry Irving cast Miss Ashwell for the part because he has not followed her career since she played Elaine in King Arthur. She was then weak, timid, subordinate, with an insignificant presence and voice which, contrasted as it was with Miss Terry's, could only be described—if one had the heart to do it—as a squawl. Since then she has developed precipitously. If any sort of success had been possible for the plays in which she has appeared this year at the Duke of York's and Shaftesbury Theatres, she would have received a large share of the credit of it. Even in Carmen, when, perhaps for the sake of auld lang syne, she squawled and stood on the tips of her heels for the last time (let us hope), her scene with the dragoon in the first act was the one memorable moment in the whole of that disastrous business. She now returns to the Lyceum stage as an actress of mark, strong in womanly charm, and not in the least the sort of person whose sex is so little emphasized that it can be hidden by a doublet and hose. You might as well put forward Miss Ada Rehan as a boy. Nothing can be more absurd than the spectacle of Sir Henry Irving elaborately playing the uncle to his little nephew when he is obviously addressing a fine young woman in rational dress who is very thoroughly her own mistress, and treads the boards with no little authority and assurance as one of the younger generation knocking vigorously at the door. Miss Ashwell makes short work of the sleepiness of the Lyceum; and though I take urgent exception to her latest technical theory, which is, that the bridge of the nose is the seat of facial expression, I admit that she does all that can be done to reconcile us to the burlesque of her appearance in a part that should have been played by a boy.

289

Another mistake in the casting of the play was Mr Gordon Craig's Edward IV. As Henry VI, Mr Craig, who wasted his delicacy on the wrong part, would have been perfect. Henry not being available, he might have played Richmond with a considerable air of being a young Henry VII. But as Edward he was incredible: one felt that Richard would have had him out of the way years ago if Margaret had not saved him the trouble by vanquishing him at Tewkesbury. Shakespear took plenty of pains with the strong ruffian of the York family: his part in Henry VI makes it quite clear why he held his own both in and out of doors. The remedy for the misfit lay ready to the manager's hand. Mr Cooper, his too burly Richmond, shewed what a capital Edward he would have made when he turned at the entrance to his tent, and said, with the set air of a man not accustomed to be trifled with,

> O Thou, whose captain I account myself,
> Look on my forces with a gracious eye,
> Or you will have me to reckon with afterwards.

The last line was not actually spoken by Mr Cooper; but he looked it, exactly as Edward IV might have done.

As to Sir Henry Irving's own performance, I am not prepared to judge it, in point of execution, by what he did on the first night. He was best in the Court scenes. In the heavy single-handed scenes which Cibber loved, he was not, as it seemed to me, answering his helm satisfactorily; and he was occasionally a little out of temper with his own nervous condition. He made some odd slips in the text, notably by repeatedly substituting "you" for "I"—for instance, "Shine out, fair sun, till you have bought a glass." Once he inadvertently electrified the house by very unexpectedly asking Miss Milton to get further up the stage in the blank verse and penetrating tones of Richard. Finally, the worry of playing against the vein tired him. In the tent and battle scenes his exhaustion was too genuine to be quite acceptable as part of the play. The fight was, perhaps, a relief to his feelings; but to me the spectacle of Mr Cooper pretending to pass his sword three times through Richard's body, as if a man could be run through as easily as a cuttle-fish, was neither credible nor impressive. The attempt to make a stage combat look as imposing as Hazlitt's description of the death of Edmund Kean's Richard reads, is hopeless. If Kean were to return to life and do the combat for us, we should very likely find it as absurd as his habit of lying down on a sofa when he was too tired or too drunk to keep his feet during the final scenes.

Further, it seems to me that Sir Henry Irving should either cast the play to suit his acting or else modify his acting to suit the cast. His playing in the scene with Lady Anne—which, though a Punch scene, is Punch on the Don Giovanni plane—was a flat contradiction, not only of the letter of the lines, but of their spirit and feeling as conveyed unmistakeably by their cadence. This, however, we are used to: Sir Henry Irving never did and never will make use of a play otherwise than as a vehicle for some fantastic creation of his own. But if we are not to have the tears, the passion, the tenderness, the transport of dissimulation which alone can make the upshot credible—if the woman is to be openly teased and insulted, mocked, and disgusted, all through the scene as well as in the first "keen encounter of their wits," why not have Lady Anne presented as a weak, childish-witted, mesmerized creature, instead of as that most awful embodiment of virtue and decorum, the intellectual American lady? Poor Miss Julia Arthur honestly did her best to act the part as she found it in Shakespear; and if Richard had done the same she would have come off with credit. But how could she play to a Richard who would not utter a single tone to which any woman's heart could respond? She could not very well box the actor-manager's ears, and walk off; but really she deserves some credit for refraining from that extreme remedy. She partly had her revenge when she left the stage; for Richard, after playing the scene with her as if he were a Houndsditch salesman cheating a factory girl over a pair of second-hand stockings, naturally could not reach the raptures of the tremendous outburst of elation beginning

Was ever woman in this humor wooed?
Was ever woman in this humor won?

One felt inclined to answer, "Never, I assure you," and make an end of the scene there and then. I am prepared to admit that the creations of Sir Henry Irving's imagination are sometimes—in the case of his Iachimo, for example—better than those of the dramatists whom he is supposed to interpret. But what he did in this scene, as well as in the opening soliloquy, was child's play compared to what Shakespear meant him to do.

The rest of the performance was—well, it was Lyceum Shakespear. Miss Geneviève Ward was, of course, a very capable Margaret; but she missed the one touchstone passage in a very easy part—the tenderness of the appeal to Buckingham. Mr Macklin, equally of course, had no trouble with Buckingham; but he did not give us that moment which makes Richard say:

None are for me
That look into me with considerate eyes.

Messrs Norman Forbes and W. Farren (junior) played the murderers in the true Shakespearean manner: that is, as if they had come straight out of the pantomime of The Babes in the Wood; and Clarence recited his dream as if he were an elocutionary coroner summing up. The rest were respectably dull, except Mr Gordon Craig, Miss Lena Ashwell, and, in a page's part, Miss Edith Craig, the only member of the company before whom the manager visibly quails.

END OF VOL. II